D0216453

CREATING A CONSTITUTION

Creating a Constitution

LAW, DEMOCRACY, AND GROWTH IN ANCIENT ATHENS

FEDERICA CARUGATI

PRINCETON UNIVERSITY PRESS

PRINCETON & OXFORD

Copyright © 2019 by Princeton University Press

Published by Princeton University Press
41 William Street, Princeton, New Jersey 08540
6 Oxford Street, Woodstock, Oxfordshire OX20 1TR

press.princeton.edu

All Rights Reserved

Library of Congress Control Number 2019931720
ISBN 978-0-691-19563-6

British Library Cataloging-in-Publication Data is available

Editorial: Rob Tempio and Matt Rohal
Production Editorial: Jill Harris
Jacket Design: Pamela L. Schnitter
Production: Merli Guerra
Publicity: Alyssa Sanford and Amy Stewart
Copyeditor: Brittany Micka-Foos

Jacket image: The fragmentary fourth roll containing the Constitution
of the Athenians. Papyrus 131, f 5v. Egypt (near Hermopolis), ca. 100 AD.
Copyright © The British Library Board

This book has been composed in Arno

Printed on acid-free paper. ∞

Printed in the United States of America

10 9 8 7 6 5 4 3 2 1

CONTENTS

FIGURES

ACKNOWLEDGMENTS

IT IS commonplace to say that a book has been long in the making. This one is no exception. It was born as a dissertation submitted to the Stanford Department of Classics. It is now a book that hopes to reach a much broader audience. This transformation would not have been possible without the many eyes, ears, and minds that have accompanied me from Stanford, to Bloomington, and back.

The ideas that make up the bulk of the book were first hammered out on the Farm where many colleagues and friends offered suggestions, direction, and mentorship. These include Scott Arcenas, Edwin Carawan, Steve Haber, Foivos Karachalios, James Kierstead, Ian Morris, Andrea Nightingale, Josiah Ober, Dan-el Padilla Peralta, Tomer Perry, Mark Pyzyk, Walter Scheidel, Matt Simonton, and Barry Weingast.

Many of those ideas were revised, refined, and expanded thanks to the exposure to discussions with my wonderful coauthors and at a number of conferences. For believing early on in the value of ancient Greece as a case study, my heartfelt thanks go to Randy Calvert and Gillian Hadfield. For helping me think through the details of my argument, I would like to thank fellow panelists and participants in the following conferences and workshops: the Leventis Conference on Ancient Greek History and Contemporary Social Science (University of Edinburgh); the Conference on the Political Economy of Judicial Politics (Center for the Study of Democratic Politics, Princeton University); the Colloquium on Law Economics and Politics (NYU); the Midwestern Consortium of Greek Historians and Political Theorists (University of Michigan); the Conference Political Theory in / and / as Political Science (McGill University); the World Justice Project Scholars Conference (Stanford and Duke); the Society for Institutional and Organizational Economics Annual Meeting (SciencesPo, Paris); the Public Choice Society Annual Meeting (Charleston, SC); the American Political Science Association Annual Meetings (San Francisco and Boston); and the Institutional and Organizational Economics Academy (Corsica, France). Finally, many thanks to the organizers and participants of the many gatherings at Indiana University Bloomington that offered an exceptional sounding board at various critical stages: these include Lee Alston at the Ostrom Workshop; Will Winecoff at the World Politics Research Seminar;

Susan and David Williams at the Center for Constitutional Democracy; and Victor Quintanilla at the Center for Law, Society, and Culture.

I owe an immense debt of gratitude to the participants in the book conference I hosted at the Ostrom Workshop in September 2017. Their willingness to read a very early, very inchoate, transitional version of this book, and their ability to see the good in it and help me figure out the next steps was outstanding and humbling. These are Lee Alston, Sara Forsdyke, Tom Ginsburg, Andy Hanssen, Jeffrey Isaac, Cyanne Loyle, Lauren MacLean, Eric Robinson, Jessica Steinberg, and Gustavo Torrens. A particular shout-out goes to the staff of the Ostrom Workshop who not only helped me organize this important event, but also shared a great deal of my experience at Indiana University: Emily Castle, Gayle Higgins, Patty Lezotte, David Price, and Allison Sturgeon.

Many others along the way offered critical insights and suggestions. Some of their names are scattered in the pages that follow. Others include Daron Acemoglu, Eric Alston, Rob Fleck, Matthew Landauer, Margaret Levi, Adam Littlestone-Luria, Joel Mokyr, Ken Shepsle, John Wallis, Jeremy Weinstein, and Susan Williams.

Two excellent reviewers, one of them being Melissa Schwartzberg, saved me from mistakes big and small, refined my language and made the book immeasurably better. I hope to have done justice to their suggestions. If I didn't, and if other errors remain, it is wholly my fault. A special thanks also goes to the team at Princeton University Press: to my editors, Rob Tempio and Matt Rohal, for their advice and guidance throughout the publication process, to Dimitri Karetnikov for his help in drawing the map, to Brittany Micka-Foos for copyediting, to Jill Harris for steering the book through the production phase, and to everyone else who contributed behind the scenes.

Now to the special people of my life. Two friends have meant so much to me and to this project. These are Jessica Steinberg and Cyanne Loyle, my dear friends. It has not always been easy to see the many steps that took the project to its current form. Without them, I am not sure this book would exist. And not much of value would exist at all without my partner, Artemis Brod, who is my best friend and the source of all happiness.

This book is dedicated to two groups of people. My family, Franca, Felice, Andrea, Giulia, and Alice, who have been an enduring source of support for the choices that I made in the last decade. And my intellectual mentors, Josh Ober and Barry Weingast, whose pervasive influence in my work and in my life is the greatest gift I have ever received.

CREATING A CONSTITUTION

Introduction

IN EARLY August 2016, I traveled to Yangon, Myanmar, to attend a meeting with representatives of some of the country's ethnic minorities. The subject: constitutional reforms. Myanmar has a tough history of conflict between the central government and the ethnic states. In some parts of the country—for example Karen State—a civil war has been ongoing since independence in 1948. In other parts, the conflict has formally ceased, but ethnic demands have hardly been heeded. A mere three weeks after the ratification of the Nationwide Ceasefire Agreement (NCA) in October 2015, the party of Nobel Peace Prize winner Aung San Suu Kyi—the National League for Democracy—won in a landslide election. Since then, three peace conferences were held, in August 2016, May 2017, and July 2018. They are referred to as "21st Century Panglong," after the historical 1947 Panglong agreement between Aung San (Aung San Suu Kyi's father) and representatives of Kachin, Shan, and Chin ethnic groups. The Panglong agreement established the principle of "full autonomy in internal administration for the Frontier Areas" (Tinker 1983: 404–5). But no full autonomy ever materialized for Myanmar's ethnic groups. Aung San was assassinated in his office five months after Panglong. Within a year, parts of the country had devolved into civil war. In 1962, the military (Tadmadaw) took power—and kept it for almost half a century. Today, the relationship between the government and the ethnic groups remains fraught, despite the transition to electoral democracy. Not all ethnic groups have signed the NCA, and there is frustration around the lack of progress of the 21st Century Panglong.

Myanmar's path to peace and prosperity faces many obstacles. One of these is the 2008 constitution. The preamble captures the problem concisely, where it states that "We, the National people, firmly resolve that we shall steadfastly adhere to the objectives of nondisintegration of the Union, nondisintegration of National solidarity, and perpetuation of sovereignty." These objectives justified half a century of military rule, and they are tightly enshrined in constitutional provisions that endow the military with an enormous amount of power, provide for a strong centralized control of the country (largely through the Office of the President and the General Administration Department), and pay little more than lip service to federalism and other forms of devolution of power (Williams 2014). These objectives are hard to square with ethnic demands for meaningful forms of self-determination. For Myanmar to achieve a lasting peace, the 2008 constitution will have to be significantly, if not completely, rewritten.

We live in an era of constitution-making. More than half of the world's constitutions have been drafted in the last half century. Of these, forty-two were born since the dawn of the new millennium.[1] The trend is not likely to end any time soon. At the time of writing in April 2019, some countries are discussing major constitutional amendments to curtail the influence of all-powerful actors, like the Tadmadaw in Myanmar and the Office of the President in Liberia. Other countries are waiting to formulate permanent constitutional agreements, like South Sudan, and Yemen. Others yet have pursued constitutional change as a vehicle to shake ossified democratic institutions, like Italy—but failed.

In response to this trend, the study of constitutions has also burgeoned. But one question remains elusive to scholars and practitioners in the field, despite its centrality to the design of governance institutions: How do stable, growth-enhancing constitutional structures emerge and endure?

The existing literature does not provide a comprehensive answer to this question. In part, this is due to a lack of interdisciplinary engagement. We have a wealth of descriptive historical accounts of how particular constitutions have emerged; a number of positive theoretical analyses of the conditions that foster constitutional stability; and a growing set of empirical studies of the relationship between constitutional provisions and economic performance. A parallel literature in political economy explores the institutional foundations of political and economic development, but pays little attention to the role of constitutions.

In this book, I combine tools and methodologies from institutional analysis, political economy, and history. I argue that the creation of a stable, growth-enhancing constitution requires a set of steps. These include a *consensus* on a shared set of values capable of commanding support over time, a *self-enforcing*

---

1. These are Hungary, Kyrgyzstan, Turkmenistan, Kosovo, Montenegro, Dominican Republic, Ecuador, Bolivia, Tunisia, Egypt, Syria, Morocco, Iraq, Afghanistan, Qatar, Bahrain, Chad, Cote d'Ivoire, Central African Republic, Congo, Zimbabwe, Somalia, Kenya, Angola, Guinea, Niger, Madagascar, DRC, Swaziland, Burundi, Mozambique, Rwanda, Senegal, Comoros, Nepal, Bhutan, Maldives, Pakistan, Thailand, Myanmar, East Timor, and Fiji. The number grows to forty-six if we count the interim constitutions of Libya, Yemen, South Sudan, and Sudan. Data: Comparative Constitutions Project (accessed Feb. 5, 2019).

institutional structure that reflects those values, and regulatory mechanisms for policy-making that enable *trade-offs of inclusion*. By trade-off of inclusion, I mean a process whereby institutional access is extended differentially across the domains of politics, economics, law, and society to increase prosperity without jeopardizing stability.

I.1. Existing Accounts

Positive accounts of constitutional stability from the field of institutional analysis focus on the role of self-enforcing rules—that is, rules that make all parties better off, eliminating the need of a third-party enforcer tasked with sanctioning violations.[2] These rules impose limits on the government, provide incentives for actors to acquiesce, and create institutional mechanisms to punish those who renege (Hardin 1989; North and Weingast 1989; Ordeshook 1992; Greif 1998; Gonzales de Lara, Greif and Jha 2008; Mittal and Weingast 2013).[3] Self-enforcing constitutional *equilibria* are thus, by definition, stable. They are also associated with increases in economic performance (see especially North and Weingast 1989; Greif 1998). The notion of self-enforcing constitutions is therefore a useful heuristic to investigate how constitutions may support political stability and economic growth.

However, analyzing constitutional stability as a product of self-enforcing rules tells us nothing about the processes that brought those rules into being. One example will suffice. North and Weingast's (1989) influential study of the Glorious Revolution in seventeenth-century England focuses on the Crown's arbitrary and confiscatory power as the driver of constitutional breakdown, and describes the fiscal and institutional changes that successfully addressed that problem as the elements of a self-enforcing pact (1989: 808–12, 815–17). But how did actors with profoundly different interests and preferences (the Crown and the Parliament) come to agree to those changes? North and Weingast's story does not say.[4]

---

2. On self-enforcing democracy: Przeworski (1991; 2006); Weingast (1997; 2004); Boix (2003); Acemoglu and Robinson (2006); North, Wallis, and Weingast (2009); Fearon (2011). On self-reinforcing institutions: Greif and Laitin (2004).

3. Like Hardin (1999) I highlight the relevance of processes of consensus-building for a coordination theory of constitution-making. But consensus here is not mere acquiescence. It is instead a positive (because it aids coordination) and normative (because it is grounded on a shared view of the basic elements of good government—what I later refer to as legality) building block of constitution-making.

4. Similarly, Mittal and Weingast's (2013) theory of self-enforcing constitutions posits consensus as one of the conditions for stability but does not explain how the consensus emerges.

Scholars in other disciplinary fields have similarly downplayed this preconstitutional stage. In some important respects, the trend began as early as 1651, when political philosopher Thomas Hobbes postulated the existence of an original covenant, a "unity of . . . all," at the heart of the foundational act of government—the establishment of Leviathan (1994 [1651]: 109). But Hobbes never addressed the question of how exactly humankind would reach this foundational agreement, given the obstacles to cooperation that doom people to live in the state of nature to begin with.[5] More recent studies of constitution-making also begin, so to speak, when the struggle ends. The Comparative Constitutions Projects (CCP) relies on the existence of constitutions as documents (Elkins, Ginsburg, and Melton 2009: 6 and ch. 3; Ginsburg and Huq 2016). Indubitably, constitutional provisions reflect compromises, but then again it remains unclear why the parties chose the option to compromise in the first place. Similarly, constitutional political economy (CPE) moves from the existence of constitutions to assess the impact of different provisions on various political and economic outcomes (Persson and Tabellini 2003; Voigt 1997; 2011).[6] Comparative constitutional analyses have shed much-needed light on

---

In the authors' application of the theory to America's early constitutional struggles, the focal solution is derivative of the equilibrium constitutional rules. The 1787 constitutional pact in the United States imposed limits on the power of the federal government—including separation of powers, federalism, enumerated powers, the bill of rights, and parity between North and South (2013: 290–91). Those limits constituted "bright lines focal solutions defining for citizens the appropriate use of governmental power" (2013: 291). But it remains unclear how federalist and anti-federalists came to agree on a particular set of bright-lines rules that satisfied their differing views of what an optimal constitutional solution would look like.

5. More specifically, by appealing to reason, individuals can understand that it is in their long-term interest to establish Leviathan. However, it is unclear that rationality can trump other features of human nature (e.g., competition, greed, and diffidence) and that it can do so for all at the same time. These objections concern the commonwealth by institution more than the commonwealth by acquisition. Many thanks to Arash Abizadeh for helping me clarify this important distinction.

6. Constitutional political economy emerged as a field in the 1980s as part of the revival of institutional analyses connected with the New Institutional Economics of Douglass North. The founders of the discipline, James Buchanan and Gordon Tullock (1962), pioneered the normative approach to constitutional political economy, stressing the relevance of consensus. For Buchanan and Tullock, consensus required unanimity as a means to achieve, at great costs, a Pareto-optimal result. The positive strand of the literature began with an assessment of whether constitutional rules affect economic and political outcomes, including macroeconomic, fiscal policy, and governance variables (cf. Voigt 2011: 210). Other contributions have focused on the procedures for choosing or amending constitutional rules. Elster (1993) focused on constitutional conventions, and later analyzed the motivations guiding framers (1995; 2000). Riker

constitutions as critical determinants of state performance. But like studies of institutions-as-*equilibria*, these analyses fail to account for the processes that bring constitutions into being.

To say that the question of constitutional origins has been downplayed in some branches of the literature does not mean of course that the question has never been asked. An influential theory attributes constitutional origins and design to processes of diffusion and imitation across countries (Simmons and Elkins 2005; Tushnet 2009). Another explanation focuses on the role of framers (Ackerman 1991; Elster 1995; 2000; Schofield 2006).[7] These studies concentrate on the processes that bring constitutions into being, but tend to downplay the question of constitutional endurance.[8]

The goals of this book are twofold. First, to weave these strands of the literature to provide a theoretically rigorous and empirically new account of constitutional emergence and endurance. Second, to connect the study of constitutions to the study of the conditions that foster political and economic development.[9]

(1983; 1984) focused on the role of creative processes (herestetics) in structuring bargaining among actors. More recent work in constitutional political economy has sought to endogenize constitutional provisions, but no comprehensive theory of constitutional emergence and performance has yet been developed (on presidentialism vs. parliamentarism: Aghion et al. 2004; Robinson and Torvik 2016; cf. Voigt 2011: 246–47).

7. On cooperative vs. distributional models of framers' behavior: Negretto (2013: 49–53). Negretto's own account of constitution-making processes in Latin America blends a choice model with endogenous and exogenous drivers of constitutional emergence. For Negretto, constitutional choice depends on preexisting constitutional structures, partisan interests, and the relative power of reformers. My account is compatible with Negretto's approach in that it highlights actors' choices, as well as exogenous shocks and endogenous processes. However, the case of Athens highlights a different set of factors driving constitutional choice.

8. Ackerman's (1991) discussion of constitutional change is of course related to the question of constitutional endurance, but endurance is not the focus of his contribution (on constitutional change and popular constitutionalism, see also Griffin (1996); Kramer (2004)). Similarly, Ginsburg and Huq (2018: ch. 6) focus on constitutional design to minimize the risk of democratic backsliding. Finally, a number of studies of political transitions, peace processes, and interim constitutions address, if tangentially, the question of constitutional process (see, e.g., Alston and Ginsburg 2017).

9. My account is compatible with Alston et al.'s (2018) recent analysis of constitutional change as driven by changes in what they term "core beliefs" (see also Alston et al. 2016). By "core beliefs" the authors mean beliefs about how the world works, to be distinguished from "behavioral beliefs," defined as beliefs about other people's behavior. In their model, constitutional change occurs when core beliefs become malleable as a result of a gap between expectations and outcomes. Malleable beliefs, in turn, create "windows of opportunity" for leaders.

Recent work in political economy has highlighted the critical role of inclusive institutions for development (North, Wallis, and Weingast 2009; Acemoglu and Robinson 2012; 2016). Existing theories, however, remain rather vague on the causal mechanisms driving the emergence of inclusive institutions. For Acemoglu and Robinson (2012), inclusive institutions develop at "historical conjunctures" that jumpstart "virtuous cycles."[10] North, Wallis, and Weingast's theory of social orders provides somewhat more detail, but the question of how a polity moves through stages of development—from natural state to the doorstep conditions and finally to open access, where inclusion is more fully realized—remains undertheorized.[11]

We know, therefore, relatively little about how inclusive institutions emerge. But we know that constitutions matter. Findings from the CCP suggest that constitutional endurance is correlated with constitutions that are more flexible, more inclusive, and more specific—that is, constitutions that can adapt to changing circumstances, include relevant social and political actors, and incorporate more detailed provisions (Elkins, Ginsburg, and Melton 2009: 8, ch. 4). The CCP thus suggests an important correlation between inclusivity and constitutional endurance. I further probe this correlation by analyzing how constitutional structures may support the emergence of inclusive institutions.

Core beliefs create a new institutional structure during "constitutional moments," and take root through a process of "institutional deepening." This book provides a more fine-grained lens to understand the processes that take place during the critical stages of "window of opportunity" and "institutional deepening."

10. Acemoglu and Robinson (2012) suggest that economic development relies on the establishment of inclusive political institutions. Inclusive political institutions, in turn, rely on state capacity and on a broad distribution of power in society. More recently (2016: 41), the authors argued that the processes of building state capacity and fostering a broad distribution of power occur in a "basin of attraction," and understanding this basin of attraction is a key to "understanding the emergence of inclusive political institutions." Here, the authors take up the case of ancient Athens at the time of the transition to democracy, suggesting that the institutionalization of informal social norms within the polis' central structure enabled the Athenians to strengthen the state while maintaining a broad level of citizen control over state institutions.

11. North, Wallis, and Weingast (2009) speak of development as the transition from a natural state to an open-access order via three doorstep conditions: perpetuity for the state and other organizations, rule of law for elites, and political control over the sources of violence. An open access society, for the authors, features impersonal, perpetual, and inclusive political and economic institutions.

I.2. Constitution Building in Ancient Athens

To explore the conditions that enable stable, growth-enhancing constitutions to emerge and endure, I analyze the case of ancient Athens.

Many readers will be familiar with the fact that, in the classical period (roughly from 508 to 322 BCE[12]), the ancient city-state (*polis*; pl. *poleis*) of Athens created the world's first large-scale experiment in democratic governance. For almost two hundred years, the Athenians governed themselves through institutions that featured the active participation of the entire adult male population (ca. forty thousand to sixty thousand people).[13] Some readers may even be familiar with the fact that, in the same period, Athens sustained remarkable levels of economic and social development (Morris 2004; Ober 2015a; Bresson 2016): economic growth matched that of the most successful polities on the eve of the Industrial Revolution;[14] the population was healthy and urbanized (Morris 2004; Lagia 2015; Hansen 2006a; 2008); real wages were surprisingly high by premodern standards (Scheidel 2010); and inequality—in terms of wealth, landholding, and income—was low, indicating a reasonably fair distribution of the proceeds of prosperity (Kron 2011; 2014; Morris 1998; Ober 2015a; 2017).[15]

But classical Athens was not always democratic, stable, and prosperous. In the late fifth century, the polis' democratic institutions succumbed to the joint pressure of coups and institutional erosion, the two leading causes of contemporary democracies' death (O'Donnell 1973; Linz 1978; Levitsky and Ziblatt

---

12. All dates are BCE unless otherwise specified.

13. A complete history of Athens' constitutional development would encompass the original transition to democracy, as well as the events that I discuss here. Tracking this development in its entirety, however, goes beyond the scope of the present book. I focus on the events that took place in the late fifth and fourth centuries for two reasons: first, Athens' democratization has been the object of much recent social scientific scholarship (e.g., Fleck and Hanssen 2006; Lyttkens 2006; Ober 2008; McCannon 2012; Hanssen and Fleck 2013; Acemoglu and Robinson 2016); second, in the fourth century, the absence of the empire provides a cleaner case for an analysis of Athens' institutions.

14. Population growth measured at 0.4% per annum; aggregate consumption measured at 0.6–0.9% per annum (as compared to Holland's 0.5%); per capita consumption measured at 0.15% per annum (as compared to Holland's 0.2% and Rome's 0.1%): Morris (2004; 2005); Saller (2005); Ober (2010; 2015a). Ober (2015a) modifies Morris' earlier estimate of per capita consumption (as ranging between 0.07 and 0.14%).

15. Gini coefficients for wealth, landholding, and income have been estimated at 0.708; 0.382–0.386; and 0.40–0.45, respectively. The last measure includes slaves and resident foreigners.

2018; Ginsburg and Huq 2018). In the span of a decade, roughly from 413 to 403, Athens experienced five constitutional transitions, lost the empire that was the foundation of its economic structure, was bereaved of half of its citizen population, and ultimately devolved into civil war. After the civil war, the Athenians reestablished democracy. The new democracy remained in place until the Macedonian conquest of Greece eighty years later. During this period, Athens was once again stable and remarkably prosperous (Ober 2008).

Why was democracy reestablished, after it had failed? Why was the new democracy stable, after a decade of instability? And how did the polis manage to restore prosperity, after such a tremendous shock to its economic structure?

I argue that Athens' political and economic development owed to the creation of a new constitutional order that shaped the direction of institutional change, social choices, and economic policy throughout the fourth century. By "constitution," I do not mean a written document laying out detailed principles of government. Athens produced no such document. Instead, following Ordeshook (1993: 232), I define the Athenian constitution, minimalistically, as a "mechanism . . . to guide the formulation of legislation and law."[16]

Athens' constitution was grounded on a consensus on legality that opposing parties hammered out during a decade of violent constitutional struggles.[17] The consensus inspired the creation of a set of new, self-enforcing institutions. These included the creation of a written law code; an additional legislative institution; new procedures to regulate the process of lawmaking; and measures to protect people's freedom, property, and dignity. As such, the new institutions defined both a series of substantive rights—or, with Ober (2000), "quasi-rights"[18]—as well as the rules for making rules. The rules for making rules regulated the decision-making process in ways that encouraged policy innovation without threatening the social order. Throughout the fourth century, bargaining under the constitution enabled a gradual expansion of institutional access to economically productive noncitizen actors in the spheres of law, the economy, and society. Access to political institutions, and thus to the

16. This definition does not mean to suggest that we should understand the Athenian constitution as a small-c constitution (constitution qua constitutional order: Elkins, Ginsburg, and Melton 2009; or core beliefs: Alston et al. 2018). Instead, as I explain below, despite the absence of a written document, the Athenian constitution laid out both substantive rights and procedural rules for making rules.

17. My reading offers support to recent arguments concerning the importance of consensus in Athenian politics and deliberative settings (Canevaro 2018b), regardless of whether majority rule was or was not the decision-making mechanism of choice (Schwartzberg 2013b).

18. With the label "quasi-right," Ober (2000: 30) distinguishes between the modern definition of right as "natural, innate and inalienable," and the Athenian notion of rights as "performative and contingent."

decision-making process, remained instead restricted to Athenian citizens. The constitution therefore enabled a trade-off of inclusion between political, economic, legal, and social institutions that fostered prosperity without jeopardizing stability.

The case of ancient Athens allows us to take an additional step in the exploration of the institutional bargains that lie on a country's road to development. The existing paradigm focuses on political inclusion as the precondition for access to other goods. This process is well captured in North, Wallis, and Weingast's "incorporation of citizens" (2009: 118–21). In their account, political inclusion in England, as well as in France and the United States, yielded access to the rule of law, infrastructure and education, labor protection, and social insurance programs.[19] The practice goes back at least as far as the Romans, who extended citizenship as a result of both conquest and emancipation.[20] But in postulating the primacy of the political, the existing paradigm obscures the possibility of a series of intermediate steps. The story of Athens suggests that meaningful forms of welfare-enhancing inclusion need not await the high-stakes bargains that compel dominant elites to share power (Carugati 2019b).

I.3. Methodology

Ancient Athens provides a remarkable laboratory to study the determinants of successful constitution building. First and foremost, Athens' constitution was, like Athens itself, relatively simpler in its institutional make-up compared to modern constitutions. Second, constitution building in Athens was a thoroughly experimental process not driven by external models or preexisting commitments to a given normative or institutional structure—it was constitution building, so to speak, in the wild.[21] Third, insights derived from considering

19. The expansion of access to nonpolitical institutions is not unique to ancient Athens. In France, for example, economic rights for women preceded the franchise, but still may have had empowering effects (Dermineur 2014). Similarly, enforceable property rights existed for merchants in many parts of medieval and early modern Europe (Milgrom, North, and Weingast 1990; Kadens 2015). Athens provides a particularly suitable laboratory to study these processes for reasons that I discuss below.

20. By the beginning of the first century BCE, all those residing in the Italian peninsula were Roman citizens. The process continued during the imperial period, and culminated in Caracalla's edict of 212 CE, which extended citizenship to all free men in the Roman Empire.

21. Athens' previous democratic structure should not lead us astray. As I argue in chapter 2, Athens' commitment to democracy was shattered in the late fifth century. If democracy was restored, it was due in part to the failure of alternative constitutional options, and in part to the Athenians' ability to adapt democratic institutions in response to the crisis.

consensus mechanisms within a population are arguably much clearer than those derived from analyzing consensus mechanisms within a group that weakly represents a population. Bargaining among elites necessarily implicates the organizations and groups they represent, which in turn implicates complex theories of political representation (see e.g., Wallis, in progress; Alston et al. 2018: ch. 8). For all these reasons, ancient Athens offers a cleaner case for analysis, enabling the study of the *minima* of successful constitution building.

Another reason to select ancient Athens as a case study is that constitution building there was strikingly successful. According to the CCP, the average lifespan of a modern constitution is nineteen years, and only a handful of constitutions have survived for more than fifty years (Elkins, Ginsburg, and Melton 2009: 1–2). Athens' constitution lasted for over eighty years, presiding over a period in which the polis rose from the ashes of a civil war to reach the zenith of Greek prosperity.[22]

Finally, Athens provides a remarkably well-documented case of constitution-making and development. First, we have a number of literary accounts of the constitutional struggles and reforms, written by firsthand witnesses of the events (like the orator Andocides and the historian Thucydides), as well as later commentators (like the philosopher Aristotle). The literary sources are complemented by a wealth of epigraphic and archaeological evidence regarding, first and foremost, inscribed laws and policies. In addition, two recent landmark books have compiled and distilled this evidence (Shear 2011; Carawan 2013), providing new and compelling accounts of many aspects of this important period of Athenian history. Alongside primary and secondary accounts of the constitutional struggles, there are a number of new interdisciplinary studies of Athenian politics and economics. Indeed, this ancient case study is rapidly becoming a favorite among political economists (e.g., Acemoglu and Robinson 2016; Fleck and Hanssen 2006; forthcoming; Hanssen and Fleck 2012; 2013; Tridimas 2011; 2012; 2014; 2015; 2016; 2017), economists and economic historians (e.g., Bergh and Lyttkens 2014; Lyttkens 1991; 2008; 2010; 2013; Kaiser 2007), and legal scholars (e.g., Lanni and Vermeule 2012; 2013; Werhan 2012; Gowder 2014; 2016).[23]

22. In this context, it would be interesting to systematically compare the average lifespan of constitutions among what North, Wallis, and Weingast (2009) call "open access orders." The constitutions of open access orders in Western Europe and North America, arguably the most developed countries in the world, average eighty-seven years. It is harder to determine which countries are open access in other regions of the world, but it is nevertheless clear from the data that the average lifespan of constitutions in other regions is much shorter.

23. The list is not meant to be exhaustive. In the course of the book, I will return to these contributions and add many others, including the work I conducted with my coauthors in

There are, of course, gaps in the historical record. As we will see, in order to track the development of Athenian policy in the fourth century, I support the existing ancient evidence with a model of decision-making. The model allows me to reconstruct the incentives regulating the behavior of actors in the public institutions of the polis, even if we do not have a complete record of the policies passed during the eighty years in which the constitution was in place. Additionally, two types of evidence would be ideal to establish a causal relationship between the constitution and political and economic development. First, comparative evidence from other Greek poleis suggesting that similar arrangements yielded stability and growth elsewhere and, conversely, that the absence of such arrangements yielded unrest and stagnation. But because we know so little about other Greek poleis, this investigation is unfeasible. Second, evidence that the collapse of the constitutional structure in Athens coincided with a decline in political and economic development. This evidence exists, but is largely inconclusive. After the Battle of Amorgos against the Macedonians in the year 322, the institutions that sustained the fourth-century constitutional order—most notably the law-making institution of *nomothesia* (on which more in chapter 2)—were dismantled and never resurfaced (Canevaro 2011: 58). The collapse of the constitutional structure coincided with frequent constitutional transitions and a slow, yet ineluctable decline in Athens' prosperity.[24] It would however be preposterous to push this evidence too far. Massive changes affected Athens' stability and prosperity after 322, which go well beyond the demise of its constitutional structure. The year before the Battle of Amorgos, Alexander the Great had conquered the entire known world, and the Macedonian Empire reached as far as India. In the vastly expanded Hellenistic world, the Greek poleis became pawns in the endgame of world conquest—first with Alexander himself, and later with his successors. As the epicenter of the Mediterranean shifted abruptly toward the East, the loss of the polis' constitutional structure remains an important, but perhaps only a secondary factor in its political and economic decline. To address these evidentiary constraints, in chapter 5 I collect and analyze the available comparative and

---

economics, political science, and law: Randy Calvert, Robert Fleck, Gillian Hadfield, Andrew Hanssen, and Barry Weingast.

24. Greek economic growth declined in the third century compared to the peaks reached in the fifth and, particularly, in the fourth (Ober 2015a: 3), though perhaps not as abruptly as previous scholarship suggested. Athenian prosperity followed the general trend, though the city's prosperity may have declined somewhat more abruptly than that of other Greek poleis (compare Ober 2015a: 3 with Ober 2008: 293). Note, however, that development proxies are different in the two studies: Ober (2008) measures Athenian state capacity as proxied by military power, public buildings, and domestic programs, while Ober (2015a) measures development in terms of population and consumption.

counterfactual evidence to show that, in the absence of the new constitution, Athens' development in the fourth century would have lagged.

The case-study approach raises the important question of the generalizability of the results presented here. While there are obvious limits to what ancient Athens can teach us about constitution-making today, any in-depth case study would be subject to similar limitations. Constitutions are indeed written under special circumstances, but that does not mean that endogenizing them is a "nearly impossible" task (Voigt 2011: 246–47). After all, if we take this historicist-sounding argument to its logical extreme, the whole field of comparative politics (including positive constitutional political economy) would cease to exist.

There is much to learn from this unique historical case study. Indeed, the features that make Athens the perfect case to study the question that animates this book—how do stable, growth-enhancing constitutional structures emerge and endure?—also make it unparalleled in comparative politics. While I discuss several contributions to a number of different disciplinary fields below, one preliminary point deserves specific mention here. Studying constitution-making in ancient Athens is not meant to yield a set of institutional outcomes to be replicated in modern nations. The question for the people of Myanmar, to return to the case with which I opened this introduction, is not so much whether to choose between the models of, say, the United States, Germany, or ancient Athens. Whereas the details of Athens' case cannot and should not be generalized—for example, as we will see, the specific content of Athens' consensus on legality was rooted in Athens' legal culture and traditions—the case of Athens suggests a series of minimal conditions for successful constitution-making that consider both institutional structures and the values that sustain them. Moreover, Athens' case shows that the goals that contemporary societies seek to achieve by designing complex formal constitutional arrangements—namely, democracy and economic growth—were historically achieved in the absence of such arrangements. As such, Athens offers a new body of theoretical and empirical evidence that we can build on to spur theory development and testing.

I.4. Alternative Explanations

In this book, then, I argue that a new constitution fostered political and economic development. But what other variables could have caused Athenian development in the fourth century?

To begin, Athens' development could have been indebted to geographic or cultural factors—the two alternative leading explanations for differential developmental outcomes in the literature (Acemoglu and Robinson 2012).

Geographic explanations are the easiest to rule out. Athens was not always democratic, and it was not always stable. As to the city's prosperity, the classical peak was not replicated until the twentieth century (cf. appendix B; Ober 2015a). As we will see in chapter 5, geography did play a role in Athens' development—particularly when it came to endowing the polis with a fine harbor—but geography alone certainly did not determine Athens' stability and prosperity in the classical period. Ruling out cultural explanations is perhaps more difficult—after all, in the fifth century, the Athenians were known for their "interventionist hyperactivism," or "busybodiness" (*polypragmosynē*, Thuc. 6.87.3). In a famous passage from Thucydides' *History of the Peloponnesian War* (1.70.2–3; trans. Strassler 1996), the Corinthians describe the Athenians as "addicted to innovation . . . adventurous beyond their power, and daring beyond their judgment."[25] So perhaps the Athenians' cultural traits are responsible for the performance of their polity. But then again, if cultural variables were to explain Athens' success, it is hard to justify why such growth- and stability-enhancing traits thrived only in the classical period. Hiving off culture from institutions makes it impossible to answer this question.

Institutions thus played a role in Athens' political and economic development. But was Athens' development simply the product of path-dependent institutional processes? Because Athens was democratic, stable, and prosperous before and after the late fifth-century crisis, critics may argue that the new constitution had no impact on stability and growth. In terms of political structure, the costs of creating nondemocratic institutions after a century of democracy were sufficiently high that it was neither in the interests of the elite, nor of the masses to incur those costs. In terms of economic structure, the imperial fifth century had placed Athens and its harbor, Piraeus, at the center of Eastern Mediterranean trade and the costs of finding another commercial hub were prohibitively high for both Athenian and non-Athenian traders, especially in the short run.[26]

25. All translations of Thucydides are from Strassler 1996, unless otherwise noted. To facilitate access to the ancient sources, throughout the book, I used translations from the online database Perseus (http://www.perseus.tufts.edu/hopper/) or other standard translations.

26. A more nuanced version of the argument runs as follows: Athens' prosperity in the fourth century depended on a relatively quick recovery (before investing in building new port facilities elsewhere became an attractive solution for rival poleis), and a quick recovery was made possible by two quite obvious factors: first, the extent of the war-led crisis, which yielded a large peace dividend in its aftermath; and second, cash from Persia, which, in an effort to curtail the rising power of Sparta after the Peloponnesian War, funded a military revolt in Greece. The question of whether Athens received money from Persia is problematic. Xenophon denies it (*Hell.* 3.5.2), but other sources confirm the disbursement (*Hell. Oxy.* VII.2ff.; Plut. *Artax.* 20; Paus. 3.9.8), and the fact is accepted by many scholars (cf. Seager, 1994: 98). Persian

Neither of these arguments is supported by the evidence. In the last decade of the fifth century, not one, not two, but three oligarchic governments ruled Athens. This fact suggests a willingness to invest in oligarchy. If we want to understand why oligarchy was not the option of choice, we must investigate the reasons for its failure—a task to which I turn in chapter 2. Similarly, path-dependent economic explanations fail to take into account the massive changes in Athens' economic structure after the loss of the empire. The harbor of Piraeus surely provided a favorable location for trade (and thus foreign merchants had conspicuous incentives to stick with Piraeus). But Piraeus was not the only such location in the Aegean (cf. chapter 5 and appendixes A and B). In fact, after the Macedonian conquest of Athens in the year 322, Piraeus ceased to provide the primary destination for Aegean trade. As Athens' power declined, Rhodes and Alexandria rose to prominence. There was nothing intrinsic to Piraeus that prevented this shift. Without the empire, Athens had to come up with an entirely new set of policies to incentivize foreign merchants to trade in Piraeus. Path-dependent explanations cannot account for these aspects of policy innovation. As such, path-dependent explanations fail to provide a robust account of Athens' fourth-century political and economic development.

In the book *Democracy and Knowledge,* Josiah Ober offers an alternative explanation of Athens' development. For Ober (2008: 37–38), "democratic Athens was able to take advantage of its size and resources . . . because the costs of participatory political practices were overbalanced by superior returns to social cooperation resulting from useful knowledge as it was organized and deployed in the simultaneously innovation-promoting and learning-based context of democratic institutions and culture." For Ober, then, Athens' development owed to the polis' democracy, and, in particular, to the ability of democratic institutions to aggregate, align, and codify useful knowledge dispersed across the population. It was because Athens knew what the Athenians knew (2008: 118) that the polis was so successful. The argument of this book is not incompatible with Ober's. Indeed, I show that if democratic institutions were critical to Athens' performance, in the fourth century the Athenian constitution was critical to the existence of democratic institutions.

The late fifth century constitutional struggles and institutional reforms have been the object of much attention among classical scholars.[27] However, the

---

money, then, played a part in Athens' recovery, as it enabled Athens to build a new fleet, construct new walls, and regain control of the grain-rich islands of Lemnos, Imbros, and Scyros. Once the polis acquired the means for its own defense and expansion, it was able to harness the advantages of its former success.

27. Despite the increasing attention devoted to classical Athens as a comparative case study, few social scientists have focused on this period. Ober (2015a) focuses on Greece as a whole.

existing literature is lacking in two respects. First, in terms of periodization, most studies concentrate on reconstructing one (or more) episode in a long chain of constitutional transitions, and keep the events before and after the end of the Peloponnesian War in the year 404 rigidly separate (e.g., Krentz 1982; Kagan 1987; Strauss 1987a; E. M. Harris 1990; but not Shear 2011, as we will see). Second, in terms of analytical focus, much has been written on the restoration of democracy in the year 403, but the assumption animating these studies is that democracy in Athens was the only game in town and oligarchy is never considered a real possibility (this assumption, as I will show in chapter 2, is mistaken). As a result, existing accounts seek to explain not why democracy was reestablished, but only why the new democracy was stable. Among these explanations, some focus on the strength of Athens' democratic culture, especially as enshrined in the amnesty agreement that put an end to the civil war (Loening 1987; Loraux 2002); others focus on the role of Sparta as a third-party enforcer of the amnesty (Todd 1985); and others yet focus on the institutional reforms that followed the restoration of democracy (Harrison 1955; MacDowell 1975; Hansen 1978; 1979a; 1979b; 1985; 1987b; 1990a; 1999; Robertson 1990; Rhodes 1980; 1991; 2010; Eder 1995; Carawan 2002; R. Osborne 2003). Few studies consider the question of the long-term stability of the new institutional structure, but rarely analyze the evidence beyond the third decade of the fourth century (Wolpert 2002; Quillin 2002).[28] None of the studies mentioned above considers the question of the relationship between Athens' new institutions and the polis' economic performance in the post-war period, let alone in the rest of the fourth century.

Acemoglu and Robinson (2016); Lyttkens (2006); Fleck and Hanssen (2006); McCannon (2012); and Hanssen and Fleck (2013) focus on the archaic period. Fleck and Hanssen (forthcoming) do take up the transition between the fifth and fourth century, suggesting that economic opportunities drove institutional change. When the loss of the empire made credible commitment necessary to Athens' ability to generate revenues, the Athenians established a set of rule-of-law institutions to constrain the power of the Assembly. One may counter that when the Athenians designed new institutions in the late fifth/early fourth century, allegedly to match new wealth-generating opportunities, such wealth-generating opportunities were not yet quite obvious. But by focusing on economic opportunities, Fleck and Hanssen complement the analysis offered here, which focuses on the role of political and resource constraints in shaping the process of institutional change.

28. Carawan (2013) considers the relationship between the amnesty and the reforms, as well as the issue of stability. I discuss his contribution in greater depth in chapter 2.

I.5. Contribution

The argument that I formulate in the pages that follow differs from existing accounts in the field of classics in two major respects. First, I take seriously the possibility that oligarchy could have provided an alternative to democracy. Therefore, I seek to reconstruct the conditions that made democracy once again a viable constitutional option after the collapse of the fifth-century structure. Second, I address the question of Athens' post-imperial success as a long-term process that encompasses the reasons behind the collapse of the fifth-century democratic equilibrium, the conditions that enabled the emergence of a new equilibrium, and the sources of the new equilibrium's stability and prosperity over time. Taking a broader view of the causes and consequences of institutional change, I provide a genuinely new and testable account of the sources of Athens' political and economic development.

Moreover, the argument adds to the political economy of ancient Greece by focusing on the role of legal institutions, which are frequently ignored in the literature. Studies of the political and economic development of ancient Greece have largely followed two parallel paths. On the one hand, analyses of economic structures and performance—often focused on broad categories such as "Greece" or "the Mediterranean"—have tended to neglect their political dimension (e.g., Scheidel, Morris, and Saller 2007; Bresson 2016; E. M. Harris et al. 2016). On the other hand, research focusing on political regimes and political institutions has largely avoided the thorny question of how these institutions influence economic growth (e.g., E. W. Robinson 2011; Simonton 2017; Teegarden 2014). Only very recently, ancient political economy has begun to receive greater attention. Important contributions include Josiah Ober's *Democracy and Knowledge* (2008) and *The Rise and Fall of Classical Greece* (2015a), Emily Mackil's *Creating a Common Polity* (2013), and Monson and Scheidel's *Fiscal Regimes and the Political Economy of Premodern States* (2015). Yet, few of these studies investigate the role of laws and constitutions in supporting political and economic outcomes. This book builds a bridge across the realms of law, politics, and economics. In doing so, I move beyond the selective focus on citizen actors to uncover how citizens and noncitizens negotiated the distribution of social goods through law in the course of the fourth century. As such, the book also contributes to the growing literature that focuses on noncitizen actors and sub-polis institutions in ancient Greece (e.g., Ismard 2010; 2015; Forsdyke 2012; Kamen 2013; Kierstead 2013; Gottesman 2014; Taylor and Vlassopoulos 2015; C. Taylor 2016; 2017).

But the implications of the argument proposed here go beyond the fields of classical history and Greek political economy as such. First, the theory of how a stable, growth-enhancing democratic constitution may emerge and endure contributes to the comparative study of constitutions by identifying a series of *minima* of successful constitution building in an out-of-sample, analytically cleaner case for analysis. Second, these *minima* add a dynamic dimension to existing theories of political and economic development by highlighting the role of constitutions in fostering inclusion by enabling institutional trade-offs.

Third, although a large portion of the book is devoted to the positive analysis of institutions, the argument contributes to democratic political theory by focusing on the values that sustain a robust democracy. Political theorists, ancient and modern, emphasize equality and freedom as the hallmarks of democracy. This book stresses legality as the third fundamental attribute of democratic discourse and practice. The evidence from Athens suggests, however, that *law* need not be conceptualized as a set of rules emanating from a sovereign authority—a *state*—that is endowed with the coercive power to enforce such rules.[29] Rather than the command of a sovereign power, or a sovereign power in its own right, law in Athens is best understood as a coordination device—a tool that helped citizens solve the coordination problems that plague successful bargaining in the absence of strongly centralized coercive institutions (Hadfield and Weingast 2012; 2013; 2014; Wallis and North 2013; Wallis in progress). This nonreified notion of law-without-sovereignty and the legal and constitutional structure that was built around it, I suggest, played an important role in enabling the citizens of the world's first democracy to overcome the challenges that political theorists, ancient and modern, have traditionally seen as preordaining the fate of democracy as a system of governance. These include the erosion of the democratic advantage in times of crisis, which requires delegation of the demos' authority to an all-powerful executive (Schmitt 2004); the necessary devolution of democracy into tyranny (Plato); and the likelihood that a democratic constituency—especially when made up by laymen sitting on a hill—will eventually make some awful policy mistake (Thucydides). The Athenian democracy was not everlasting, but, in the long period analyzed in this book, a cooperation-enhancing consensus on legality helped the polis remain participatory, tyrant-free, and effective in promoting

---

29. For a discussion of the limits of this assumption in economic theory: Dixit (2004: ch. 1). Classical scholars have variously sought to apply modern definitions of "law" and "state" to ancient Athens. As a result, debates over the nature of Athenian law and the institutions of the polis have been framed in terms of "sovereignty," "rule of law," and Hobbesian/Weberian "statehood." On sovereignty: Hansen (1975); Ober (1989 a and b); Ostwald (1986); and Sealey (1987). On rule of law: E. M. Harris (2006 a and b; 2007a; 2013); Gowder (2014; 2016); contra Lanni (2004; 2006; 2009; 2016). On the statehood of the polis: Berent (1996; 1998; 2000a and b; 2004); Anderson (2009); Hansen (2002). For an overview of these debates: Carugati (2015). I return to some of these issues in the conclusion of chapter 2.

policies conducive to stability, growth, and the well-being of many, if not all of its residents.

Finally, Athenian legality as reconstructed in this book shares many elements with the modern notion of rule of law. Indeed, as I show in chapter 2, Athenian legality measures well against thick definitions of rule of law—for example, the definition proposed by legal philosopher Lon Fuller (1964).[30] This finding confirms that the relationship between rule of law and political and economic development is not just a modern phenomenon. But in significant ways, Athenian legality departed from modern notions of rule of law—first and foremost in the way in which the concept was implemented in institutional practice. No privileged body of expert judges and lawyers emerged to shepherd the Athenians toward a more accurate understanding of the laws. No public prosecutor or police force appeared to bring wrongdoers to justice or punish them on behalf of the demos.[31] The Athenians developed a concept of legality very similar to our idea of rule of law, but without any of the institutions that we are familiar with. Generations of jurists steeped in the Roman tradition looked at Athenian law with contempt. Athenian law and legal institutions, I argue, provide instead a unique alternative institutional model for building the rule of law.

I.6. Outline of the Book

Chapter 1 supplies the necessary context for the discussion of institutional change that takes place in the chapters that follow. First, I provide an account of the early development of Athens' laws and legal institutions. Second, I reconstruct Athens' political and economic structure in the period that preceded the constitutional crisis. Third, I offer an analysis of the reasons behind the collapse of democracy: namely, a combination of external pressures and a crisis of legitimacy rooted in the Assembly's inability to credibly commit to policy.

In chapter 2, I focus on the constitutional crisis and the reforms that followed it. After the collapse of democracy four distinct governments—three oligarchic and one democratic—rose and fell in the span of roughly a decade. As the Athenians responded to the failures of these governments, they came

---

30. Fuller's definition of rule of law includes eight attributes: generality, publicity, prospectivity, clarity, noncontradiction, constancy, possibility to obey, and general applicability.

31. Athens did employ small groups of individuals who performed various police functions, but the polis lacked an organized police force (Hunter 1994: 143–49). Similarly, even if a number of magistrates were responsible for prosecuting crimes that fell under their jurisdiction, private individuals initiated most public (and all private) cases (MacDowell 1978: 62; contra E. M. Harris 2007b; 2013: ch.1).

to identify, collectively, the basic features that a governmental structure had to display to command their consent. The process of consensus-building revolved around the notion of *patrios politeia* (lit. the constitution of the fathers). The meaning of patrios politeia evolved during the struggles. If under the first oligarchic government the notion expressed a vague connection with Athens' past, by the end of the civil war, it became closely associated with the concept of legality, particularly as embodied by Athens' archaic lawgiver Solon. When the constitutional struggles came to an end, the consensus on Solonian legality inspired a set of reforms, which created a new self-enforcing democratic constitution. The reforms were self-enforcing in the sense that they made both the oligarchs and the democrats better off. The oligarchs were better off under a constitutional structure that protected their rights and curtailed the excesses of the fifth-century democracy than they would have been if the winning democrats had imposed a more radical form of democracy or chosen the path of retaliation and revenge. But the democrats were also better off. First, the new constitution was a democracy. Second, going after the oligarchs would have sown the seeds of renewed conflict. Given the challenges that the city faced after the civil war, renewed conflict was not merely a costly option, but a threat to the very survival of the polis.

Identifying a set of new rules that would prevent recurring instability and civil conflict, however, was only the first task that the Athenians faced. In fact, the problem with constitutional agreements is that, over time, things change, bargaining power shifts, and shocks destabilize existing *equilibria*. But as I mentioned earlier, the Athenian constitution proved remarkably long lasting—surpassing by a long shot the average lifetime of modern constitutions—and presided over a period of remarkable economic prosperity.

In chapter 3, I argue that the constitution fostered political stability and economic growth by imposing a set of constraints on the decision-making process based on the consensus on Solonian legality, while at the same time enabling citizens to introduce innovative new measures. To overcome evidentiary concerns, I build a model that reconstructs the incentives regulating actors' behavior under the new constitutional rules. The model yields four results: first, institutional design incentivized proposers of new measures to take into account the preferences of the median, or the average Athenian. Moreover, because the median was relatively stable throughout the fourth century, preferences did not dramatically shift, ensuring a modicum of predictability and consistency over time. Third, institutional design and actors' preferences interacted to enable proposers of new measures to depart from the status quo, sometimes in significant ways. Finally, innovation was more likely to occur when sub-elite actors were involved in politics.

In chapter 4, I show that the available evidence for fiscal and economic policy is consistent with the model's predictions. In particular, I show that fiscal and economic policy reflects growth-enhancing, innovative departures from the status quo, but departures crafted with an eye to preserving the balance of power among domestic actors. Throughout the fourth century, the Athenians sought to regulate the burden of taxation on the elite. But regulating elite taxation made it even harder for the state to generate revenues in a post-imperial era. In the first half of the century, the Athenians sought to extract rents from abroad while developing market incentives at home. After the defeat in the Social War (357–355) ruled out the coercion option, the Athenians sought to intensify the exploitation of domestic natural resources, most notably the harbor of Piraeus and the Laurion silver mines. But in order to intensify the exploitation of Piraeus and Laurion, the polis had to provide incentives to those actors that were primarily involved in such exploitation. As a result, forms of access to social, legal, and economic institutions were extended to selected categories of noncitizens. Access took a variety of forms, including honors and privileges for trade-related services, mining rights, litigation rights in maritime commercial cases, and land grants. The Athenians did not, however, extend political access to these or other actors. The evidence thus reveals the existence of a trade-off of inclusion in Athens' path to development that emerged from the conflicting demands of social order and growth.

In chapter 5, I deploy the available comparative and counterfactual evidence to show that, in the absence of the new constitution, Athens' development in the fourth century would have lagged. First, I use comparative evidence from the Greek polis of Syracuse in Sicily and from Rome under the Republic. Rome and Syracuse experienced crises similar to that of Athens, but responded in different ways. In Syracuse, recurring violence yielded frequent constitutional transitions and a boom and bust cycle where productivity gains were eroded in the long run. In Rome, civil conflict generated unsustainable growth gains for the masses, and was followed by a permanent transition to authoritarianism, which yielded political stability, but also a probable decline in prosperity and an increase in inequality. Second, I counterfactually reconstruct Athens' developmental potential under an alternative constitutional option—namely, oligarchy. I identify the commercial port of Piraeus as central to Athenian prosperity and I show that, had Athens been ruled by an oligarchy, Piraeus' potential would not have been fully tapped. I conclude that an oligarchic Athens would have looked a lot like a retrenched state with limited growth potential. In the conclusion, I summarize the main findings and discuss how the theory developed here can be productively applied to reflect on constitution-making processes today.

1

Athens before the Crisis

WHEN THE Dark Age lifted its mantle from the Mediterranean in the eighth century, Greek civilization began to flourish. After three centuries of poverty and isolation following the collapse of Bronze Age society, the Greeks were progressively woven into the Mediterranean-wide commercial network built by Phoenician traders.[1] Archeological evidence reveals striking developments in terms of both population and economic growth (Snodgrass 1980; Morris 2004; 2009a; Ober 2015a). But, as the saying goes, more money, more problems.

The archaic period (750–500) was a time of political instability in Greece.[2] Economic growth created incentives for each polis to expand their slice of the pie. If competition among the city-states drove early state formation, it also exposed each city-state to the threat of subjugation by more organized neighbors. Success in interstate war depended in large part on the poleis' ability to mobilize resources and manpower. But, as Morris (2009a) has shown, military, ideological, and economic factors contributed to the relative weakness of Greek elites. On the military side, warfare technology (the hoplite phalanx as a mass citizen army) and easy access to iron for weaponry made the elites dependent on a broader class of sub-elite individuals for their survival. On the ideological side, a "middling ideology" emerged early on in the archaic period, rooted in a tradition of homogeneous Dark Age elites. Finally, on the economic side, the resources that Greek elites could muster were limited, especially when compared to those available to neighboring elites (e.g., Near Eastern kings). Greek elites in the archaic period were thus stuck between a rock and a hard place:

1. Bronze Age society: Edwards et al. (1973), vol. 2, parts 1 and 2; Renfrew (1985); Dickinson (1994); Shelmerdine (2008); Morris and Powell (2006: 46–70). Dark Age: Boardman et al. (1982), vol. 3, part 1; Snodgrass (1971); Whitley (1991; 2001); Mazarakis-Ainian (1997); Morris and Powell (2006: ch. 5.)

2. Archaic history: Murray (1993); Hall (2007); R. Osborne (2009).

because they did not control ideological, military, or economic resources, their position at the top of the political hierarchy was constantly threatened from other elites, as well as from below.

Fearing the consequences of unfettered competition, Greek elites began to devise rules to regulate their interaction. Written law appeared in this period in many parts of Greece (Gagarin 1986: 51–52). One of the earliest examples, from the law code of the Cretan city of Dreros (dated to the mid-seventh century), exemplifies the tendency of early Greek law to establish boundaries for elite competition by limiting the power of magistrates (Meiggs and Lewis 1969: 2–3; Gagarin 2005; 2008).

> The city has thus decided; when a man has been *kosmos,* the same man shall not be *kosmos* again for ten years. If he does act as *kosmos,* whatever judgment he gives, he shall owe double, and he shall lose his rights to office as long as he lives, and whatever he does as *kosmos* shall be nothing.

But written law took the Greeks only so far. The sixth century saw the rise of tyrants. The word tyrant should not lead us astray. Greek tyrants were not the sort of all-powerful, brutal rulers that the English word conjures up, or at least not always. Tyrants were members of the elite who took advantage of factional struggles to impose themselves as sole rulers (S. Lewis 2009: 26). As Snodgrass (1980: 96) noted, archaic tyranny was not a constitutional form in and of itself, but it was often superimposed on existing constitutional frameworks (cf. Anderson 2005: 177, who suggests that tyranny was an "unusually dominant style of leadership"). The power of the tyrants rested on their ability to buy off other members of the elite—through marriage, magistracies, or growth-enhancing policies—as well as to coopt the demos (Arist. *Pol.* 1310b11–17), usually by means of infrastructure projects and other forms of public expenditures. Greek tyranny was thus potentially a short-lived form of rule—and in fact few Greek tyrannies, at least in mainland Greece, survived more than two generations (Sicily, as we will see in chapter 5, was different). After the demise of the tyrants by the middle of the sixth century, sole rulership disappeared from mainland Greece. As Hanssen and Fleck (2013) have shown, in many poleis "tyranny paved the way for democracy." Athens was one of these.

The development of Athens' institutions in the archaic period broadly follows the path sketched above. Elite competition led to instability, instability led to written laws, the failure of law led to the rise of tyrants. The birth of democracy followed the collapse of tyranny. In this chapter, I selectively reconstruct elements of Athens' archaic development, focusing in particular on the work of the early lawgivers (1.1). I then turn to an analysis of the polis' fifth-century political system (1.2) and economy (1.3). I conclude with an analysis of the reasons behind the collapse of the fifth-century democracy.

1.1. Laws and Lawgivers: Athens' Archaic Development

In early archaic times, Athens was ruled by an elite of blood—the *Eupatridai* (lit. those with noble fathers)—from whose ranks were drawn the most powerful magistrates, the Nine Archons (Hansen 1999: 27–28). As economic growth created a new class of rich individuals and families, elite competition for power in the state intensified. The seventh century was marred by internal instability, widespread social violence, and the predation of one elite group upon another. Constant vying for power threatened the stability of the social order, but it also weakened the elites themselves. In addition, new opportunities for enrichment widened the gap between the rich and the poor. The Athenians, unlike other Greeks (e.g., the Corinthians), did not respond to increasing Malthusian pressures by founding colonies in agriculturally rich western lands (e.g., southern Italy). Although the evidence is thin, demographic growth in Attica may have led to labor surplus, lowering the value of Athenian labor (Ober 2015a: 147). By the sixth century, as we will see, many Athenians had fallen into debt bondage.

In the seventh and sixth centuries, the Athenians sought in various ways to curb the pernicious effect of socioeconomic conflict on the stability of the polis. Like other Greeks, the Athenians began to write down laws.

1.1.a. Draco

In the year 621, a man named Draco was tasked with writing the first law code for the city of Athens. Draco's homicide legislation—the only extant part of his code—institutionalized private initiative within the nascent Athenian legal system by establishing a series of procedures for the punishment of murderers. The new procedures identified the family of the victim as responsible for punishing the perpetrator, defined the procedures to be followed during and after the trial, outlined the penalties for the charge of homicide, and delineated the options for reconciliation among the parties (Stroud 1968; Gagarin 1981; 2008; Carawan 1998). Draco sought to remove homicide disputes from the cyclical logic of blood feuds, which fostered instability and hindered social and economic cooperation.

Despite the success of Draco's homicide legislation (which was retained down to the fourth century), his law code did not yield stability. Economic divisions worsened. The threat of violence did not abate. As [Aristotle] remarks (*Ath.Pol.* 5.2; trans. Everson 1996), "when the strife was severe, and the opposition of long standing, both sides agreed to give power to Solon as mediator, and entrusted the state to him."[3]

1.1.b. Solon

Solon set to work in the year 594 and produced a far-reaching program of political, economic, and legal reforms ([Arist.] *Ath.Pol.* 5–10; Plut. *Solon*; Blok and Lardinois 2006; cf. Almeida 2003; Leão and Rhodes 2015; Ober 2019).

Economic reforms included canceling debts, freeing those Athenians who had fallen into debt bondage, and prohibiting the future use of one's person as collateral. The reforms bettered the condition of the lower strata of the population, but they also curtailed some economic opportunities. In fact, in the absence of reforms like land redistribution, the inability to use one's person as collateral deprived the poorest Athenians of the only pathway to capital. However, other measures addressed the issue of citizens' economic welfare by reorienting Athenian society toward more productive uses of available resources. First, by banning the export of agricultural produce except for oil, Solon incentivized farmers to abandon the cultivation of drought-sensitive crops in a low-rainfall area and turn to the cultivation of high-value crops (such as olives). Second, to incentivize investments in human capital, Solon's legislation imposed penalties on fathers who failed to teach their sons a trade, and encouraged immigration of foreigners with specialized skills.

Solon's political reforms were equally far-reaching. He divided the population in four census classes with differential access to political participation. Members of all classes could participate in the Assembly, but only members of the three upper classes could be selected as office-holders.[4] [Aristotle] (*Ath. Pol.* 8.1) attributes to Solon the introduction of the lot to select magistrates, but some scholars doubt that the principle was introduced so early (Hansen 1999: 49–52). Solon also introduced a Council of Four Hundred, a body made up of one hundred members from each of the four tribes and perhaps tasked with preparing the agenda for the Assembly ([Arist.] *Ath.Pol.* 8.4; Plut. *Sol.* 19.1–2; cf. Hansen 1999: 30).

In the legal sphere, Solon introduced three notable reforms. First, he took Draco's concept of institutionalized private initiative for the prosecution of

---

3. All translations of [Aristotle]'s *Athenaion Politeia* are from Everson (1996), unless otherwise noted.

4. The Assembly as an institution most likely precedes the time of Solon. Evidence for all-male assemblies exists already in the Homeric poems. Simonton (2017: 10) suggests against earlier scholarship (e.g., Anderson 2005) that archaic assemblies, if not as powerful as their classical counterparts, still enabled meaningful popular participation.

murder and expanded it to a wide range of offenses, allowing any citizen who wished (*ho boulomenos*) to initiate a public prosecution (*graphē*) against wrong-doers.[5] Second, Solon introduced a court (the Heliaea) to hear appeals against the judgments of elite judicial magistrates.[6] At the same time, Solon retained the Council of the Areopagus, whose members were ex-Archons, and whose task was, among others, to oversee the laws. Last but not least, Solon produced a new, extensive law code. The laws were written down on wooden beams (*axones*) and probably displayed on the Acropolis (Sickinger 1999: 29–30).

Solon's reforms are critical to the present inquiry because of the role that Solon and his laws played during the late fifth-century constitutional struggles and throughout the fourth century. Three elements in particular are worthy of note. First, Solon's reforms stressed the importance of freedom, dignity, and the protection of property for all citizens against the abuses of magistrates and other citizens alike. Second, to enforce these protections, Solon stressed the impor-tance of law (by compiling a new law code) and courts (by instituting the Heliaea and enabling anyone to bring wrongdoers to justice). Third, Solon was neither a staunch democrat, nor an elitist reformer. In his poetry, Solon depicts himself as an impartial arbiter that stood among factions "as a wolf among dogs" (Fr. 36.31–32; trans. my own). His reforms sought to strike a bargain between competing political and economic interests and demands (Ober 2019: ch. 4).[7] As we will see, these elements powerfully shaped the Athenian constitutional debate and the new constitution.

Solon's reforms restructured Athens' political and legal systems, as well as its economy, in important ways. However, the historical record suggests that they failed to foster long-term stability. In fact, a mere thirty years after Solon, Athens fell prey to tyranny. The tyrant Pisistratus seems to have ruled Athens well: in the words of the historian Herodotus (1.59.5, trans. Strassler 2007; cf. [Arist.] *Ath.Pol.* 14.3), "he neither disrupted the existing political offices nor changed the laws. He managed the city in accordance with its exiting legal and political institutions, and he provided it with moderate and good government." Pisistratus championed the lower classes and strengthened civic identity,

5. For a detailed discussion of the distinction between public and private cases, their termi-nology, and the role of *ho boulomenos*: Harrison (1955: 74ff.); MacDowell (1978: 53ff.); Todd (1993: 98ff.).

6. On whether Solon's court heard appeals or tried cases in the first instance: Karachalios (2013: 258–59 and note 531).

7. Ober shows how Solon's reforms made both masses and elites better off. Drawing from bargaining theory, his key insight is that Solon's solution to a conflict involving a number of resources (land, debt, labor, and offices) was to trade off each resource at a variable rate.

especially through the promotion of festivals, such as the Panathenaea. But after his death, his sons proved incapable of holding on to power.

1.1.c. Cleisthenes

After the fall of the tyrants, the political struggle resumed. This time, the contenders were Cleisthenes, a member of the noble family of the Alcmaeonids (the same as Athens' famous fifth-century leader Pericles), and Isagoras, an aristocrat well connected in Sparta. But the rules of engagement for competing elites had shifted since the seventh century. Profound economic and demographic changes, paired with the welfare-enhancing reforms of previous statesmen had strengthened the position of the demos. Cleisthenes took advantage of these developments. Instead of seeking the support of other members of the elites, Cleisthenes sought the support of the people. And the people delivered. When Isagoras and the Spartan king Cleomenes tried to manipulate the Council and Assembly into passing measures that would de facto establish Isagoras in power, the Athenian demos revolted and besieged Isagoras and Cleomenes on the Acropolis, where they had taken refuge. Three generations later, in the comedy *Lysistrata*, the playwright Aristophanes reimagined the Athenian collective agent—the chorus of old men—portraying these events as follows (lines 273–82; trans. Ober 2007: 90):

> when Cleomenes seized [the Acropolis] previously, he did not get away unpunished, for despite his Laconian spirit he departed [from Athens] giving over to me his arms, wearing only a little cloak, hungry, dirty, hairy-faced . . . that's how ferociously I besieged that man, keeping constant guard, drawn up seventeen ranks deep at the gates.

The "Athenian Revolution" (Ober 1996), paved the way for Cleisthenes' reforms. First of all, Cleisthenes proceeded to a reorganization of the territory of Attica. The region was divided into 139 demes (the smallest administrative units). The demes were grouped in thirty larger administrative units (*trittyes*). The *trytties* were distributed across three major geographical areas (the inland, the city, and the coast). Three *trittyes*, one from each area, made up one of the ten new tribes. The new organization randomized tribe affiliation, weakening the control of geographically based clans.

The new administrative structure became the basis for political representation in the new Council of Five Hundred. Each year, fifty men from each tribe were selected by lot to serve in the Council. The Council set the agenda for the Assembly and also performed a series of important executive functions (on which more below). [Aristotle] (*Ath.Pol.* 22.1) also attributes to Cleisthenes the introduction of the practice of ostracism, which enabled the Assembly to exile

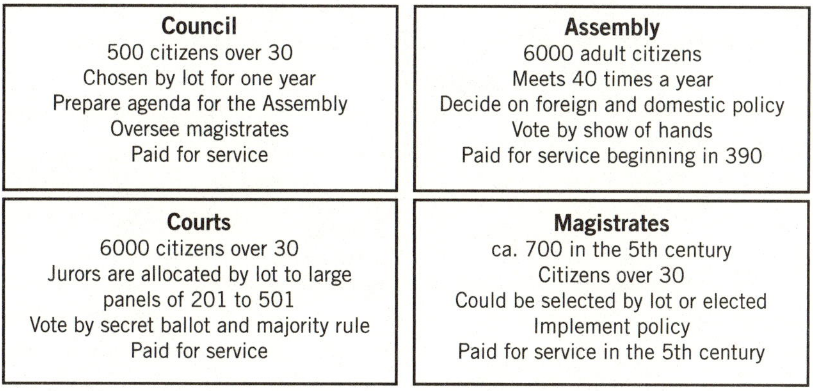

Council	Assembly
500 citizens over 30	6000 adult citizens
Chosen by lot for one year	Meets 40 times a year
Prepare agenda for the Assembly	Decide on foreign and domestic policy
Oversee magistrates	Vote by show of hands
Paid for service	Paid for service beginning in 390

Courts	Magistrates
6000 citizens over 30	ca. 700 in the 5th century
Jurors are allocated by lot to large	Citizens over 30
panels of 201 to 501	Could be selected by lot or elected
Vote by secret ballot and majority rule	Implement policy
Paid for service	Paid for service in the 5th century

FIGURE 1.1. Athens' institutions

leaders with a simple plurality vote (Forsdyke 2005). Cleisthenes may also have introduced or broadened the use of the lot to select magistrates ([Arist.] *Ath. Pol.* 22.5).

1.2. Democracy in Fifth-Century Athens

After the intense reform period in the late seventh and sixth centuries, by the end of the sixth century, the Athenians had established the four key institutions of democracy: the Council of Five Hundred, the Assembly, the Courts, and the Magistrates.[8]

1.2.a. *The Council of Five Hundred*

The Council was a representative body of the Athenian male citizen population over the age of thirty, randomly selected by lot among the ten Athenian tribes. Councilors served for one year and their mandate could only be iterated once, in a nonconsecutive year. Each tribal contingent acted as executive committee for one-tenth of the year (*prytany*), and the rotation was also randomized through the use of the lot.[9] The Council met every day with the exception of holidays—that is, roughly 275 times a year (Hansen 1999: 251). Beginning at

---

8. In what follows, I provide a summary of the functioning of these institutions. For a complete account, see Hansen (1999).

9. The selection of the presidents of the Council changed in the early fourth century: Hansen (1999): 250.

least in the mid-fifth century, councilors received an allowance of five or six obols, depending on whether they were serving on the executive committee.[10] The Council's main responsibilities included setting the agenda for the Assembly, administering the state's public finances, and overseeing the magistrates (for a full list of duties, cf. Hansen 1999: 255–65).

1.2.b. The Assembly

All adult male citizens over the age of eighteen could participate in the Assembly. For most of the classical period, the Assembly met forty times a year to discuss all aspects of foreign and domestic policy. The space where the Assembly met—the hill of the Pnyx, located just above the central square (Agora)— could seat around six thousand to eight thousand people. As Hansen (1999: 131) has shown, an average meeting probably featured six thousand participants (between 10 and 20% of the total adult male population).[11] The composition of each meeting varied as participants were allowed into the space on a first come, first serve basis.

Until the 390s, assemblymen did not receive payment for their service. After the introduction of pay for service, the allowance grew from three obols in the 390s to 1–1½ dr. in the 320s. In the fifth century, the lack of randomized mechanisms of selection and the absence of pay suggest that the composition of the Assembly may have been skewed more toward the haves than the have-nots. However, participation in the Assembly was not as burdensome as participation in the Council. In fact, meetings only lasted half a day. The Assembly's agenda was fixed in advance (by the Council) and made known to the public. So lower-class citizens who cared particularly about a given issue may choose to forfeit half a day of work in order to attend a particular meeting, but at their own expense. In the fourth century, after pay was introduced, scholars often suggest that the composition of the Assembly did not differ markedly from that of the courts, and they both broadly reflected the composition of Athens' population as a whole (Ober 1989a: 137; Hansen 1999: 127).

10. One Attic drachma (dr.) is equivalent to six obols and it corresponds to a day's wage for a soldier or unskilled laborer in the later fifth century. One talent (T) corresponds to 6,000 dr. According to Ober (2015b: 497–98), one talent approximately corresponds to "twenty-five years of gross wages (at the late fifth century wage rate of 1 drachma per day, and assuming 250 working days per year). One talent may be very roughly equated to the gross income of an ordinary working man's life (assuming average age at death of those who live to adulthood in the mid-forties)."

11. Population estimates for the fifth century vary between forty thousand and sixty thousand. In the fourth century, population has been estimated at thirty thousand (Hansen 1986).

In the Assembly, the people listened to speeches and voted on policy proposals by show of hands. Athens did not develop political parties, but the Athenians did rely on a class of expert politicians that did much, but not all (as I
discuss in chapter 3) of the talking. In the fifth century, successful politicians
tended to be skilled military leaders. In the fourth century, there occurred a
decoupling of political and military careers, such that successful leadership
began to increasingly depend on one's skills as a political and financial
advisor.

1.2.c. The Courts

The popular courts were the hallmark of the Athenian democracy.[12] At the
beginning of each year, six thousand Athenians over the age of thirty were
selected by lot to serve as jurors.[13] On each day in which the courts were in
session, panels of varying size would be assigned, again by lot, to cases.[14] Panel
size varied depending on the type of case, from 201 jurors for small private disputes to 501 jurors for public cases. Sometimes, the issues were so important
that jurors could number in the thousands (the first known case of *graphē
paranomōn*, on which more below, was judged by all the six thousand jurors).
Jurors reached decisions by secret ballot, by majority rule, and without deliberation.[15] Unlike Assembly meetings, court sessions could take up a whole day.

In the mid-fifth century, two reforms attributed to Athens' democratic leaders Ephialtes and Pericles vastly expanded the power and the reach of the
popular courts, ushering in the so-called radical phase of democracy (Hansen
1978; 1979a and b; 1987b; 1989a; 1999; cf. [Arist]. *Ath.Pol.* 27).[16] First, the elite
Council of the Areopagus was deprived of most of its powers, which were

12. The Athenians were renowned for their courts, and their litigiousness. The stock joke in
Aristophanes' comedy *The Clouds* has the protagonist stare at a map of the world unable to
recognize the location of Athens because there are "no jurors in session" (lines 207–8, trans.
my own).

13. Following common practice in classics, I use the English word jurors to translate the
Greek word *dikastai*. Scholars have also used the term judges (E. M. Harris 1994). As Lanni
(2006: 38) suggests, neither word is entirely satisfactory.

14. The courts met between 175 and 225 days a year. Hansen 1999: 186.

15. Secret ballot and lack of deliberation in the courts can be linked to two phenomena: first,
the fear that powerful and skilled orators would lead the jurors astray; and second, the fear of
the consequences of nonconformity. Both could lead to preference falsification. Many thanks
to Timur Kuran for this observation. On preference falsification: Kuran (1991; 1995).

16. I return to the labeling of the fifth-century democracy as radical in the conclusion of
chapter 2.

transferred to the popular courts. Second, the introduction of pay for jury duty enabled the lower classes to participate as jurors in the popular courts. Pay increased from two obols in the mid-fifth century to three obols during the Peloponnesian War and remained steady until the end of the fourth century.

1.2.d. The Magistrates

In Solonian times, the lowest classes could participate in the Assembly, but had no access to active political participation. However, in the classical period, all adult males (over age thirty) were eligible to become magistrates of the polis. Most Athenian magistracies used the lot to select office-holders. However, for a series of posts, office-holders were elected. These included, "all the military commanders . . . the most weighty financial officers, some persons in charge of sacred affairs . . . and a few others" (Hansen 1999: 233). [Aristotle] suggests that in the mid-fifth century, Athens had around seven hundred magistrates (*Ath.Pol.* 24.3; cf. Hansen 1999: 240). Magistrates were in office for a limited amount of time and usually could not reiterate the mandate. They served on boards where decisions were taken collectively to ensure mutual monitoring. They were also subject to scrutiny at the beginning (*dokimasia*) and end (*euthyna*) of their terms. In the fifth century, magistrates, like jurors and councilors, received remuneration for their service, but pay may have been abolished in the fourth century (Hansen 1999: 240–42).

1.3. Democracy and Empire

The Athenian democracy in the fifth century was thus a huge machine, which involved thousands of citizens in the administration of the polis—many of whom received compensation for their service. As such, the Athenian democracy was a very expensive endeavor.[17] The costs of democracy, moreover, paled compared to the costs of war.[18] In addition to democracy and war, the Athenians also spent considerable amounts on festivals and public building

---

17. For Ober (2015a: 245; 2015b: 499), the Athenians spent 100 T/yr on government and law (estimates are for the years before and during the Peloponnesian War, in 435 and 425).

For Pritchard (2015: 89), the Athenians in the 420s spent ca. 157 T/yr on the government.

18. Ober (2015a: 245; 2015b: 499) suggests that war cost the Athenians 400 T/yr before the Peloponnesian War (in 435), but peaked at 1,500 T/yr in the middle of the Peloponnesian War (in 425).

For Pritchard (2015: 97), annual spending on the armed forces in the decade between 433 and 423 averaged 1,485 T/yr.

projects.[19] In the fifth century, expenditures ranged from ca. 950 T/yr in the 430s to ca. 1,800 T/yr in the 420s. Where did the Athenians find the money to pay for all these expenses?

In the fifth century, a conspicuous part of Athenian revenues came from the empire, which the city controlled from the end of the Persian Wars in the year 479 to the end of the Peloponnesian War in the year 404. The empire was the product of the consolidation of Athens' power over the group of poleis that had fought the Persians (in 490 and in 480–479), which came together in an alliance originally led by Sparta. After the Persian Wars, the Spartans returned to the Peloponnese, while Athens and the allies met on the island of Delos to hammer out the details of a new alliance to continue fighting the Persians in the Aegean.[20] The plan, designed by Athens' general Aristides, was as follows: because no single polis could put together enough resources to fight the Persians, large poleis would contribute ships and rowers, while smaller poleis would contribute cash. In this clever structure, smaller poleis bought cheap security, and larger poleis had their navies subsidized. Quickly, membership in the Delian League swelled from a few dozens to a few hundred. Within the span of a few years, however, Athens' grip on the allies tightened. As the Persian threat receded, member poleis began to question the need for their onerous participation. But those city-states that tried to quit the league were brought back in line with the use of force. This was the fate of Naxos in the year 476, and of Thasos in the year 465. The consolidation of the league into an empire sped up the tempo of state formation in Greece (Morris 2009b). In the year 454, allegedly for fear of the Persians reappearing in the Aegean after destroying Athens' contingent in Egypt, the Athenians moved the league's treasury from Delos to Athens (Samons 2000: 92–106). Moreover, at some point in the third quarter of the fifth century, the Athenians imposed a common currency—the Athenian owl—on commercial transactions throughout the empire, along with Athenian weights and measures (Figueira 1998). Finally, Athens mandated that all disputes between Athens and the allies be tried in Athens.

According to Morris (2009b), the Athenian empire was not a coercion-wielding organization in the mold of the Persian, Roman, or other ancient (and modern) empires. Its stability relied on the use of force against allied

19. Both Ober (2015a: 245; 2015b: 499) and Pritchard (2015: 49) assess expenditures on festivals at ca. 100 T/yr. Ober adds expenditures on public building projects: 350 T/yr in the 430s with the Acropolis building program; 100 T/yr in the 420s.

20. Sparta's reluctance to leave the Peloponnese is a recurring theme in Herodotus' *Histories*. Because of the tendency of the helots (the serf population of Messenia) to revolt when Spartan soldiers left the Peloponnese, the reluctance was justified.

poleis. But the empire also provided many benefits to member states: the Athenian navy cleared the Aegean of pirates; Athenian coinage, weights, and measures facilitated the exchange of goods; and Athenian courts provided a homogeneous structure for the resolution of disputes. The allies benefited from these social goods. But especially as the allies began to shift the nature of their contribution from rowers and ships to cash (Thuc. 1.99.3), Athens found itself at the receiving end of a conspicuous and steady source of revenue.

The empire contributed to Athenian prosperity by providing revenue in the form of both tribute and rents. In the *Anabasis*, Xenophon assesses imperial income at 1,000 T/yr (of which 600 T/yr or 400 T/yr came from the tribute alone, according to Thucydides and the Athenian Tribute List, respectively: Xen. *Anab.* 7.1.27; Thuc. 2.13.3).[21] Imperial rents flowed to Athens in the form of indirect taxes levied on commercial exchange (such as toll and harbor taxes) and other imperial dues (such as confiscations of property, fees for the maintenance of garrisons and legal fees: Ober 2015b). The silver mines of Laurion were another conspicuous source of revenue not directly connected with the empire (Burke 1984; 1990; 2010; Faraguna 1992; 2003; van Alfen 2000; Kroll 2011). According to Thucydides, before the beginning of the Peloponnesian War in the year 431, the Athenians had accumulated a reserve of 9,700 T, of which 3,700 T were expended to construct the Parthenon and other buildings on the Acropolis (Thuc. 2.13.3). From the extant 6,000 T, Pericles set aside 1,000 T (and one hundred ships) as a rainy-day fund.

If the empire was largely responsible for Athens' fifth-century prosperity, it was also in meaningful ways responsible for the polis' stability. In fact, the empire may have assuaged class conflict, providing enough resources to turn a zero-sum game between masses and elites into a win-win situation. Resentment toward the democracy existed among the elite (and in fact, it punctuates the writings of our sources: Ober 1998), but as the elite writer known as the Old Oligarch noted (2.20; trans. Forsythe 2001),[22] some elite were quite happy to live under the democracy, either "to smooth [their] own path towards iniquity," or because they profited from it in legitimate ways (Finley 1981[1978]). Following [Aristotle] (*Ath.Pol.* 24.3), Finley suggests that the masses benefited from "land confiscated from subjects and distributed . . . among Athenians . . . the navy . . . [where] thousands of Athenians earned their pay for rowing in the fleet . . . [and] the work in the dockyards." (1981[1978]: 58). Moreover, the empire provided "both the necessary cash and the political motivation" for

21. Ober (2015b: 506), Finley (1981 [1978]: 48–49), and Burke (1992) accept the figure of 600 T for imperial tribute.

22. All translations of the Old Oligarch are from Forsythe (2001), unless otherwise noted.

pay for public office. Upper-class Athenians benefited from the acquisition of property in subject territories and from new outlets for investment (Finley 1981[1978]: 52; Ober 1989a: 23–24).[23]

The empire, then, brought wealth, prestige, and stability to the polis. It attracted revenues through both commerce and tribute-paying allies. It funded the polis' democratic institutions, its military might, and conspicuous public building programs. And it contributed to justify democratic culture before the eyes of (at least some) rich Athenians who may have preferred a different type of government.

1.4. Pitfalls of Democracy

In the course of the sixth and fifth centuries, then, the Athenians created a stable set of participatory institutions that enabled an unprecedentedly large section of the population to take active part in collective self-governance. The Athenians also made important strides towards establishing elements of what we may today call a rule of law. Forsdyke (2018: 186) suggests that the Athenians recognized the principles of legal supremacy—that is, "the principle that society should be regulated through authoritative rules rather than violence"—and legal equality—that is, "[the] principle that laws are to be applied equally to all and that no one—not even a monarch or magistrate—is above the law." If these principles emerged early on in the legislation of Draco and Solon, they were more fully crystallized in the complex system of accountability mechanisms of the mature fifth-century democracy—from the practice of ostracism, to magistrates' scrutinies, to the selection by lot of councilors and jurors (Lane 2016).

Why did this complex and highly developed institutional structure collapse? There are several reasons behind the collapse of the fifth-century democracy (Carugati and Ober 2020). The pressure of the long, difficult Peloponnesian War and a terrible military disaster (in Sicily) certainly played a role in straining Athens' institutions. A powerful and rich elite with strong

---

23. Other explanations of the resilience of democracy in the fifth century include the denial that Athens was a democracy (Pearson 1937; de Laix 1973); the reliance on slavery (Jameson 1978); the existence of a large middle class (A.H.M. Jones 1957) and a "middling ideology" (Perlman 1963; 1967); the fact that Athens was a face-to-face society (Finley 1973); and that its leaders were democratic geniuses (Gomme 1951; Ehrenberg 1950). These positions are discussed and rejected in Ober (1989a: 20–35). Ober's own explanation—that rhetoric helped mediate between the power of the masses and the privileges of the elites—applies to the fourth century. I return to Ober's explanation in chapter 3. R. Osborne (2010: 286), argued that "the strongest defence of democracy in the fifth century had been that it worked." We still need to explain why that may have been the case.

sympathies for oligarchy and the resources to organize for collective action also played a role. But the Athenian democracy did not collapse solely because of external forces.[24] As I argue in chapter 2, among the reasons for the collapse of democracy was also a crisis of legitimacy that led both elites and masses to turn their back on democracy. The crisis stemmed from an underlying design defect:[25] the inability of the Assembly to credibly commit to promises made via legislation.[26] This problem depended on two main factors: first, no other institution existed to check the legislative power of the Assembly; second, there were no systematic procedures to collect and archive Assembly decisions (laws and decrees).[27] As a result, decisions made by the Assembly on one day

24. Athens experienced many dire military defeats in the course of its democratic history, but democracy did not always collapse. Equally, anti-democratic sentiments and actors were quite widespread among the elite throughout the fifth and the fourth century. These reasons alone are therefore insufficient to explain the collapse.

25. This defect had its roots in the democracy's emergence from a past of tyranny and elite infighting. Against these forces, a powerful Assembly was established as a counterweight (Forsdyke 2005). But as time went by, this design proved detrimental to the stability of democracy. This design defect alone is also insufficient as an explanation for collapse: in fact, if that were the case, it is hard to explain why it took almost a century for democracy to break down. In the end, then, democracy collapsed after Sicily and not before (or after) due to a combination of the aforementioned factors: design defects, organized opposition, and military pressures.

26. On the importance of credible commitment for the stability and performance of institutions: North (1993). For an application of economic theory drawn from the tradition of new institutional economics to Athens, and an account of the relevance of credible commitment: Lyttkens (2013).

27. In the fifth century, the Athenians sought to address the problem of credible commitment through entrenchment clauses. Schwartzberg (2004; cf. 2007) documents their use in alliances and treaties and in some financial decrees. In line with my interpretation, Schwartzberg stresses the perception (especially prominent among oligarchic sympathizers) that large democracies like Athens are not to be trusted because they lack internal checks in the decision-making process (2004: 315). In the fifth century, entrenchment clauses were important signals, but, in the absence of robust enforcement mechanisms, they could be reneged on at a later time (as it happened to the entrenchment clauses protecting the Periclean emergency fund: Schwartzberg 2004: 317). In the fourth century, the use of entrenchment clauses diminished, especially for domestic legislation. As Schwartzberg herself notes (2004: 322–23), this may have been due to the reforms that are the object of the next chapter, which enhanced the credibility of Athens' commitments. Interestingly, the use of entrenchment clauses continued for legislation directed toward external actors (especially in the case of alliances), which nicely corroborates the argument I propose in chapter 4 regarding Athens' concerns with making its commitments credible vis-à-vis noncitizens that lived or worked in Athens. On entrenchment clauses see also D. Lewis (1974); Boegehold (1996); Rhodes and Lewis (1997).

were valid on the next as long as the demos was willing to respect its previous pronouncements.[28] Two examples clarify this point: the Mytilene affair in the year 427 and the Arginusae trial in the year 406.

In the midst of the Peloponnesian War against Sparta (which lasted from 431 to 404), the Athenian Assembly voted to punish a revolting ally—the city of Mytilene, on the island of Lesbos—by killing all adult males and selling women and children as slaves (Thuc. 3.36–49). When they realized the harshness of their pronouncement, the Athenians summoned another Assembly the next day to reevaluate, and eventually modify the decision. Thucydides recounts that the trireme carrying the second decision arrived in Mytilene just in the nick of time to avoid the massacre. Down to the year 427, then, the only way to reverse or modify an Assembly decision was to call another meeting and begin the discussion anew. This method of reevaluation and correction was rather cumbersome and not likely to be of much use in settings with a passionate, committed majority.

At some point after the Mytilene affair, the Athenians devised a new procedure, known as graphē paranomōn.[29] The graphē paranomōn allowed any participant (*ho boulomenos*—lit. whoever wishes) in the course of any given Assembly to indict a proposed measure as against the laws (*paranomon*) or inconvenient (*asymphoron*) to foster the interests of the Athenian demos. The indictment transferred the matter from the Assembly to the courts where a large panel of lay citizen jurors, usually numbering 501, judged the dispute. Did the graphē paranomōn provide an efficient mechanism to revise Assembly decisions?[30]

---

28. The absence of credible commitment was not limited to an area of policy—for example, commitment to not expropriating wealth (although that played a conspicuous role in the democracy's demise, as we will see in the next chapter). Instead, it was a design defect that affected policy-making as a whole. To address this problem, the postwar reforms focused, first and foremost, on providing a check on the Assembly through new institutions and procedures and on producing a coherent body of publicly available rules.

29. We do not know precisely when the graphē paranomōn was introduced. Sundahl (2000) provides a discussion of the various positions. Its absence in the Mytilenean debate may be used as indirect evidence that the procedure was introduced between 427 and 415 (Wolff 1970).

30. Because a large number of extant cases concern honorary decrees (seventeen out of forty-four, ca. 40%), and because we know that some politicians were routinely subject to the procedure (Aesch. 3.194), classical scholars have long debated whether the graphē paranomōn performed the function of political (Cloché 1960) or judicial review (Goodell 1893–94; Goodwin 1895; Bonner and Smith 1938; Wolff 1970). Most interpreters recognize that the graphē paranomōn performed both functions at once, though the relative emphasis varies: Hansen

In the year 406, the Athenian navy managed to obtain an important victory against Sparta in the Battle of Arginusae (Xen. *Hell.* 1.6.27–7.35). But in the aftermath of battle, a sudden storm made it impossible for the Athenian generals to rescue the survivors. When the news was relayed to the Assembly, Callixenus proposed to condemn the ten generals to death, en masse and without trial. Euryptolemus indicted Callixenus' proposal by graphē paranomōn. Shouted down and under threat that he join the generals' fate, Euryptolemus retracted his indictment. The Athenians executed the generals. As Adriaan Lanni and Adrian Vermeule (2013) suggest, the graphē paranomōn was a futile procedure because it was not supported by credible commitment—in other words, the people in the Assembly were unwilling, at the time of action, to be constrained by the procedures they had devised at an earlier time.[31]

The absence of reliable constraints on the decision-making power of the Assembly magnified the threat that, particularly under severe military pressures, the demos might make rash or uninformed decisions. This happened most consequentially in the year 415, when the Assembly enthusiastically voted to send a massive military expedition to Sicily. The rogue general Alcibiades rallied the demos, presenting a false image of the Sicilian poleis as extraordinarily rich, but weak and fragmented—a land of opportunities for the ever-ambitious Athenians. The moderate leader Nicias called for caution suggesting instead that, under the strains of war, the Athenians should better look after their possessions instead of seeking new ones (Thuc. 6.9–23). Within two years, the monumental expedition was utterly defeated. As

---

(1974; 1987a; 1999); Yunis (1988); Sundahl (2000; 2003); Carawan (2007). In recent years, Lanni (2010) and Schwartzberg (2013a) have put pressure on the analogy between the graphē paranomōn and judicial review, suggesting that bicameralism may be a more apt, if still imperfect, parallel. I agree that bicameralism shares many features with Athenian judicial review (most notably, the fact that the composition of the Assembly differed from that of the courts), but it does not capture the peculiarly constitutional aspects of the graphē paranomōn. As I show in chapter 3, the graphē paranomōn did not merely ask jurors to choose between two legislative options (a new proposal and the status quo) or to evaluate a new proposal in the second stage of a two-stage process. Instead, the procedure has specifically constitutional connotations: these emerge clearly in the procedural requirements that the new legislative proposal conform with existing laws, and with the normative requirement that the new proposal conform with the spirit of the constitution, especially as embodied in the figure of Solon (cf. Carugati, Calvert, and Weingast 2019). This interpretation of course applies to the fourth century.

31. Lanni and Vermeule's analysis may apply to the fifth century. But it does not, I suggest, apply to the fourth century, when the graphē paranomōn became the central mechanism to protect the new constitution, raising tremendously the costs of abusing the procedure. I return to this point at the end of chapter 2.

Thucydides (7.87.6) put it, "they were beaten at all points and altogether; all that they suffered was great; they were destroyed, as the saying is, with a total destruction, their fleet, their army—everything was destroyed, and few out of many returned home."[32] The defeat in Sicily plunged Athens into a severe financial crisis, triggering political instability. It took the Athenians a decade to restore order in the city.

32. According to Hansen's estimates (1988: 15–16), as many as ten thousand Athenians may have died in Sicily. For Thucydides (6.43.1; 7.16.2; 7.20.2), Athens lost 170 ships during the campaign.

2

Constitution and Consensus

THE SICILIAN disaster was the beginning of the end for Athens' fifth-century democracy (R. Osborne 2010: 274). Within two years, the city's political institutions collapsed and a decade-long quest for a new constitutional equilibrium began. In the year 411, the oligarchy of the Four Hundred rose to power, only to disintegrate four months later. The Four Hundred were replaced by another oligarchy—the Five Thousand, who lasted for eleven months. Democracy was reestablished in the year 410/409 and remained in place until the end of the Peloponnesian War in the year 404. After the defeat in the war, a Spartan-friendly oligarchic regime—the Thirty—ruled Athens for about eight months. To rid the city of the oligarchs, whose violent rule earned them the appellation "Thirty Tyrants," the Athenians took up arms against one another in a brief, but bloody civil war.

Comparative evidence from other large-scale, prosperous, ancient polities suggests that such periods of unrest often yield recurring instability or permanent transitions toward authoritarianism (cf. chapter 5). Neither occurred in Athens. Instead, when the civil war came to an end, the Athenians reestablished a democratic form of government. The new democracy, however, was different from the one that had collapsed a decade earlier. First, the Athenians introduced an additional legislative institution (nomothesia). Second, new measures were put in place to more clearly define and enforce people's rights to freedom, property, and dignity after the civil conflict. Third, a series of new rules came to regulate the legislative process. We find these rules summarized in a passage from the orator Andocides (1.89, trans. Maidment 1968): "Now you decided that the laws were to be revised and afterwards inscribed [;] that in no circumstances were magistrates to enforce a law which had not been inscribed [;] that no decree, whether of the Council or the Assembly, was to override a law [;] that no law might be directed against an individual without applying to all citizens alike [;] and that only such laws as had been passed since the Archonship of Euclides were to be enforced."

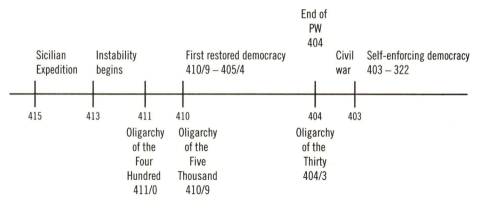

FIGURE 2.1. Political instability in Athens (413–403)

How did these new rules and institutions come about? And how did they manage to return stability to the divided polis, after a decade of constitutional turmoil? This chapter offers a new reading of the ancient sources that analyzes the causes, process, and outcome of institutional change in late fifth-century Athens. I show that the collapse of the fifth-century democracy was due to external pressures as well as to a crisis of legitimacy rooted in the Assembly's inability to credibly commit to policy. In the aftermath of Sicily, lack of credible commitment triggered fear of expropriation among the elite. The demos, for its part, began to question its own ability to make sensible decisions, particularly under the pressure of conflict. The time for constitutional change had come. Oligarchy, however, failed to provide a viable alternative to democracy. The ruling oligarchs' foreign policy record proved abysmal. In an attempt to stay in power, the oligarchs systematically disregarded Athens' laws, which led to abuses of citizens' personal and property rights.

As the constitutional struggles unfolded, the Athenians reacted to the excesses of both democratic and oligarchic governments. In the process, they collectively identified the minimal conditions that a government had to display to command their consent. These conditions are reflected in the debate over the patrios politeia—the constitution of the fathers.[1] Both oligarchs and

---

1. The phrase patrios politeia here encompasses its synonyms, including "the ancient laws" (*archaioi nomoi*), "the laws of the fathers" (*patrioi nomoi*), and also "the laws of Solon" (*Solōnos nomoi*). Patrios politeia was not a late fifth-century invention (Hansen 1989b), but its use in the constitutional debate marks the beginning of a period in which the Athenians began to perceive the past as an age of stability and prosperity, in contrast with the fifth-century view—expressed

democrats used the notion of patrios politeia to legitimize their claims to power. The meaning of this notion, I argue, evolved during the debate. If under the Four Hundred, patrios politeia is perhaps best understood as a vague connection with Athens' past, by the time of the first restoration of democracy it became imbued with the concept of legality. By the end of the civil conflict, patrios politeia expressed a consensus on principles of legality that harkened back to Athens' archaic lawgiver Solon. Symbolic of this connection is the emphasis on the principles of personal freedom, dignity, and property security for all citizens; on the role of the city's laws and courts to enforce these principles; and on the need to strike a bargain between competing demands in order to secure political stability (cf. chapter 1).

Based on the consensus on Solonian legality, the Athenians passed a series of reforms that made up a self-enforcing constitution. The new constitution was self-enforcing, in the language of institutional analysis, because it imposed limits on the government, successfully addressing the causes of previous governments' instability (including lack of credible commitment and abuses of citizens' rights); it created incentives for both oligarchs and democrats to choose institutional channels to resolve disputes, instead of resorting to retaliation and violence; and it provided mechanisms for punishing those who sought to renege.

The notion of a self-enforcing constitution provides a rigorous and testable heuristic to explain how a set of apparently haphazard pieces of legislation managed to return stability and prosperity to a city that had just emerged from a decade of constitutional instability, a dire economic crisis, and a divisive civil conflict. But if we neglect the role of the consensus in shaping actors' preferences, it is difficult to explain why those pieces of legislation were chosen vis-à-vis others. First, the reforms were not an obvious response to instability. In fact, they imposed significant departures from the fifth-century status quo and were, as far as we know, unparalleled anywhere else in Greece. Second, the new reforms enshrined a compromise between oligarchic and democratic interests that is otherwise hard to justify in light of the historical sequence of events. The democrats won the civil war and were therefore in a better position to pass reforms that would uniquely benefit them. But instead of doing so (or instead of retaliating against the losers), the democrats established new institutions to tie their own hands. On this combination of consensus and constitutional reforms, I argue, the stability of democracy rested.

---

most cogently by Thucydides in Pericles' funeral oration—that the past was great, but the present is better (Thuc. 2.35–46).

The chapter proceeds as follows. I begin by describing how my reading of the ancient sources differs from existing accounts in the field of classics. I then turn to the constitutional debate. In the last section, I analyze the reforms.

2.1. A New Reading of the Ancient Sources

The restoration of democracy in Athens has been the object of much attention among classical scholars. Previous studies have greatly contributed to our understanding of the new institutions' basic features (e.g., Harrison 1955; MacDowell 1975; Hansen 1978; 1979a; 1979b; 1985; 1987b; 1990a; 1999; Robertson 1990; Rhodes 1980; 1991; 2010; Eder 1995; Carawan 2002; 2013; R. Osborne 2003); others have sought to explain the stability of the new democracy, focusing in particular on the role of the amnesty agreement ratified after the civil war (Loening 1987; Loraux 2002; Quillin 2002; Wolpert 2002; Carawan 2013; Lanni 2016: ch. 6), and Athens' fear of Spartan intervention (Todd 1985).

But with one exception, which I discuss more fully below, studies concerned with the restoration of democracy neglect the constitutional struggles that preceded the rise of the Thirty.[2] This is at least in part due to issues of periodization. The end of the Peloponnesian War in the year 404 has traditionally been viewed as a watershed in Athenian political history such that the events before and after 404 are often considered in isolation from one another. There is however another reason. Classical scholars tend to perceive the restoration of democracy in the year 403 as a given outcome of the constitutional struggles. As a result, the possibility that oligarchy could have provided a viable alternative to democracy is never taken seriously.[3] This view might at first appear justified. Athens was ruled by a democracy for almost a century before the late fifth-century constitutional crisis, and for eighty years afterward. Moreover, the oligarchic regimes that rose in Athens between the years 411 and 403 all lasted for only a handful of months. Oligarchy, then, may look like a blip in Athens' long-term relationship with democracy. But if we take a closer look at the events that followed the Sicilian expedition, a different picture emerges.

First, democracy was not the only game in town. The defeat in Sicily exposed the polis to an unprecedented level of danger by devastating Athens' human and

---

2. Two additional accounts deserve mention: Ostwald (1986) and Gowder (2016: ch. 5–6). Both accounts see the restoration of democracy in view of the struggles that preceded it and stress the increasing importance of law for the stability of democracy. Ostwald focuses on changing notions of sovereignty, while Gowder focuses on the emergence of the rule of law. I return to their contributions in greater detail in the conclusion of this chapter.

3. A partial exception is Osborne (2010), but the main focus remains on the crisis of democracy, rather than on the viability of oligarchy.

financial resources, thus dwarfing the polis' chances of prevailing over Sparta in the Peloponnesian War. As the demos lost trust in democracy, the elites began to fear that the demos would expropriate their wealth in a desperate attempt to fund the war. Under these circumstances, it was not preposterous to suggest that democracy had to be replaced.

Second, there is no reason to rule out a priori the possibility that oligarchy could have provided a viable alternative to democracy. Oligarchy was a stable form of government elsewhere in Greece. As Simonton (2017: 7) argues, oligarchy "was likelier to survive, all else being equal, when oligarchs implemented specialized social and political institutions that kept the elite united while discouraging the demos from collective action." As we will see, Athenian oligarchs implemented many of the institutions that Simonton identifies as being conducive to oligarchic stability. Why, then, did oligarchy fail to provide a viable constitutional alternative to democracy in Athens?

To identify the sources of democratic stability in the post-war period, we must focus on the instability that preceded the reforms. This requires analyzing the reasons behind the failure of oligarchy and identifying the challenges to democratic stability after the collapse of the fifth-century structure. In these respects, my account differs from previous studies. I also provide a different reading of the cardinal concept of the Athenian constitutional debate: the notion of patrios politeia.

For long, classical scholars associated the phrase patrios politeia with the moderate oligarchic faction (Fuks 1953; Finley 1975). But in 1986, Martin Ostwald observed that, in fact, individuals from different political backgrounds used it to legitimize constitutional change in the years between 413 and 403. The observation that both oligarchs and democrats appealed to patrios politeia, however, contributed to its dismissal as a propagandistic slogan, whose manipulation was made possible by what Stephen Todd called "a very considerable confusion over the nature and authority of the law of Athens" (1996: 107; cf. Simonton 2012a). But in an interdisciplinary tour de force, Julia Shear (2011) has challenged this view. Through an analysis of the available literary, epigraphic, and archeological evidence, Shear shows that, in the last decade of the fifth century, the Athenians were engaged in a debate on the best constitution for the polis that revolved around the notion of patrios politeia. In her reading, the appeals to patrios politeia were not mere slogans. Conversely, "these discussions made the city's past into an important focus of attention and the past was used to legitimize the oligarchs and their actions" (Shear 2011: 20).

My reconstruction of the role of patrios politeia in the constitutional debate owes much to Shear's account. In particular, I agree that patrios politeia was not just a slogan, and that its appropriation as a legitimizing tool is key to interpreting the constitutional debate. However, my interpretation differs from Shear's in two relevant respects. First, patrios politeia was not merely a tool to legitimize oligarchy, but also to legitimize democracy. Second, if patrios politeia may have initially expressed a vague association with Athens' past, by the end of the constitutional debate, it expressed a consensus on legality that formed the normative pillar of the new democracy.[4]

If Shear is right in arguing that patrios politeia was employed to legitimize the oligarchic governments, then the oligarchs ought to have assumed that, whatever patrios politeia precisely meant, the notion was widely associated with legitimate government. The critical aspect of this appropriation, then, is that the oligarchs believed that *everyone else,* upon hearing patrios politeia, would have trusted the reformers to establish a legitimate, *patrios* government. The same goes for the democrats. Shear assumes that democracy did not need legitimizing in the eyes of the Athenians. Instead, I suggest that, after the failure of the fifth-century structure, a stable democracy had to address, at a minimum, the problem of credible commitment. If the oligarchs needed to legitimize their rule in the eyes of the demos, the democrats needed to legitimize democracy in the eyes of all, and especially those of its most powerful (and rich) members—that is, the elite.

The notion of patrios politeia conjured up a past whose defining features were, by and large, lost in the mists of time. As such, patrios politeia was particularly well suited to enable institutional experimentation. But the fact that we cannot assess whether patrios politeia can be more readily identified with the archaic statutes of Solon, Cleisthenes, or Draco, does not mean that the notion itself remained vague. If, under the Four Hundred, patrios politeia expressed a connection with Athens' past that helped the oligarchs legitimize constitutional change, its meaning evolved during the debate. In particular, the evidence suggests that the notion was progressively associated with the laws of the city as a bulwark against governmental abuses, and with the figure of the archaic lawgiver Solon as the symbol of a new commitment to legality. If we disregard this long and contentious process of experimentation and debate,

4. Overlooking critical institutional distinctions between the forms of government that rose and fell in Athens between 411 and 403, Shear misses the evolving association between patrios politeia and legality. For example, Shear (2011: 167) considers the democracy established in 410 to have been the same as the fifth-century democracy, arguing that, "evidence for political reforms is strikingly absent from the period between 410 and 404." As we will see, this was definitely not the case. Moreover, the connection between patrios politeia and a nebulous past both fails when tested against the evidence (particularly the evidence from the reign of the Thirty, on which more below) and lacks analytical poignancy, leading to an inability to connect the features of the new democracy with the debates that preceded it. I discuss my debt to Shear's analysis and the ways in which my interpretation differs from hers more fully in Carugati (2015).

we cannot understand why the Athenians eventually restored democracy. If we disregard the evolving meaning of the cardinal concept of the debate—which was not democracy per se, but legality—we cannot understand the focus on law or the bipartisan spirit of the new constitution.

The next section presents an in-depth examination of the extant ancient evidence. For those readers that may be less interested in my discussion of the sources, I summarize the main findings at the end of the section (see also Carugati 2019a). Before I delve into the analysis, however, a methodological caveat is in order. It is impossible to track the evolution of the meaning of patrios politeia between the years 413 and 403 directly in the literary sources, given their paucity.[5] For this reason, my argument about the evolution of the meaning of patrios politeia rests largely on the analysis of what the reformers did, rather than what they said. More explicitly, I track the evolution of patrios politeia in the reforms that oligarchic and democratic governments passed while pledging a return to the patrios politeia. The reforms attest clearly, if indirectly, to the relationship between patrios politeia, legality, and the figure of Solon.

2.2. The Patrios Politeia Consensus

When the news was brought to Athens, for a long while they disbelieved even the most respectable of the soldiers who had themselves escaped from the scene of action and clearly reported the matter, a destruction so complete not being thought credible. When the conviction was forced upon them, they were angry with the orators who had joined in promoting the expedition, just as if they had not themselves voted it, and were enraged also with the reciters of oracles and soothsayers, and all other omen-mongers of the time who had encouraged them to hope that they should conquer Sicily (Thuc. 8.1.1).

5. In relation to the events narrated in this chapter, the phrase "patrios politeia" appears nine times: in a fragment of Thrasymachus (85 BI (DK[6]); cf. Shear 2011: 42–43); in Lys. 34 (quoted in Dion. Hal. *Lys.* 32); twice in [Arist.] *Ath.Pol.* 34.3; in [Arist.] *Ath.Pol.* 35.2; twice in Diod. 14.3; in Diod 14.32; and in Schol. Aesch. 1.39.2). The phrase *"archaios nomos"* appears only once (in Xen. *Hell.* 2.4.42). The phrase *"patrios nomos"* appears three times (in Thuc. 8.76.6; in [Arist.] *Ath.Pol.* 29.3; and in Xen. *Hell.* 2.3.2). Finally, the phrase *"Solōnos nomos"* appears five times (in Lys. 30. 2 and 26; in Andoc. 1.81, 82, and 83). Of these, three refer to the Four Hundred (Thrasymachus' fragment; [Arist.] *Ath.Pol.* 29.3; and Thuc. 8.76.6), two refer to the revision of the laws (Lys. 30.2, 26), eight to the reign of the Thirty (the two references in [Arist.] *Ath.Pol.* 34.3; [Arist.] *Ath.Pol.* 35.2; the two references in Diod. 14.3; and Diod. 14.32; Schol. Aesch. 1.39.2; and Xen. *Hell.* 2.3.2); four to the democracy established in 403 (Xen. *Hell.* 2.4 42; and Andoc. 1. 81, 82, and 83); and one to events after the restoration of democracy (Dion. Hal. *Lys.* 32).

When the news of the Sicilian disaster spread in Athens, democratic institutions began to crumble. The expedition to Sicily had been enthusiastically acclaimed and heavily funded by the assembled demos only two years before. But, as Thucydides insinuated in his reconstruction of the debate in the Assembly (6.8–26), the fateful decision was the product of the unrestrained power of a demos too often inclined to uncritically follow the lead of self-interested and badly informed politicians. Now these politicians, and anyone else who encouraged the demos to vote in favor of the expedition, became the targets of the Athenians' anger, "just as if they had not themselves voted it." To handle the crisis, the Athenians took the extraordinary decision to elect a board of elders (*probouloi*) "to advise upon the state of affairs, as occasion should arise," and passed a series of emergency economic measures (Thuc. 8.1.3).[6] These efforts proved insufficient to stabilize the vacillating democracy.[7]

As the demos lost trust in democracy, the elite began to fear that the demos would expropriate their wealth to continue funding the war against Sparta. For Thucydides (8.48.1) "the most powerful citizens . . . suffered most severely from the war" because military expenditures fell largely on them. After Sicily, the burden could only have increased. By how much, no one knew, because whatever the Assembly may have decided one day could be reneged on the next day through a simple majority vote.[8]

An oligarchic platform emerged at this juncture, featuring a set of solutions to the difficulties that the defeat in Sicily had engendered. For both Thucydides

6. The election of the *probouloi* in 413 marked the beginning of a decade of constitutional upheavals: their role in the establishment of the Four Hundred provides an important link between the Sicilian disaster and the rise of the Four Hundred. On the functions of the *probouloi*: Andrewes (1954); Ruze (1974). On the *probouloi* elected in 413: Ostwald (1986: 338–43); Kagan (1987: 5–8).

7. Since at least the 420s, the conspicuous resources accumulated during the heyday of empire had begun to dry up (Samons 2000). In the year 412, the Athenians tapped into the reserve of 1,000 T set aside by Pericles before the beginning of the war (Thuc. 8.15.1). They also substituted the imperial tribute with a 5% tax on import and export by sea (7.28.4). In addition, Thucydides speaks of a communal effort to reduce unnecessary expenses (8.4). Athens' financial crisis after Sicily is crystallized in such acts as the melting down of golden statues (*nikai*, in 407/406) to mint a temporary gold coinage: Aristoph., *Frogs*, 718–26; Gardner (1913); Thompson (1965; 1966); Kraay (1976); Grandjean (2006). Athenian finances during the Ionian War: Blamire (2001: 114–22).

8. On elite fear of expropriation as the hallmark of mass and elite relationship in Athens: Ober (1989a: ch. 5). Collapse of democracy due to credible commitment problems: Lyttkens (2013: ch. 4); Fleck and Hanssen (forthcoming). On financial pressures as the triggers of constitutional change: Gabrielsen (1994: 173).

(8.65.3) and [Aristotle] (*Ath.Pol.* 29.5), this platform included proposals to abolish pay for magistracies, direct state resources to the war effort, and limit the franchise to five thousand citizens who could serve the state "in person and in purse." If the Athenians were to agree to constitutional change, the supporters of oligarchy further argued, the King of Persia would look favorably towards Athens and provide resources to the city ([Arist.] *Ath.Pol.* 29.1; Thuc. 8.53.1). Oligarchy was thus presented as a government that could successfully secure a deal with Persia, stabilize Athenian finances, and constrain the demos' power. The proposal was not without merit. As Thucydides remarks (8.48.3; cf. [Arist.] *Ath.Pol.* 29.1),

> The multitude, if at first irritated by these intrigues, were nevertheless kept quiet by the advantageous prospect of the pay from the king.

> Things, however, did not pan out smoothly for the oligarchs.

2.2.a. The Four Hundred (411–410)

To legitimize constitutional change, the Four Hundred appropriated the notion of patrios politeia.[9] As Shear has shown, these appeals were not empty slogans. In fact, during their rule, the Four Hundred appropriated institutions, buildings, and traditions that connected their government with that of Athens' forefathers, particularly Solon and Cleisthenes (2011: 49–51).[10] The Four Hundred also implemented many of the institutions that, according to Simonton, were conducive to oligarchic stability: these included secret extra-legal killings, the manipulation of Assemblies, and the use of informants (2017: 112, 115, 126, and 141). If the oligarchs went out of their way to present themselves as a legitimate government, and if they did everything by the book to maintain their hold on power, why did they collapse after a mere four months?[11]

Indubitably, the oligarchs faced a difficult challenge. As Thucydides put it, establishing an alternative form of government in Athens after a century of

---

9. On the Four Hundred, see esp. Hignett (1952); Ostwald (1986); Kagan (1987). For a fuller bibliography see, most recently, Wolpert (2017).

10. The Four Hundred's numbers and the use of the (old) Bouleuterion as a meeting place connected their rule with both Solon and Cleisthenes.

11. For Simonton (2017), the Four Hundred failed because they were not capable of maintaining unity among their ranks (either because they fell prey to competition 77–78; or because they did not have time to "cultivate a proper sense of oligarchic equality": 257, cf. 281). I agree with Simonton's explanations, but I highlight two additional elements: that is, foreign policy failures and popular perceptions about the legitimacy of the oligarchs' rule.

democracy was "no light matter" (Thuc. 8.68.4).[12] But the government of the Four Hundred was not doomed from the start. As we saw earlier, the proposal for constitutional change was a compelling response to Athens' financial difficulties. Had the Four Hundred managed to secure a deal with Persia, we may counterfactually speculate, oligarchy might have survived longer. However, the Four Hundred failed to secure a deal with Persia (Thuc. 8. 48) and then a peace with Sparta (Thuc. 8. 70–71). In addition, they suffered the revolt and loss of Euboea, Athens' strategic ally ([Arist.] *Ath.Pol.* 33.1; Thuc. 8. 96–97). This abysmal foreign policy record likely played a role in their rapid demise.[13]

In addition to foreign policy failures, the collapse of the Four Hundred in the sources is related to the growing perception that they were an illegitimate government. Soon after their establishment, supporters of democracy as well as partisans of a moderate form of oligarchy began to demand that the Four Hundred share power with a larger constituency of five thousand citizens. The opposition began to mobilize from Samos, where the Athenian fleet was deployed. The Four Hundred sent two embassies to Samos, to "reassure the army, and to explain . . . that there were five thousand, not four hundred only, concerned" (Thuc. 8.72.1; cf. 86.3). At the second gathering, the populist leader Alcibiades replied that, "he did not object to the government of the Five Thousand, but insisted that the Four Hundred should be deposed" (Thuc. 8.86.6). When the ambassadors returned to Athens, they delivered Alcibiades' message to the Four Hundred. After hearing that the army in Samos supported the establishment of a government of five thousand, the opposition to the ruling oligarchs began to mobilize in Athens as well.[14] According to Thucydides (8.89.1–2),

> the majority of the members of the oligarchy, who were already discontented and only too much inclined to be quit of the business in any safe way that they could . . . banded together and strongly criticized the administration, their leaders being some of the principal generals and men in office under the oligarchy, such as Theramenes, son of Hagnon, Aristocrates, son of Scellias, and others . . . . [These men] urged that the Five Thousand must

12. The words uttered by Pisander (at Thuc. 8.53.3) suggest that the oligarchs were walking on eggshells to present their preferred constitutional option as something different than plain oligarchy, but as a "more moderate (*sōphronesteron*) form of government."

13. Closer to home, the oligarchs also failed to secure the support of the Athenian soldiers stationed on Samos (on which more below).

14. For Teegarden (2012), the "revolutionary bandwagon" was first set in motion by the assassination of Phrynichus, a member of the Four Hundred.

be shown to exist not merely in name but in reality, and the constitution placed upon a fairer basis.

As the opposition in Athens grew stronger, the moderate oligarchic leader Theramenes coordinated a concerted reaction against the regime (cf. [Arist.] *Ath.Pol.* 33.2). The first blow was the demolition of the wall of Eetionea.[15] Theramenes called upon those "who wished the Five Thousand to govern instead of the Four Hundred" (Thuc. 8.92.11) and collected a motley crew that encompassed both oligarchic and democratic sympathizers or, in Thucydides' words, "the hoplites and a number of the people in Piraeus" (Thuc. 8.92.10).

Why did so many Athenians come to perceive the Four Hundred as illegitimate, and a government of five thousand as legitimate? To answer this question, we must investigate the circumstances of the Four Hundred's establishment—a task that is complicated by major inconsistencies in the sources.[16] In what follows, I discuss first the constitutional Assembly as described by Thucydides and [Aristotle]. I then turn to Thucydides' narrative depicting the circumstances surrounding the rise of the Four Hundred.

[Aristotle]'s and Thucydides' accounts of the constitutional Assembly that ushered in the rule of the Four Hundred are consistent in one respect: the Assembly was characterized by the manipulation of Athens' laws and procedures. According to Thucydides' brief account, the meeting was peculiar as to its location and constituency. First, the Assembly was held at Colonus (a deme about one mile northeast of Athens) and not on the Pnyx (that is, within Athens' defensive walls) at a time when the Attic countryside was not a safe place. Spartan armies occupied strategic locations there, making movement outside of the walls extremely dangerous. The poorer members of Athens' political body, who could not afford to buy their own armaments, would have been wary of

15. The wall of Eetionea in Piraeus had been built by the Four Hundred to more easily control access to the port (Thuc. 8.90.2–5).

16. [Aristotle] (*Ath.Pol.* 29–32) describes the establishment of the Four Hundred as the result of an orderly constitutional assembly in the course of which two different constitutions were ratified: a constitution for the present, which featured the participation of four hundred individuals, and one for the future, which extended the franchise to five thousand individuals. By contrast, Thucydides (quoted below) plunges the constitutional proceedings in the midst of violent confrontations in the city between the supporters of oligarchy and the rest of the population. Shear (2011: 20) reads the diverging accounts of Thucydides and [Aristotle] not as evidence of the Four Hundred's actions, but as "constructed responses to the events." The two constitutions in [Aristotle]'s account "come directly out of the fierce contemporary debates over the correct *politeia* for Athens and its relationship to the city's past." Instead, Thucydides' portrait of violence in the city "reflects strategies used in the lawsuits brought against the oligarchs and their supporters after the fall of the Four Hundred."

venturing into the countryside to participate in the meeting. Moreover, when the Colonus Assembly took place, many lower class Athenians were stationed on Samos, serving in the fleet.[17] According to [Aristotle]'s detailed narrative (*Ath.Pol.* 29.4), the meeting was characterized by the abolition of major constitutional safeguards, including indictments for illegal proposals, impeachment proceedings, and summons.

> They suspended the statute of indictments for illegal proposals (*graphai paranomon*) and all impeachments (*eisangeliai*) and summonses (*prosklēseis*)[18] so that any Athenian who wished could make proposals about what was being discussed. If anyone punished, summonsed or brought before a court anyone for doing so, he should immediately be indicted and brought before the *strategi*, and they should hand him over to the Eleven for execution.[19]

In sum, according to both [Aristotle] and Thucydides, the shift from democracy to oligarchy was brought about by the manipulation of Athens' laws and procedures. Depending on which account we follow, the Colonus proceedings may have been perceived as illegitimate either because of interference with the polis' constitutional safeguards, or because the decisions ratified at the meeting could not but achieve, at best, a limited consensus. However, whether the Athenians assembled at Colonus perceived these actions as illegitimate, and whether those that were not at Colonus (e.g., the soldiers stationed on Samos) had a detailed knowledge of the proceedings, remains unclear in the sources.

Thucydides' larger narrative (8.65.2–66.5) paints a very different picture of the circumstances surrounding the Colonus meeting. When supporters of oligarchy arrived in Athens to set up the constitutional Assembly,

> they found most of the work already done by their associates. Some of the younger men had banded together, and secretly assassinated one Androcles, the chief leader of the commons. . . . There were also some other obnoxious persons whom they secretly did away with in the same manner. . . . The Assembly and the Council . . . still met notwithstanding, although they discussed nothing that was not approved of by the conspirators, who both

17. The Assembly that brought the fifth-century democracy to an end was very similar to the Assembly that brought it into being. According to Plutarch (*Cim.* 15), in 464, Ephialtes introduced the reforms that transferred political power from the Areopagus to popular institutions in an assembly that was decimated by the absence of nearly four thousand hoplites who were serving abroad under Cimon.

18. *Prosklēsis* is a summons to appear before the competent magistrate (Thür 2006).

19. Thucydides (8.67.2) reports only the suspension of the graphē paranomōn.

supplied the speakers, and reviewed in advance what they were to say. Fear, and the sight of the numbers of the conspirators, closed the mouths of the rest; or if any ventured to rise in opposition, he was presently put to death in some convenient way, and there was neither search for the murderers nor justice to be had against them if suspected; but the people remained motionless, being so thoroughly cowed that men thought themselves lucky to escape violence, even when they held their tongues. An exaggerated belief in the numbers of the conspirators also demoralized the people, rendered helpless by the magnitude of the city, and by their want of intelligence with each other, and being without means of finding out what those numbers really were. For the same reason it was impossible for any one to open his grief to a neighbor and to concert measures to defend himself, as he would have had to speak either to one whom he did not know, or whom he knew but did not trust. Indeed all the popular party approached each other with suspicion, each thinking his neighbor concerned in what was going on, the conspirators having in their ranks persons whom no one could ever have believed capable of joining an oligarchy; and these it was who made the many so suspicious, and so helped to procure impunity for the few, by confirming the commons in their mistrust of one another.

If the details of the Colonus Assembly must remain obscure, the violent picture that Thucydides paints is confirmed by independent evidence—namely, the forensic speeches that deal with the trial of members and supporters of the Four Hundred (Shear 2011: 60–67). When the Four Hundred collapsed, many Athenians were prosecuted on account of their association with the regime. During their trials, some of them were able to clear their name by shifting the blame on a small cadre of extremists. In other words, they claimed that the supporters of oligarchy aimed to establish a legitimate government, but their plan succumbed under the actions of a violent fringe. It is these extremists, not the supporters of a moderate oligarchic regime, that were responsible for the violence in the city.

———

In light of the evidence discussed above, we may reconstruct the reign of the Four Hundred as follows. The Four Hundred came to power in the midst of a severe political and financial crisis. Pledging to secure a deal with Persia that would have funneled much-needed resources to the war effort and assuaged the elite's fear of expropriation, the Four Hundred succeeded in replacing the democratic constitution with an oligarchic one. To present oligarchy as a legitimate governmental option, the Four Hundred appealed to the notion of patrios politeia and proceeded to refashioning Athens as an oligarchic city. But their commitment to the past as a symbol of legitimate governance soon proved hollow. Whether it was because they failed to restore Athens' finances (through a deal with Persia or otherwise), or because they failed to respect the constitutional mandate they had received (as [Aristotle] suggests), or because they employed violence to secure their position in power (as Thucydides suggests), a large section of the population came to perceive the new government as illegitimate. The violence perpetrated by the Four Hundred made coordination difficult, until the opposing groups learned that there was broad support (in Athens as well as on Samos) to replace the Four Hundred with a government in which the franchise was extended to five thousand citizens. Whereas the Athenians perceived the Five Thousand as legitimate because their rule was actually ratified in Colonus, or because they were willing to support the oligarchic platform that was discussed in the aftermath of Sicily, however, we will probably never know.

2.2.b. The Five Thousand (410–409)

After the collapse of the Four Hundred, the Athenians gathered on the Pnyx to establish the rule of the Five Thousand.[20] As Shear documents (2011: 51–60), the Five Thousand also employed the notion of patrios politeia to legitimize their rule and appropriated buildings and traditions associated with Athens' archaic lawgivers, especially Cleisthenes.[21]

Information about the Five Thousand's time in power is woefully scarce. However, the sources at our disposal suggest that they did well. Thucydides (8.97.2; cf. [Arist.] Ath.Pol. 33.2) states that the government of the Five Thousand was a good one – a balanced mix (metria synkrasis) of democracy and oligarchy. The reconstruction I conducted above also suggests that, at the time of their establishment, many Athenians may have perceived the Five Thousand as a legitimate government. Finally, unlike the Four Hundred, the Five Thousand apparently did not engage in extra-constitutional action, they did not perpetrate arbitrary acts of violence, and they did not suffer military defeats. They actually achieved an important victory in the naval battle of Cynossema (Thuc. 8. 104–6).

20. On the Five Thousand, see esp. Vlastos (1952); de Ste. Croix (1956); Rhodes (1972a); Sealey (1975); Harris (1990); Raaflaub (2006).

21. The use of the Pnyx as a meeting place and possibly the restoration of a Council of Five Hundred connected the Five Thousand with Cleisthenes' reforms.

Why, then, did the Five Thousand disintegrate so quickly? Martin Ostwald (1986: 405) considered the Five Thousand as an "intermediate regime," responsible for a whole constitutional revolution that paved the way for the reestablishment of democracy.[22] Donald Kagan (1987: 205) argued that the exclusion from political privileges of the lower classes who manned the ships and played a strategic role in Athens' military was not a sustainable, long-term measure. Similarly, Simonton suggests (2017: 47) that the Five Thousand were "an emergency measure that looked forward to the restoration of full democracy . . . an armed caretaker of the polis until such time as the traditional democracy could be safely reinstated."[23]

All these explanations more or less explicitly assume that oligarchy was an aberration in Athens, and that all the Athenians wanted to do after the collapse of the Four Hundred was to reestablish democracy as soon as possible. However, the fact that they didn't points to a different explanation. If we take seriously the possibility that the Five Thousand were established to last, then their rapid demise was probably due to a lack of support once they got to power. As we saw above, the democratic and oligarchic opponents of the Four Hundred were able to coordinate their actions when one group knew that the other group knew that there was bipartisan support for a government of five thousand citizens. But the evidence also suggests that the groups opposing the Four Hundred—notably the soldiers on Samos and the moderate oligarchic group led by Theramenes in Athens—may have rallied behind the five thousand only to get rid of the Four Hundred, but that neither group truly supported such a solution. If the army on Samos was overwhelmingly pro-democracy (Thuc. 8.76.6), the oligarchs opposing the Four Hundred supported the five thousand merely as a "political cry" (Thuc. 8.89.3).

Borrowing an insight from bargaining theory, I suggest that the constitution of the Five Thousand was a concession that the parties made to one another rather than keeping the Four Hundred in power. As economist Thomas Schelling

22. Relying on Thucydides' (8.97.2) assertion that, "many other assemblies were held afterwards, in which law-makers were elected and all other measures taken to form a constitution," Ostwald attributes the beginning of the process of revision of the laws (on which more below) to the Five Thousand. Shear's discussion of the epigraphic evidence, however, demonstrates that the process began under the restored democracy (Shear 2011: 72–75).

23. Simonton discusses and rejects the "myth of the hoplite republic" on account of its structural inadequacy. For Simonton (2012b: 57–58) if the hoplites could choose whether "they wanted to be at the poorest end of the voting spectrum in a hoplite oligarchy, or instead be closer to occupying the pivotal middle voting position in a constitution that included all and that offered a much better chance of blocking the desires of the very wealthiest," they would unmistakably choose the latter option.

remarks in the influential book *The Strategy of Conflict* (1966: 70), "most bargaining situations ultimately involve some range of possible outcomes within which each party would rather make a concession than fail to reach agreement at all. In such a situation any potential outcome is one from which at least one of the parties, and probably both, would have been willing to retreat for the sake of agreement, and very often the other party knows it." The fact that collective action—i.e., the series of events that began with the demolition of the wall of Eetionea—occurred after the ambassadors had relayed the news that the army on Samos supported a government of five thousand points toward this interpretation. However, once the city was reunited and the threat of the Four Hundred neutralized, the costs of supporting a compromise regime that neither the democratic nor the moderate oligarchic leadership actually preferred may have quickly outweighed the benefits of maintaining the Five Thousand in power.

2.2.c. The First Restored Democracy (409–404)

The Five Thousand lasted in power for eleven months. After their demise, the Athenians restored a democratic government. Like the oligarchic governments that preceded it, the new democracy appropriated patrios politeia for its own ends and, as Shear suggests (2011: ch. 4 and 5), began to refashion Athens as a democratic city.[24] But what would a new, *patrios* democracy look like, after the collapse of the fifth-century structure?

The previous analysis suggested that the primary obstacle to democratic stability in the aftermath of Sicily was the inability of the Assembly to credibly commit to policy. To address this problem, the first restored democracy passed a series of important reforms in the areas of fiscal policy and legal institutions.

Fiscal policy reforms indicate that the demos sought to address the elite's fear of expropriation by regulating their disbursements. However, the evidence also suggests that the demos may have gone about this task only halfheartedly. One the one hand, the Athenians introduced the *syntriērarchia* (lit. co-trierarchy)—a system that allowed the wealthy to pool resources to finance the trierarchy (the tax to equip and finance a warship).[25] As Gabrielsen (1994:

---

24. The demos put its mark on the Agora and the Acropolis through construction projects and created new rituals and traditions, like the oath of Demophantus against tyranny and the new practice of announcing gold crowns at the city Dionysia.

25. The *triērarchia*—the sponsorship of a warship for a year—and the *chorēgia*—the sponsorship of a chorus during a festival—were taxes that fell on the Athenian elite (those with

173–74) suggests, "the syntrierarchy was the first known major concession made to the propertied class. It reflected the realization that the financial and personal requirements accruing from trierarchic service had become exorbitant for many individuals. By way of this innovation, the previous firm adherence to the principle "one man to a ship" was loosened, and permission was given to two or more individuals who wished to cooperate toward discharging a single service."[26] On the other hand, the Athenians passed a series of measures that benefited the demos: they reinstated pay for office; added a new disbursement to citizens—the so-called *diobelia* (lit. two obols); and levied two special taxes on the wealthy (*eisphorai*). The evidence thus suggests that, in the context of a dire financial situation, the Athenians did not shy away from extracting revenue from the wealthy, while at the same time attempting to regulate their financial contributions to the polis.

Legal reforms point to a desire to impose checks the demos' power. In this period, the Athenians set out to collect, revise, and publish the laws of the city—a process significantly referred to as the revision of the "laws of Solon" (Lys. 30.2). As Finley (1975: 39) put it, commissions of *syngrapheis* and *anagrapheis* (loosely translated as writers and recorders) were appointed "to examine the ramshackle accumulation of laws and decrees and to inscribe a tidied-up [i.e., internally coherent] code of binding law over the whole field." In order to complete this task, the *anagrapheis* received a four-month mandate, but remained in office for six years (from 410 to 404), until the end of the Peloponnesian War disrupted the proceedings.[27]

The revision of the laws is a critical step in the elaboration of patrios politeia.[28] By appropriating the "laws of Solon" and displaying them

---

assets worth three to four talents or more: Davies 1971). On the ad hoc use of the *synchorēgia* in the year 406/405, see Wilson (2000: 265).

26. Fiscal policy reforms between 410 and 404: Blamire (2001: 117–22); Burke (2010: 404–5); Davies (2004: 505–6).

27. The process resumed under the new democracy in 403 and ended in 399. On the terms used to describe the office: Harrison (1955); Ostwald (1986); Sealey (1987); Rhodes (1991); Carawan (2002).

28. Here, my interpretation differs markedly from Shear's. For Shear, the laws are a manifestation of the demos' power. In her words (2011: 71), the laws that were inscribed and prominently displayed "allowed the demos to write its control of the city firmly on the topography and particularly on the Agora." But the strong emphasis on the demos is limited to the oath of Demophantus and to the law pertaining to the power of the Council (concerning actions that cannot be taken "without the approval of the full demos"). In the other laws that Shear discusses (including the law of Draco, the naval law, the text about taxes, and the sacrificial calendar) the same strong emphasis on the demos is absent. In my reading, instead, the laws are self-imposed

prominently where the power of the demos was exercised—that is, in the Agora—the democracy also displayed a commitment to respecting those laws. The laws were a bulwark against violations such as the ones perpetrated by the Four Hundred. The laws were also a signaling device toward those groups whose fear of an unchecked demos had brought down the fifth-century democracy. The demos that asserted its power in the year 410/409, then, was not the fifth-century demos, but a demos *surrounded by laws*.

The fact that "the laws of Solon" that were inscribed between the years 410/409 and 404 were not, strictly speaking, "of Solon," as they were not "of Draco" or "of Cleisthenes," does not necessarily mean that patrios politeia expressed an imperfect connection with all of these figures, and by extension a vague connection with Athens' past. Instead, I suggest that the phrase "laws of Solon" indicated something less specific than an appropriation of a set of measures that can be (or could be, by the Athenians) directly attributed to the polis' early lawgiver(s). In collecting, revising, and prominently displaying the laws of the city and attributing them to Athens' early lawgivers, the first restored democracy established a connection between the patrios politeia, which they were avowedly reestablishing, the legitimate nature of their rule, and the fundamental concept on which such legitimacy was grounded: the concept of legality.

If we analyze the first restored democracy through the lens of the problem of credible commitment, we might conclude that democracy collapsed in the year 404 because the emerging commitment to law was not woven into the polis' institutional structure in a way that made it credible to all actors involved. The package of fiscal reforms sent, at best, a mixed message to the wealthy. As to the revision of the laws, it was one thing for the demos to write the laws, another to systematically enforce them. The problem emerged clearly after the Battle of Arginusae, when an enraged demos voted to sentence its generals to death, en masse and without trial (cf. chapter 1). However, the extent to which the collapse of democracy in the year 404 was triggered by the external shock brought about by Athens' loss in the Peloponnesian War recommends the use of caution.

After the Battle of Aegospotami in the year 405, the Spartan navy appeared in Piraeus, while enemy armies occupied the countryside. The siege forced Athens to capitulate in the year 404. The victorious Spartans imposed the terms of the peace treaty: Athens "should destroy the long walls and the walls of

---

checks on the demos' power. In other words, before being symbols of the demos' power, the laws that the Athenians collected, inscribed, and displayed were just that—laws. These laws regulated the behavior of individual Athenians, as private citizens and magistrates.

Piraeus, surrender all their ships except twelve . . . , count the same people friends and enemies as the Lacedaemonians did, and follow the Lacedaemonians both by land and by sea wherever they should lead the way" (Xen. *Hell.* 2.2.20; trans. Brownson 1921).[29] In addition to determining foreign policy, Sparta also intervened in Athens' domestic policy, establishing the most infamous of Athens' oligarchies—the regime of the Thirty Tyrants.[30]

2.2.d. The Thirty (404–403)

The debate on patrios politeia resumed as soon as the Thirty came to power and shaped their reconstruction of Athens as an oligarchic city.[31] Once again, the process involved appropriating buildings and institutions traditionally associated with Athens' forefathers, particularly Cleisthenes (Shear 2011: 167–80).[32] But the oligarchs' program did not stop at buildings and institutions. Soon after their establishment, the oligarchs turned to the laws of the city. As [Aristotle] (*Ath.Pol.* 35.2; trans. my own) suggests,

> [the Thirty] took down from the Areopagus the laws of Ephialtes and Archestratus about the Areopagites; they also repealed such of the statutes of Solon as were obscure (*osoi diamphisbētēseis eschon*), and abolished the authority vested in the jurors (*to kuros o ēn en tois dikastais katelusan*).

The Thirty, then, proceeded to their own "revision of the laws." First, they removed the statutes of the democratic leaders Archestratus and Ephialtes, which in the mid-fifth century had curtailed the authority of the elite Council of the Areopagus by transferring its powers to the popular courts. If the Thirty

29. All translations of Xenophon's *Hellenica* are from Brownson (1921), unless otherwise noted.

30. On the Thirty, see esp. Hignett (1952); Krentz (1982); Ostwald (1986); Wolpert (2002); Osborne (2010).

31. If Sparta's imprimatur on the establishment of the Thirty is hardly to be doubted (Diod. 14.3.4–7), the evidence indicates that the Thirty's subsequent actions did not stem from Spartan authority. Both Xenophon and Diodorus suggest that the Thirty, rather than bowing their head to the Spartans, exploited them for their own purposes (Diod.14.4.1–4; cf. Xen. *Hell.* 2.3.13).

32. Shear argues that the Thirty's appointment of a council of five hundred *bouleutai* recalled the Cleisthenic system (Shear 2011: 171). However, if the Council of Five Hundred was originally created by Cleisthenes, it was also the key institution of the fifth-century radical democracy for a century, a fact that was perhaps more obvious to an Athenian in the late fifth century. It is even harder to see how the appropriation of the New Bouleuterion as the Thirty's meeting place, and therefore the appropriation of a space recently built under the democracy, may fit a plan to appropriate "the past."

sought to appropriate Athens' past to set themselves apart from the fifth-century democracy, then it made sense to remove the laws that ushered in the democracy's most radical phase (cf. chapter 1).

But why repeal the statutes of Solon, one of the fathers whose past the Thirty were supposedly appropriating?[33] In the passage above, [Aristotle] specifies that, of the laws of Solon, the Thirty removed "those that were obscure" (*osoi diamphisbēteseis eschon*). Earlier in his account (*Ath.Pol.* 9.2), [Aristotle] had stated that, "some people think that Solon purposely made his laws obscure (*amphisbēteseis*), *in order that the people might have power over the verdict*" (trans. my own). The use of the same adjective (in Greek strengthened by the particle *dia*) establishes a connection between the passages, suggesting that, in the passage quoted above, [Aristotle] is saying that the Thirty removed the obscure laws of Solon as a necessary step toward abolishing the power of the courts or, as he puts it, "the authority vested in the jurors."[34] The Thirty's legal reforms, then, were explicitly directed against Athens' laws regardless of their author, and particularly against the popular courts as the ultimate arbiters of legal interpretation.[35]

Rather than an appropriation of Athens' past, then, the Thirty's attack on the city's laws is best understood as a response to the demos' appropriation of the city's laws in the period between the years 410 and 404. In appropriating patrios politeia to legitimize their power, the Thirty also appropriated the connection, forged by the first restored democracy, between patrios politeia, legitimacy, and legality. From this perspective, it does not matter exactly which past the Thirty's reforms appropriated or discarded. A legitimate, *patrios* government after the first restored democracy was a government surrounded by laws. The Thirty, then, set out to surround themselves with laws—but only those that would support their position in power.

The Thirty not only eliminated statutes unpalatable to their style of rule. They also implemented a set of institutions conducive to oligarchic stability (Simonton 2017). These included consensus-building among their ranks (by isolating Theramenes: 84); extra-legal killings to cow the population (112; 116); the use of the open ballot to control Assemblies (128); the use of cooptation, informants, and the destruction of monuments to manipulate the flow of

33. A scholion to Aeschines (*Schol. Aesch.* 1.39.2; trans. Shear 2011: 173) reports that "when they [i.e., the Thirty] had overthrown the *patrios politeia* of the Athenians, they maltreated the laws of both Draco and Solon."

34. And in fact, the Thirty's prosecution of opponents was carried out before the Council, not before the popular courts (Xen. *Hell.* 2.3.12; Lys. 13.35–36).

35. As Osborne noted (2010: 281), the Thirty's reforms agenda focused on the laws and the courts, unlike the Four Hundred's agenda, which focused on the Assembly and Council.

information (136; 142; 216); and finally, the control of public spaces (156; 161). So why did the Thirty, like the Four Hundred, collapse after a mere handful of months?

Two similarities between the regime of the Four Hundred and that of the Thirty are striking. First, both governments' loss of legitimacy arose from a refusal to share power with a larger constituency. Second, both regimes were undermined by an opposition that encompassed their own ranks.

The literary sources differ again on what exactly was ratified during the constitutional Assembly that established the rule of the Thirty. For Diodorus and Xenophon, the Thirty were tasked with drafting a new constitution and new laws with which to administer the state—which they didn't do (Diod. 14.4.1–2; Xen. *Hell.* 2.3.11). For [Aristotle], the Thirty received a specific constitutional mandate—but they ignored it ([Arist.] *Ath.Pol.* 35.1). Wholly unconstrained, their rule soon degenerated into arbitrary violence and expropriations of citizens and noncitizens alike. The chronology of events is complicated by inconsistencies in the sources, but all accounts suggest that the violence of the Thirty escalated as time went by. [Aristotle] writes (*Ath.Pol.* 35.3–4; cf. Diod. 14.4.2–3; Xen. *Hell.* 2.3.12, 21),

> at the outset . . . they got rid of the informers and the wicked mischief-makers who flattered the people to their disadvantage. The people were delighted, thinking they made these changes for the best of motives. When the Thirty had tightened their grip on the city, there was no type of citizen they did not attack. They killed those remarkable for wealth, family or reputation, aiming to remove any potential threat and to lay their hands on their property. After a short time they had killed no less than fifteen hundred men.

Moreover, the sources seem to suggest that the support of Sparta may have allowed the Thirty to engage in acts of violence and expropriations more thoroughly, and more brazenly, than the Four Hundred ever could.[36]

However, like the Four Hundred seven years before, the Thirty also had to come to terms with an unexpected breed of opponents: individuals from their own ranks. As he did when the Four Hundred were in power, the moderate leader Theramenes criticized the Thirty's use violence and their refusal to share

---

36. Xenophon and Diodorus see the escalation of violence as a consequence of the arrival of a Spartan garrison. In Xenophon's (*Hell.* 2.3.24–26) account, Critias justifies the violence as a necessary tool for protecting the oligarchy. The oligarchy, in turn, is necessary to preserve the favor of Sparta. [Aristotle] (*Ath.Pol.* 37.2) places the request of the garrison later on in the narrative, after Thrasybulus' occupation of Phyle and the death of Theramenes.

power with a broader section of the populace. In the words of [Aristotle] (*Ath. Pol.* 36.1; cf. Xen. *Hell.* 2.3.17),

> Theramenes was angry at what was happening; he urged the Thirty to stop behaving so outrageously, and to give the best citizens a share in government.

This time, Theramenes was promptly eliminated.

After the death of Theramenes, opposition to the Thirty could not have been mobilized in the city. Widespread and protracted armed violence, and the fear that such violence generated, prevented the Thirty's opponents from coordinating. However, that very fear also contributed to swell the ranks of the opposition. Theramenes' last speech, as Xenophon (*Hell.* 2.3.38–39, 42) reconstructs it, puts this process in plain words:

> up to the time when you became members of the [Council] and magistrates were appointed and the notorious informers were brought to trial, all of us held the same views; but when these Thirty began to arrest men of worth and standing, then I, on my side, began to hold views opposed to theirs. For when Leon the Salaminian was put to death—a man of capacity, both actually and by repute—although he was not guilty of a single act of wrongdoing, I knew that those who were like him would be fearful, and, being fearful, would be enemies of this government. . . . And further, when I saw that many in the city were becoming hostile to this government and that many were becoming exiles, it did not seem to me best to banish either Thrasybulus or Anytus or Alcibiades; for I knew that by such measures the opposition would be made strong, if once the commons should acquire capable leaders and if those who wished to be leaders should find a multitude of supporters.

When the democratic leader Thrasybulus seized the stronghold of Phyle in northwestern Attica, an increasing number of exiles joined him (Xen. *Hell.* 2.4.5, 10, 25).[37] From Phyle, Thrasybulus moved to occupy the harbor of Piraeus. Epigraphic and literary evidence reveals that Thrasybulus' army included a diverse group of Athenian citizens, resident aliens, and slaves (Xen. *Hell.* 2.4.25; [Arist.] *Ath.Pol.* 40.2).

The civil war was brief, but bloody. The major battle, the Battle of Mounichia, was fought primarily between the democrats under Thrasybulus and the

---

37. Despite the lack of decisive military actions taking place in Phyle, the tradition that looked back to the civil conflict identified Phyle with the origin of the insurgency: e.g., Isoc. 8.108; Ar. *Pl.* 1146; Andoc. 1.80; Lys. 13.77; Dem. 19. 280; and IG II2 10.

supporters of the Thirty. The battle resulted in the success of the democratic faction (Xen. *Hell.* 2.4.11-19; [Arist.] *Ath.Pol.* 38.1; Diod. 14.33.2–3).[38] Only Xenophon among our sources reports a second battle in Piraeus, which was born as a skirmish, but soon turned into a full-blown encounter. In this second battle, the Spartans, who had been recalled by the Thirty, were victorious (Xen. *Hell.* 2.4.31–43).[39] After the battle, the Spartan king Pausanias brokered a reconciliation between the democratic faction in Piraeus and the supporters of oligarchy in the city. The terms of the reconciliation brokered by Pausanias were breached two years later (on which more in a moment). But the reconciliation agreement—the amnesty—was only one element in a larger process of institutional reforms that began after the end of the civil conflict. On this process, which I describe in greater detail in the next section, the Spartans had no say.

In this section, I reconstructed the Athenian constitutional struggles in the period between the years 413 and 403. In what follows, I summarize the main points of the analysis.

The collapse of the fifth-century democracy was triggered by the disastrous defeat in Sicily, but it was ultimately traceable to a crisis of legitimacy that stemmed from an institutional design defect: namely, the Assembly's inability to credibly commit to policy. Lack of credible commitment led the elites to fear that the demos would expropriate their assets to fund the war against Sparta. The emergency election of an advisory board of elders also indicates that, at this critical juncture, the demos lost trust in its own ability to guide Athens through the crisis. The supporters of oligarchy now began to advocate for replacing the democracy with a form of government in which the major asset-holders would also be the primary decision-makers.

To legitimize their rule, the first oligarchic government—the Four Hundred—appropriated the notion of patrios politeia, forging a critical connection between patrios politeia and legitimacy. Foreign policy fiascoes and a growing domestic opposition heightened the pressure on the oligarchs. As the Four Hundred proved unable to maintain order and security, the appeals to patrios politeia as a source of legitimacy proved hollow. Manipulation of the

---

38. [Aristotle] and Xenophon agree on the presence of a small Spartan contingent in support of the oligarchic faction. Diodorus does not mention the Spartans.

39. According to Xenophon, after the first battle, the Thirty took refuge in Eleusis and from there they sent envoys to Sparta to ask for help. The entrepreneurial naval commander Lysander set out to collect a force of hoplites, but King Pausanias, jealous of Lysander, marched on Athens himself to broker a peace. The skirmish and the battle ensued (Xen. *Hell.* 2.4.28–30).

city's laws and procedures, the unwillingness to share power with a larger constituency, and the widespread use of violence enabled the mobilization of a wide constituency of opponents, which coalesced under the moderate oligarchic leader Theramenes. When Theramenes learned that the army stationed on Samos would support the establishment of a broader-based regime of five thousand citizens, he spearheaded the effort to remove the Four Hundred from power.

The government of the Five Thousand came to power enjoying the support of the soldiers on Samos and of the moderate oligarchs in Athens—at least in words. The sources also suggest that the Five Thousand handled themselves well in both foreign and domestic policy. The reasons of their rapid demise are, however, shrouded in the paucity of our evidence. Previous scholarship identified the Five Thousand as an intermediate regime, created with a view to reestablishing democratic rule. My interpretation suggests instead that there is no reason to doubt that the Athenians wanted to establish a broad-based oligarchy when they did so. However, because it was born as a compromise government for the purpose of removing the Four Hundred, the Five Thousand lacked critical support once in power. Hence, their rapid demise.

When the Five Thousand collapsed, the Athenians restored democracy. The new government appropriated patrios politeia for its own ends and elaborated on the connection, forged initially by the Four Hundred, between patrios politeia and legitimacy. After the failure of the fifth-century democracy, a legitimate democratic government had to tackle the problem of credible commitment. Accordingly, the first restored democracy promoted reforms in the area of fiscal policy to regulate the fiscal burden on the wealthy by allowing them to pool resources to discharge Athens' most onerous tax: the trierarchy. Moreover, the new government sought to constrain the decision-making power of the demos by undertaking a vast program of collection, revision, and publication of the laws of the city—a program notably referred to as the revision of the laws of Solon. In doing so, the first restored democracy elaborated on the connection between patrios politeia and legitimacy by adding a third element: legality.

After the crippling defeat in the Peloponnesian War, Athens was once again ruled by an oligarchy. Although established by the victorious Spartans, the Thirty still had to present themselves as a legitimate government in the eyes of the Athenians in order to stay in power. To do so, they appropriated the notion of patrios politeia, like previous governments had done. But patrios politeia meant something different in 404 than it did in 411. After the first restored democracy, a *patrios* government was, at a minimum, a government capable and willing to respect the laws of the city. Accordingly, the Thirty promoted their own revision of the laws to eliminate those statutes that threatened their position in power, including some of the laws of Solon. As the Thirty began to remove their political opponents and to persecute, kill, and expropriate asset-holders—citizens as well as noncitizens—the Athenians took up arms against them under the leadership of Thrasybulus.

Against the Thirty, as against the Four Hundred, the opposition encompassed a broader group than just "the democrats." Thucydides says plainly that the opposition to the Four Hundred included supporters of democracy as well as partisans of oligarchy that had grown weary of the abuses of the ruling oligarchs. The army that joined the democratic leader Thrasybulus first in Phyle and then in Piraeus was a motley crew of citizens, foreigners, and slaves. We do not have direct evidence for former supporters of oligarchy joining Thrasybulus' army. However, the Thirty's persecutions may have persuaded those who found it in their interest (because of their wealth) to live under an oligarchy to support democracy instead.

The bipartisan nature of the opposition to the oligarchs' violations, like the collective dismay toward the democracy that had led the demos to Sicily (Thuc. 8.1.1), favored the elaboration of a broad-based consensus on the basic features of legitimate government. But what was the consensus about? If, as Shear suggests, under the Four Hundred, patrios politeia expressed a connection with Athens' past aimed at legitimizing constitutional change, at least since the first restoration of democracy patrios politeia became associated with the concept of legality—a concept germane to patrios politeia as the constitution of Athens' early lawgivers. Among Athens' lawgivers, one stood out: Solon. The first restored democracy referred to the revision of the laws as the "laws of Solon;" the Thirty's attack on the city's laws, at least according to [Aristotle], singled out Solon's laws. The decree that ushered in the new democracy also referred explicitly to the laws of Solon as the pillar of the new structure (Andoc. 1.83).[40] These references in the sources may simply reflect ex-post preferences. Yet, as we will see in the next section, the new constitution was markedly Solonian.

On the consensus on patrios politeia qua Solonian legality, the Athenians built a new, self-enforcing democratic constitution.

2.3. The Athenian Self-Enforcing Constitution

In the year 403, Athens hit rock bottom. The defeat in the Peloponnesian War had left the city without walls, ships, and allies (Xen. *Hell.* 2.2.20), Athenian finances were at an all-time low (Strauss 1987a: ch. 2; Burke 1990; Blamire 2001),

---

40. The decree itself has recently been shown to be a later forgery (Canevaro and Harris 2012; 2017). However, as many scholars suggest, and as I show in the next chapter, the laws of Solon played an important role in the new constitutional structure.

and about half of the male population was dead (Strauss 1987a: ch. 3; Hansen 1988: ch. 3; Akrigg 2007). For the first time since the establishment of democracy in the late sixth century, the worst of all evils—civil war—had ravaged the city. After a decade of divisions, and after the violence of the oligarchs and the civil conflict, restoring a stable government was no small task. As I show in chapter 5, comparative evidence suggests that after such large-scale episodes of internal unrest, Athens could have experienced recurring civil conflict, as it happened to Syracuse throughout the classical period, or a permanent transition toward a form of government where a sovereign third party enforces the rules that everyone must follow, as in Rome under Augustus. The Athenians, however, did not take either of those paths. When arms were laid down, winners and losers sat down at the negotiating table, ratified an amnesty, and drafted a series of institutional reforms.

The scholarly tradition has often analyzed the amnesty and the institutional reforms in isolation from one another. Efforts to study the reforms have concentrated on settling evidentiary problems (e.g., Harrison 1955; MacDowell 1975; Hansen 1978; 1990a; Robertson 1990; Rhodes 1991), while the amnesty has long been regarded as a categorical commitment to forgive and forget past wrongs (Loening 1987; Loraux 2002; Wolpert 2002)—the brightest product of Athens' democratic culture.[41]

Against this tradition, Edwin Carawan (2013) suggested that the amnesty expressed not a moral commitment to remembering and forgetting, blaming and forgiving, but a contractual agreement that concerned restitution of property, compensation for losses, and restoration of legal rights. Moreover, for Carawan (2013: 19), the "success of the Athenian amnesty had much to do with the legislation that reinforced the original agreement; for this process endowed 'the ancestral laws' with a new sense of contractual obligation . . . Whatever forgiveness they felt in their hearts, it was this more rigorous reckoning with the laws that kept the peace and sustained the new democracy." The legislation that "reinforced the agreement" was the product of a negotiation conducted "across ideological lines" (2013: 8) and informed by the notion of the ancestral laws.

After a decade of division and turmoil, why was the negotiation conducted across ideological lines? Carawan (2013: 68–9) follows a number of ancient and modern scholars in attributing the resilience of the amnesty to the role of Sparta as a third-party enforcer. But as we will see in a moment, the evidence does not support this explanation. Instead, I suggest that the effort to strike a balance among competing demands and interests, which pervades the amnesty

41. On the meaning and importance of the phrase *mē mnēsikakein* (lit. not to recall wrongs): Carawan (2012; 2013); contra Joyce (2008; 2014; 2015).

agreement as well as the institutional reforms, owed to the long process of elaboration of a collective consensus on patrios politeia understood as a form of Solonian legality. As Solon had done through his legislation, so the postwar amnesty and reforms sought to make all parties better off (Ober 2019), and focused on protecting citizens' freedom, dignity, and property and on strengthening Athens' laws and courts (cf. chapter 1).

In this section, I analyze the amnesty and the institutional reforms as constitutive parts of a new self-enforcing constitutional structure. Borrowing from the language of institutional analysis, I argue that the stability of the constitution rested on three factors: the constitution imposed limits on the government; it created incentives for the parties to abide by the rules; and it provided institutional mechanisms to punish violations without devolving into violence.[42]

2.3.a. Limits

The Athenians imposed limits on the previously unrestrained decision-making power of the demos in the Assembly by introducing another legislative institution—the nomothesia (lit. lawmaking) and by specifying a series of procedures to be followed in the process of legislation. The reforms enhanced the credibility of the demos' commitments.

Many aspects of the process of nomothesia are debated.[43] But two features deserve attention. First, the nomothesia created multiple veto points in the process of lawmaking. According to Canevaro's recent reconstruction (2013a: 150; 2015), the nomothesia involved four institutions—the Council, the Assembly, the law-courts, and the *nomothetai* (lit. lawgivers)—and seven stages. These included a preliminary vote in the Assembly to allow new proposals, a period for the publication of the new proposals in front of the monument of the Eponymous Heroes concomitant with readings in subsequent assemblies, the summon of nomothetai, the repeal of existing laws that contradicted the new proposal, and an approval stage. Second, whether this final approval stage took place in the courts before jurors selected by lot from the body of those who had sworn the jurors' oath (e.g., MacDowell 1975: 62–74; Hansen 1985: 363–65, 371; Rhodes

---

42. As Wolpert (2002) has shown, multiple attempts to punish the oligarchs were made. My reconstruction does not suggest that the self-enforcing pact was successful because it eliminated the possibility of conflict. Instead, I suggest that the success of the reforms lay in the fact that conflict was channeled through the courts and that it did not lead to violence.

43. Debates focus on the composition of boards of nomothetai and on the steps involved in the process of nomothesia: MacDowell (1975); Hansen (1985; 2016); Pierart (2000); Rhodes (2003); Canevaro and Harris (2012); Kremmydas (2012); Canevaro (2013a; 2015; 2016; 2018a); Carawan (2013: 269–70).

2003: 124–25; Kremmydas 2012: 16–31, 350–51; cf. Canevaro 2016: 46–48) or in an assembly labeled nomothetai (Piérart 2000), the many steps that preceded the final stage made it very difficult for a proposer of new legislation to predict, ex ante, how each different body would vote on a given proposal and manipulate the proceedings.[44]

Moreover, a complex system of checks and balances was created to coordinate the legislative process and define the relative spheres of influence of the two institutions. First, the Assembly maintained the power to pass decrees (*psēphismata*), subject to the provision that decrees could not contradict existing laws (*nomoi*). Second, laws were the domain of the nomothetai, but their power to pass legislation was in turn limited by the provision that the nomothetai could only be convened by the Assembly.[45] Finally, both decrees of the Assembly and laws of the nomothetai had to conform to the body of existing laws, which were collected and republished between the years 410 and 399 (cf. section 2.2.d).[46]

But in addition to limiting the power of the Assembly, in the aftermath of the civil conflict the Athenians had to deal with the threat of recurring violence. Pacifying Athens required establishing robust institutional channels to defuse the hostility that prevailed among citizens who had suffered violence, expropriation, exile, and disenfranchisement at the hands of the Thirty and during the civil conflict.[47] For this purpose, the amnesty agreement included a right-of-return clause whereby Athenian citizens (i.e., Athenians who were citizens

44. In the Council and in the law-courts, participants were selected by lot (cf. ch. 1). If the final stage of nomothesia was in fact in an assembly setting and not in a court setting, the lot did not apply. Assembly participants would be perhaps easier to persuade (though surely not to bribe), but before a new proposal could reach the final approval stage, it had to go through the other bodies.

45. The Athenians may have been the first to establish a distinction between laws and decrees as two levels of man-made law. The locus classicus for the distinction between laws (general rules) and decrees (rules that apply to specific cases) is Arist. *NE* 1137b13–32. The distinction was customary in fourth-century Athens (MacDowell 1978: 43–46), and respected in fourth-century legislation (Hansen 1978).

46. As part of this package of reforms, the old elite Council of the Areopagus acquired the power to supervise the administration of the laws by the magistrates (Hansen 1999: 290). The expansion of the power of the Areopagus continued throughout the fourth century. I discuss this process in chapter 4.

47. On the role of the courts in dealing with the threat of interpersonal violence: Wolpert (2002); Quillin (2002); Lanni (2016: ch. 6); Gowder (2016: ch. 6). I note here that Quillin's explanation—that oligarchic sympathizers managed to avoid the demos' judicial backlash in the courts by arguing that the stakes of reneging on the amnesty were tantamount to threatening to resume civil conflict—nicely dovetails with the one I propose here.

before the year 403) could reclaim political and legal rights, and whereby both citizens and noncitizens could reclaim their property. To protect the legal system against a wave of disputes that threatened to crush it, the Athenians also defined a series of procedures to determine which claims could and which couldn't go to court.[48]

In the fifth century, the Assembly's power was unchecked by laws or other institutions, leading to a critical inability to credibly commit to policy, which, under the pressure of war, brought down the entire constitutional structure. In the fourth century, legislation became the product of a complex and highly regulated mechanism of checks and balances among decision-making institutions. The reforms established the principle of divided government through coordination in lawmaking; and the amnesty helped define and enforce personal and property rights for all who voluntarily subjected themselves to the new constitutional rules—elites as well as nonelites, democrats as well as supporters of oligarchy.

2.3.b. Incentives

What incentives did the parties have to abide by the new rules? A long scholarly tradition rooted in the ancient sources suggests that the process of pacification succeeded because Sparta acted as a third-party enforcer of the amnesty (Todd 1985; Xen. *Hell.* 2.4.38; Diod. 14.33.6; [Arist.] *Ath.Pol.* 38.4). To challenge this view, we must pause to analyze the events that followed the civil conflict as they unfolded. The initial settlement that put an end to the civil conflict, overseen by Sparta, created a safe haven in the neighboring polis of Eleusis for the Thirty and those of their supporters who chose to leave Athens (Xen. *Hell.* 2.4.38).[49] Personal and property rights of both factions were protected under the

---

48. These procedures involved: first, a distinction between arrangements concluded under the democracy and those concluded under the Thirty, whereby the former were valid and the latter were not. Second, a distinction between private claims and liabilities to the polis, whereby the former were valid if concluded under the democracy (subject to a bar against suits in matters that the parties had already decided) and the latter were valid from the archonship of Euclides (that is, the year 403). Third, a distinction between offenders (*autocheires* and *authentai*) and informers, whereby *autocheires* were liable, informers (or denouncers) were not, and *authentai* were the object of a long legal struggle that pans out in the cases against Callimachus, Agoratos, and Eratosthenes (Carawan 2013: chs. 5, 6, 7). The reconstruction that I provide here is highly synchronic. For a diachronic perspective: Carawan (2013: ch. 4).

49. Under the settlement, the city of Athens belonged to the "men of Piraeus," that is the supporters of democracy under the leader Thrasybulus. The Thirty could relocate at Eleusis, and the settlement enabled them to acquire property there. The "men of the city," that is the

settlement, but the solution physically separated the warring factions, reducing the likelihood of protracted conflict. After ratification, King Pausanias and
his military contingent returned to Sparta (Xen. *Hell.* 2.4.39). This initial settlement failed two years later, around 401/400, when the Athenians heard that the
former partisans of the Thirty at Eleusis were hiring mercenaries to resume hos-
tilities and marched on Eleusis to defeat them (Xen. *Hell.* 2.4.43). At this crucial
juncture, the Spartans were nowhere to be seen. After the fall of Eleusis, a process
of reunification began in earnest, unassisted by Sparta (Lanni 2016: 185).

The evidence therefore suggests that the Spartans were not the key to the
stability of Athens' post-conflict agreement. However, the presence of Sparta
may have resolved a critical coordination problem in the immediate aftermath
of the civil conflict. In other words, Sparta acted as the first-mover, forcing the
Athenians down the path of reconciliation. By the time the first settlement
failed, conspicuous resources had already been committed toward building institutions to facilitate the process of pacification, which raised the stakes and
the costs of resuming conflict. If Sparta played an important role as first-mover,
but only a limited role in actually enforcing the agreement, then we must still
explain what kind of incentives the parties in Athens had to uphold the agreement. The question is all the more pressing in light of modern scholarship on
civil war suggesting that negotiated settlements fail to end civil wars, especially
in the absence of a third-party enforcer (Toft 2010; contra Nathan and Toft 2011;
Walter 1997; 2002).[50]

Were both democrats and oligarchs better off under the new rules than they
would have been under alternative constitutional options? Answering this question requires a measure of counterfactual speculation. Because the supporters

---

supporters of oligarchy, could decide whether to remain in the city and live under the rules
imposed by the new democratic constitution, or to relocate to Eleusis (Carawan 2013: 70–81).
Many stayed ([Arist.] *AthPol.* 40.1). Top oligarchic officials who wanted to remain in Athens
could do so only if they passed a scrutiny (*euthyna*) before a court. The spirit of reconciliation
emerges clearly from the provision that, contrary to common Athenian practice, the jurors in
this court were citizens with taxable property ([Arist.] *Ath.Pol.* 39.6).

50. The comparison is problematic insofar as we cannot assess whether the Athenian civil
war fits modern definitions of civil war. For example, following Fearon and Laitin's (2003) influential definition, Athenian combatants were "agents of (or claimants to) a state and organized
groups who sought . . . to take control of a government." The available evidence, however, does
not provide reliable measures of war casualties. According to Xenophon, ca. 370 men died in
the civil war. Of these, ca. 180 were either supporters of the Thirty or Spartan soldiers. (Xen.
Hell. 2.4.6, 19, 32, 34). These numbers, if reliable, meet only one of the other two criteria of
Fearon and Laitin's definition (at least one thousand deaths, of which one hundred are on the
government side).

of democracy had prevailed in the civil war against the supporters of oligarchy (cf. section 2.2.d), oligarchy was no longer a viable constitutional option. But various forms of democracy could have emerged. In particular, the democrats could have chosen two alternative paths to the constitutional reforms discussed earlier. First, they could have restored the fifth-century democracy, imposing once again no checks on the people's power. This choice would have likely alienated the supporters of oligarchy, who would have then faced three potential responses: to acquiesce, to resume fighting, or to relocate elsewhere in Greece. While fight and flight implied conspicuous costs, acquiescence was likely to prove unsustainable in the long run. Second, the democrats could have turned against the supporters of oligarchy more openly, for example by choosing the path of retribution and expropriation. This path would have increased the risk that the oligarchs would choose fight or flight. Compared to these alternatives, the new reforms made the supporters of oligarchy better off. Indeed, the new constitution provided conspicuous protections to the vanquished. But were the democrats better off?

The democrats were better off under the new constitutional structure than they would have been under the counterfactual options outlined above for three reasons. First, the consensus on patrios politeia qua Solonian legality embodied a solution that would enable the democrats to maintain their preferred constitutional structure (i.e., democracy), while limiting the excesses of the fifth-century democracy. Second, reneging on this solution meant alienating a section of the population (the supporters of oligarchy), thus sowing the seeds of renewed civil conflict.[51] Third, given the challenges that the city faced after the civil war, protracted civil conflict was not merely a costly option, but a threat to the very survival of the polis. In the year 403, the financial crisis that began in the first phase of the Peloponnesian War and worsened in the aftermath of Sicily had never been so dire. The emergency fund that the fifth-century democratic leader Pericles had put aside for rainy days was long gone. And so were other forms of stored wealth (e.g., golden statutes) that were melted down during the second phase of the Peloponnesian War (between the years 412 and 404). The defeat at the hands of Sparta in the year 404 meant the loss of the city's walls, ships, and allies. Adding insult to injury, the Thirty had compromised the infrastructure of Athens' military and commercial hub—the harbor of Piraeus (on which more in chapter 4). The Laurion silver mines, a conspicuous source of revenue in the fifth century, were shut down due to the

51. The civil war had just shown how costly repression could be. It is unclear if, at this juncture, the democrats could muster enough manpower and resources to both expropriate and repress. Many thanks to Bob Keohane for this observation.

Spartan takeover of key strongholds in the Attic countryside (between the years 412 and 404). The countryside lay idle, after a decade of Spartan occupation.[52] Since the beginning of the Peloponnesian War, Athens had suffered a plague (in the years 430 and 429), twenty-seven almost consecutive years of war, and a civil war. The casualties had decimated Athens' adult male citizen population.[53] The losses compounded each other. Without workers, Laurion and Piraeus were useless; without Laurion and Piraeus resources were scarce. Under these conditions, the possibility that Athens' neighbors—Sparta, but also Thebes and Corinth—would exploit Athens' divisions to take over control of the city was very real.[54]

2.3.c. Enforcement Mechanisms

The new constitutional structure revolved around the principle of coordination between the Assembly and the nomothetai. Coordination could only be preserved by policing the integrity of the corpus of laws, to which both Assembly decrees and nomothetai's laws had to conform. If the Assembly or the nomothetai passed new decrees and laws that contradicted existing statutes, then the institutional balance of power would crumble, allowing the proposers of contradicting measures to elevate themselves above the laws. Such behavior, associated with the experience of oligarchy, was among the threats that the Athenians sought to inhibit.[55]

To police the integrity of the corpus, the Athenians brushed up an old procedure: the graphē paranomōn. Because the reforms had introduced a

---

52. Throughout the Peloponnesian War and the civil war, Athens' countryside bore the brunt of military conflict: during the Archidamian War (the first phase of the Peloponnesian War, from 431 to 421), Spartan armies periodically ravaged the territory surrounding Athens; in 413 and during the following decade, the Spartans occupied key strongholds in Attic territory—notably Decelea—preventing Athens from tapping into its (scarce) agricultural and (abundant) mineral resources; finally, additional destruction was wrought by marching armies in the northern territory of Attica during the civil war. On the success of the Spartan destruction of Attic crops and farms see Hanson (1998); contra Thorne (2001).

53. War casualties did not affect all social classes in the same way. For Strauss (1987a: 78–81), during the Ionian War (412–404), the Athenian lower classes had suffered disproportionately compared to the upper classes. The natural constituency of Athens' democracy was therefore numerically weak, which would have contributed to lowering their violence potential.

54. Indeed, according to Xenophon (Hell. 2.2.19), after the Peloponnesian War the Corinthians and the Thebans had urged Sparta to raze Athens to the ground.

55. A parallel development, analyzed in Teegarden (2012; 2014), is the emphasis on anti-tyranny legislation.

distinction between laws and decrees, the Athenians maintained the graphē paranomōn to challenge decrees and devised a new procedure to challenge laws: the *graphē nomon mē epitēdeion theinai*—a public action against an unsuitable law. The stability of the constitution thus rested on the mandate bestowed equally on every adult male citizen to police the corpus of the city's laws.

But this was a risky move. First, the two procedures technically allowed whoever wished (ho boulomenos) of the roughly six thousand Athenians sitting in the Assembly to bring a public action against the proposer of a new legislative measure.[56] Second, the grounds for indictment were rather loose. Although one had to show that the new proposal contradicted an existing statute, the vague substantive nature of Athens' laws left ample room to articulate the *inconvenience* or *unsuitability* of new proposals. Third, these types of public actions slowed down the legislative process. If someone brought an indictment, the whole procedure was transferred from the Assembly to the courts for adjudication. Especially at a time when the city was divided and personal resentments were heightened by the recent experience of protracted political instability and civil war, the chance that people would use the graphē paranomōn and graphē nomon mē epitēdeion theinai to prosecute *proposers*, rather than *proposals*, was extremely high. Because indictments could be brought against just about any proposal (including various highly time-sensitive policies, such as military actions), had the Athenians frequently used these procedures to pursue personal feuds, the legislative process would have ground to a halt. Systematic abuse, in sum, would have jeopardized the entire constitutional structure.[57]

To prevent abuses, the Athenians relied in part on penalties. The use of the graphē paranomōn and graphē nomon mē epitēdeion theinai was regulated

56. A graphē paranomōn could be brought before or after the Assembly had passed the measure (Hansen 1974: 49) and against any proposal, with the exception of proposals that dealt with the appointment of magistrates.

57. One could argue that my reading overemphasizes the vagueness of the notions of "inconvenience" or "unsuitability" on the grounds that a graphē paranomōn required actual written laws to be presented as evidence that the indicted proposal was, in fact, against existing legislation. Yet, there are reasons to doubt that legal charges alone were sufficient to guarantee a conviction, as the fate of Aeschines' legal charges against Demosthenes illustrates. One could also argue that even if any individual in the Assembly could, in theory, bring a graphē paranomōn, it was highly unlikely that the vast majority of them ever did so, given the costs of failure (see below). However, as I show in chapter 3, there are reasons to believe that a larger section of the population beyond the elite was involved in these procedures. Moreover, even if one believes that it was the elite who were predominantly involved in the procedure, we must still explain why feuding elites, each aiming primarily at personal advantage by defeating their political opponents, would not bring about legislative failure.

through a system of fines and other forms of punishment for litigants who engaged in frivolous litigation. As in other public cases, punishment awaited a prosecutor who failed to gather one-fifth of the votes. The proposer of new legislation was also fined if the graphē paranomōn was successful, but only within a year from the proposal.[58] The fear of punishment thus acted as a deterrent for those who sought to abuse these procedures.[59] But the one-year limit and the quasi-unanimity requirement were actually quite lax forms of deterrence. Moreover, this punishment regime was already in place in the fifth century, when the Athenians brazenly disregarded it after the Battle of Arginusae (cf. chapter 1).

The new constitution also played an important role in preventing abuses of these procedures. In fact, the constitution raised the stakes for would-be abusers by conjuring up the threat of civil conflict. If the graphē paranomōn was futile in 406 (Lanni and Vermeule 2013; cf. chapter 1), in the fourth century, the new constitution made the commitment to prosecute wrongdoers under the terms of the procedure credible.[60]

2.4. Conclusion

The last decade of the fifth century was a watershed in Athenian political history. The constitutional crisis confirmed the perils of oligarchy, but it also revealed the limits of unconstrained democratic rule. Accordingly, the democracy established in the year 403 was different from the one that collapsed in the year 411.

Classical scholars have paid a great deal of attention to these changes. Some scholars distinguish between a fifth-century *radical* democracy and a fourth-century *moderate* democracy, and evaluate the latter by reference to the former.[61] This method, I suggest, yields an incomplete picture. The fourth-century structure emerged in response to a number of practical challenges, only some of which can be traced back to the fifth-century democracy. These challenges

---

58. Fines ranged from relatively small sums (e.g., 25 dr.) to very large ones (usually in the amount of 1,000 dr., but we also have evidence for higher sums: Hansen 1974: 28–43). I return to the penalty regime associated with the graphē paranomōn in the next chapter.

59. In a decentralized system of coercion, deterrence worked because enforcement was incentive-compatible for punishers (Carugati, Hadfield, and Weingast 2015).

60. The problem of credible commitment was not a problem only for the democrats, as Gowder (2016: 105) assumes. Instead, in order for the democracy to be stable, everyone needed to trust their fellow citizens. The next chapter delves deeply into how the constitution regulated the use of the graphē paranomōn (and cognate cases).

61. Hansen (1978; 1979a; 1979b; 1987b; 1989a; 1999); Strauss (1987b.) The history of the "labeling" of Athenian democracy (and Hansen's position) is discussed in Millett (2000).

include lack of credible commitment, the breakdown of political order, and the need to protect citizens' freedom, dignity, and property from arbitrary rule. Analyzing the fourth-century democracy as an adaptation to these challenges, as opposed to a blind response to the structure of the fifth-century democracy, sheds light on important questions of long-term stability.

Other scholars have interpreted this period as introducing new concepts of "sovereignty of law" (Ostwald 1986) or "rule of law" (Gowder 2016). Neither interpretation is satisfactory. The notion of sovereignty of law is highly problematic in the Athenian context. In fact, it makes little sense to argue that a demos that articulated, debated, repealed, and replaced the city's laws was not, in a meaningful way, a sovereign agent.[62] As to the rule of law, the Athenians did not discover it after the civil war. As Forsdyke (2018) compellingly argues, the fifth-century democracy had already made significant strides toward establishing legal supremacy and equality—critical pillars of the contemporary notion of rule of law.

A more nuanced interpretation suggests that the late fifth-century reforms advanced the process of establishing a form of rule of law in significant ways. If we define the rule of law, with legal philosopher Lon Fuller (1964), as including attributes such as generality, publicity, prospectivity, clarity, noncontradiction, constancy, possibility to obey, and general applicability, then the fourth-century Athenian democracy measures well even against "thick" modern definitions. Generality and constancy were ensured through the decoupling of the legislative process into two separate institutions (the Assembly and nomothesia) and the introduction of a distinction between two levels of man-made rules: laws (*nomoi*) and decrees (*psēphismata*). General applicability rested on the ban on laws *ad personam* (Andoc. 1.89). The codification and publication of a new code of laws, to be preserved in the archives (Sickinger 1999), enhanced both publicity and clarity. The principle of noncontradiction was perhaps the cardinal principle of the new order, elevating the importance of the integrity of the corpus of laws. Assembly decrees had to be consistent with all the laws, and new laws had to be consistent with other laws. Any citizen who considered a proposed measure to be against the laws could indict the measure through the procedures of graphē paranomōn and graphē nomon mē epitēdeion theinai. Finally, prospectivity was secured through the establishment of a date after which the new rules applied—that is, the archonship of Euclides in the year

62. On the problematic nature of the notion of unitary sovereignty as a heuristic to understand the nature of Athenian law and politics: Ober (1989a: 22 and note 49); Ober (1989b); Carugati (2015; cf. Introduction note 29).

403/402.[63] Moreover, the reforms of the late fifth century contributed greatly to rooting these ideas of rule of law more firmly within an institutional structure that clearly defined the boundaries of acceptable behavior and provided mechanisms to punish wrongdoers.

Certainly, then, a century of democratic practices played a role in the restoration of democracy. But the fact that the Athenians would agree on a set of new institutions after the crisis of the late fifth-century was neither predetermined, nor obvious. A decade of experimentation and failure yielded a consensus on a form of Solonian legality that established a connection between the new constitution and a shared tradition, a past that was clearly not a form of authoritarian rule of one or a few men over others. It was, instead, a form of rule where each Athenian could look to the city's laws to guide their behavior. If someone broke the laws, by behaving or proposing new measures contrary to their spirit or letter, it was in the interest of every citizen, and by extension of the demos as a whole, to bring the wrongdoer to court. It was only if each Athenian committed to preserving the constitution by acting as its guardian that the Athenians could, individually and as a group, hope to see their person, property, and dignity protected. The framers of the new constitution must have realized early on that this form of consensus was extremely demanding of a populace that had just fought a civil conflict. The consensus therefore needed an institutional carapace that would give everyone incentives to abide by the new rules and make it extremely costly to renege.

The consensus on legality did not require that everyone agree on everything. Indeed, supporters of oligarchy and of democracy continued to disagree on fundamental issues: for example, the question of citizenship. On the oligarchic side, a proposal war aired in the year 403/402 that favored a property qualification for citizenship, but it was defeated (Lys. 34). Around the same time, the democrats sought to extend citizenship to slaves and resident aliens who had fought to oust the Thirty ([Arist]. *Ath.Pol.* 40.2). That proposal was also defeated. Yet, these differences did not lead to violence. Instead, they were resolved in the courts, and according to law.[64] The burgeoning antidemocratic literature of the fourth century points to the same conclusion: not everyone in

63. We do not have any explicit indication in the sources regarding whether the new rules were possible to obey, but also no indication that they were not.

64. The evidence is not beyond doubt, but it seems that Phormisius' proposal to restrict the franchise was indicted by graphē paranomōn because it was contrary to the patrios politeia (Dion. Hal. *De Lysias* 32; cf. Ostwald 1986: 504–5; Fuks 1953: 40–48). We are on firmer grounds with Thrasybulus' proposal, against which Archinus brought a graphē paranomōn ([Arist.] *Ath. Pol.* 40.2). Archinus is earlier identified by Aristotle as one of the proponents of the patrios politeia, alongside Theramenes ([Arist.] *Ath.Pol.* 34.3).

Athens came to embrace the democratic ethos. In fact, the government and its pitfalls continued to be the object of intense scrutiny—as it emerges most notably from the writings of the giants of the Athenian intellectual tradition: Plato, Aristotle, and Isocrates.

The institutional structure that emerged at the end of the fifth century created incentives for individuals to choose the polis' institutions to resolve conflict and make collective decisions, rather than take matters in their own hands. Those institutions also imposed constraints on the range of possible policy outcomes. Those constraints, however, did not produce a rigid, ossified constitutional order. Instead, they enabled negotiation across a wide range of interests. In the next chapter, I reconstruct the microfoundations of policymaking in fourth-century Athens to show how the constitution regulated interactions among actors in ways that fostered both stability and innovation.

3

Stability and Innovation in Athenian Policy

IN THE fourth century, as in the fifth, Athens was stable and remarkably prosperous. The crisis of the late fifth century, one might surmise, did little to undermine Athens' performance. This view, however, overlooks the fact that the institutional sources of both stability and prosperity changed dramatically from the fifth to the fourth century. As I showed in chapter 1, in the fifth century, the empire was responsible for a conspicuous part of Athens' revenue. Imperial rents played an important role in lowering the threat of destabilizing violence, making both the elites and the masses better off. The crisis of the late fifth century, and particularly the defeat in the Peloponnesian War, shattered the fifth-century equilibrium. As I showed in the previous chapter, a long process of experimentation followed the collapse of democracy. The Athenians struggled for a decade to restore a stable form of government. In the process, they elaborated a consensus on legality that inspired the creation of a new, self-enforcing constitutional structure. The Athenian constitution offered conspicuous incentives for the parties emerging from the civil war to abide by the new rules.

But the problem with constitutions is that things change. As Elkins, Ginsburg, and Melton (2009) have shown, constitutional endurance is difficult to achieve. The average lifespan of a modern constitution is, in fact, a mere nineteen years. Athens' constitution survived for eighty-one years, from its establishment in 403 until the Macedonian conquest in 322. Throughout this period, Athens had to fend off many external threats. In fact, the Greek poleis were constantly at war among each other in the fourth century, weakening one another while Persia in the east and Philip of Macedon in the north sought to destabilize and control them. The stability of the constitution in the post-war period, moreover, faced another threat arising from within. Democracy was a costly form of government, and war was becoming costlier by the day with the introduction of more expensive military techniques, such as siege engines.[1] But revenues were scarce. The empire was gone. The silver mines had a rough start in the fourth century, after being shut down for over a decade.[2] The amnesty had enshrined personal and property rights, ruling out the option of expropriating the wealth of those who owned assets in Attica. The institutional reforms had made that commitment credible, by creating a decision-making process where the demos could no longer do "whatever they wished" (Xen. *Hell.* 1.7.12).

The new constitutional structure thus returned stability to a divided polis. But it also created a big problem: how were the Athenians to pay for their wars and their government? The city's long-term stability, as well as its prosperity, required an entirely new strategy to generate revenues without compromising the constitutional pact.

The question of the sources of Athens' stability in the fourth century has lain dormant for almost three decades. In 1989, Josiah Ober provided a compelling answer in the influential book *Mass and Elite in Democratic Athens*. For Ober, the stability of the Athenian democracy depended on how the Athenians solved the tensions between masses and elites. How did the masses come to accept elite leadership? And how did they limit the concentration of power in the hands of the elite without driving them into revolt? For Ober, the balance between the interests of masses and elites was struck on the ideological plane, and must be found in the vocabulary of social mediation deployed in the public institutions of the polis: that is, the Assembly, the theater, the Agora, and particularly the law-courts. In Ober's own words (1989a: 306), "the complex of rhetorical strategies successfully deployed by elite litigants over time helped to create a

---

1. Pritchard (2015: 89) estimates the cost of democracy in the fourth century as ranging from 98 T in the 370s to 128 T in the 330s. Ober (2015a: 245; 2015b: 499) estimates the cost of democracy as fluctuating from 140 T in the 370s, to 105 T in the 350s, and to 220 T in the 330s. For war, Pritchard (2015: 111–13) estimates a steady outlay of ca. 522 T for the 370s and into the 360s. For Ober (2015a: 245; 2015b: 499), instead, war expenditures required 350 T in the 370s, plummeted in the 350s to 130 T, and rose again in the 340s (200 T) and in the 330s (400 T). In addition to the costs of democracy and war, both Pritchard (2015: 49) and Ober (2015a: 245; 2015b: 499) include another 100 T for festivals (which for Ober rose to 150 T in the 330s). Ober also adds fluctuating amounts for infrastructure expenditures, which ranged from no expenditures in the mid-fourth century to 200 T in the 330s.

2. The mines were shut down at the end of the fifth century due to the Spartan occupation of strongholds in the Attic countryside. They probably slowly resumed operations soon after the end of the civil war (Kroll 2011; contra van Alfen 2000 for whom the mines did not resume operations until the middle of the fourth century). Their contribution to Athenian state revenue in the first half of the century is hard to assess. I return to these issues in chapter 4.

vocabulary of social mediation which defined the nature of mass-elite interaction for the Athenians and legitimated both the power of the masses and the special privileges of the elite." Ober thus locates the sources of Athens' stability in the social realm.

I build on Ober's account in order to explain another facet of Athenian development in the fourth century: the polis' remarkable prosperity. Previous scholarship that analyzed the institutional sources of Athens' economic success in the fourth century has focused on individual pieces of legislation aimed at lowering transaction costs and ensuring the credibility of commitments in the Athenian marketplace. For example, Nikophon's law set up coin-testers in the Agora and Piraeus to guarantee the value of Athens' coinage (Stroud 1974; Ober 2008: 220–26); the *dikai emporikai*—commercial tribunals where noncitizens had standing—enabled Athenian and non-Athenian merchants to enforce maritime contracts (Lanni 2006); and decrees extending honor and privileges to foreign merchants for trade-related services promoted Athens as a primary commercial destination (Engen 2010).

I will return to these important reforms in chapter 4. Here, I take a step back to tackle a prior set of questions. How did these pieces of legislation, some of which imposed significant departures from the status quo, come about?[3] And why didn't change destabilize the social order? To answer these questions, we need to bring institutions back into the picture and analyze how institutional constraints affected actors' behavior.

The task of reconstructing Athenian law and policy in the fourth century from the primary sources is problematic. While a thorough study of extant laws and decrees is a task well beyond the scope of this book, I am not convinced that such a study would take us very far. In fact, the epigraphic record yields a high number of honorary decrees and a very limited number of laws (Hansen 1978; Canevaro 2015). When we turn to the literary sources, we similarly encounter major gaps. According to Ober's categorization (1989a: 349), in the period between 403 and 322, we have seventeen speeches delivered before the Assembly. Of these, fourteen are delivered by one man—Demosthenes—in the decade between 350 and 340 (and another one is also by Demosthenes, dated to the year 336). Five speeches were delivered before the Council, but one concerns an honorary crown (Dem. 51), and two are official scrutinies of magistrates

3. The dikai emporikai, for example, enabled non-Athenian traders to seek redress in the Athenian law-courts. The introduction of these new cases signals a major innovation from a fifth-century status quo in which only metics and allies had (sporadic) access to the courts: metics' access was restricted to private cases, which were heard by a separate court (that of the Polemarchus); for the allies, the requirement to appear in Athens to settle cases was a form of judicial control (Lanni 2006: 34; Whitehead 1977: 92–97).

before entering office (*dokimasiai*: Lys. 26; 31). Of the eighty extant speeches delivered before the law-courts, forty-four have no political background, leaving a total of only thirty-six politically relevant speeches to cover a period of over eighty years.

The extant law-court speeches represent only a minuscule fraction of the cases heard in the courts. The Athenians litigated, conservatively, two thousand cases a year, and each case must have featured at least two speeches.[4] Therefore, the eighty extant law-court speeches amount to 0.025% of the total. Moreover, accidents of publication and transmission have skewed the sample by overrepresenting elite litigants. In fact, only the best speechwriters would have published their work, work which they most likely produced for rich and powerful individuals (often themselves), whose disputes would have most likely captured the attention of later authors (many of whom were Hellenistic copyists interested in rhetoric) to whom we owe the speeches' very survival.[5] Later authors did not care much about the subtleties of Athenian politics. But they cared a great deal about the clash of personalities. The point is best exemplified when we analyze the extant cases of graphē paranomōn and graphē nomon mē epitēdeion theinai. Within the constitutional structure, these procedures enabled the Athenians to make and change laws and policies. And yet, of the thirty-eight cases that we glimpse in the sources, 50% (nineteen cases) concern honorary decrees, and of six we do not even know why they were brought. Only seven complete speeches are extant (Hansen 1974, these are Demosthenes 18, 20, 22, 23, 24, Hyperides 2, and Aeschines 3). Of these seven speeches, only three deal with actual laws and policies (Dem. 20; 23; 24). The rest deal with honorary crowns.

In sum, the evidence for political decisions in the law-courts is incomplete and biased, and the evidence for political decisions in the Assembly and the Council is largely limited to the actions of one politician in one decade. If the Attic orators can shed light on Athenian political ideology, they provide much less guidance when it comes to understanding Athenian politics.

To study Athenian law- and policy-making, and to analyze change over time, we need a different methodology. In this chapter, I build a model of decision-making in the law-courts. I focus specifically on the law-courts for the following reasons. A complete account of decision-making in ancient Athens would track the process in its entirety—from the deliberations of the Council, which put agenda items on the Assembly's calendar, to the negotiations that took place

4. Two thousand cases per year is a conservative number based on Hansen's calculations of the volume of litigation (Hansen 1999: 186–88; Lanni 2009: 711). Two thousand cases over eighty years yields a total number of at least 160,000 cases and at least 320,000 speeches.

5. See, most concisely, *The Oratory of Classical Greece*, series introduction.

in the Assembly itself, and finally into the law-courts, where new and contro-versial pieces of legislation were ultimately rejected or approved.[6] However, our knowledge of procedural rules regulating Council and Assembly meetings is limited (at least compared to the law-courts). Moreover, tracking a process that involves three institutions of which we know relatively little would mag-nify the margin of error, compromising the soundness of the entire endeavor. As more work continues to illuminate the rules regulating the decision-making process in the Council and in the Assembly (see esp. Canevaro 2018b), others will take up the task. But the law-courts offer a promising starting point.

Focusing on the law-courts enables me to cast a wide net over the legisla-tive process, as well as to capture the mechanisms that regulated the high-end domain of law- and policy-making, where change was more likely to occur. Under the new constitutional rules, the law-courts did not deal with all legisla-tion passed in Athens, but they dealt with laws (through the nomothesia and the graphē nomon mē epitēdeion theinai), while the Assembly dealt with de-crees. But if a decree presented in the Assembly was challenged as unconstitu-tional, it ended up in court though the graphē paranomōn. Therefore, the courts dealt with both laws and policy. Most importantly, assuming that leg-islation that promoted major departures from the status quo would be more likely to be challenged, the courts remained the locus where controversial mea-sures (both decrees and laws) were debated and decided upon.

How, then, did the new constitutional rules shape decision-making in the law-courts? The model that I present in this chapter is a variation on the median voter theorem (Hotelling 1929; Black 1948; Downs 1957) based on the work of Randall Calvert (1985). Political scientists have used the median voter theorem extensively to study the dynamics of decision-making under majority rule, especially in the electoral context. The basic version of the theorem assumes that voters have ideal outcomes and full information and that candidates want to win office. Based on these assumptions, the model predicts that candidates will converge on the out-come preferred by the median voter. Calvert modified these assumptions by in-troducing two forms of uncertainty, which I replicate here. First, candidates (here, litigants) are uncertain about the position of the median voter (here, the median juror) on a given policy issue. Second, candidates want to win office (here, honor), but also have preferences over policy outcomes.[7]

6. I come back to these stages in more detail in section 3.3.a.

7. As I explain more fully in section 3.2.b, I define "honor" (timē) as a form of social capital that enables a litigant to solidify his position of leadership to the detriment of his opponent. The word and the concept do not easily match commonsensical meanings in English, but derive from debates in the field of classics concerning Athenian litigants' utility functions (that is, the reasons why they entered litigation).

The validity of these two assumptions in the Athenian context is supported by the evidence that I lay out in section 3.1. Drawing from recent studies of Athenian social networks and political sociology, I suggest that litigants and jurors interacting in the law-courts brought to the fore meaningfully pluralistic preferences that included, but were not limited to, those produced by their individual identities as adult, male—mass or elite—citizen. This evidence adds greater texture to the traditional view of Athenian litigation as a game played by elite litigants and mass jurors (Ober 1989a; D. Cohen 1995: 193–94; Herman 1995; 1996; Christ 1998: 32–33; Johnstone 1999: 19; Lanni 2006: 34; Kamen 2013: 100).

I also build on the social scientific literature on the median voter theorem by introducing an additional assumption derived from the features of the Athenian institutional environment. In the law-court cases that I model here (graphē paranomōn, graphē nomon mē epitēdeion theinai, and the repeal stage in the process of nomothesia),[8] only one player can move their platform along the policy continuum: the proposer of legislation can choose what kind of measure to present, but his challenger's position is fixed at the status quo (he can only challenge the proposal without providing an alternative that can be voted on, therefore de facto advocating for the status quo). My model therefore assumes the existence of a status quo.

There are several reasons to build a model to study the behavior of Athenian actors. The first concerns the state of our sources. As I mentioned earlier, we lack fine-grained evidence that would allow us to track the development of Athenian policy over time; moreover, the available evidence offers no information about an important set of actors—namely, sub-elite Athenians—that, as we will see, played an important role in politics. Second, a model affords a high degree of clarity in terms of identifying the actors and their preferences: I turn to these tasks in sections 3.1 and 3.2 b and c. Third, a model reveals the logical consistency of arguments, enabling readers to follow each step of the argument and identify its potential weaknesses. Fourth, a model may reveal counterintuitive, unexpected results. And finally, a model enables the analyst to predict patterns. I elaborate on these last two claims in section 3.3.e The model that I present here is not meant to supplant existing evidence but to provide a testable, verifiable account of decision-making in the Athenian law-courts based on a set of assumption rooted in the ancient evidence.

---

8. The repeal stage, where existing laws that conflicted with a new proposal had to be discussed and repealed, took place in a law-court and therefore fits the assumptions of the model. The inconsistencies about the nature of the last stage of nomothesia, where new legislation was approved by the nomothetai, make it difficult to determine a possible fit between the procedure and the model. I therefore prefer to suspend judgment.

The model suggests that bargaining under the new constitutional rules fostered a balance between stability and innovation in Athenian policy-making. In particular, I lay out four results. First, the graphē paranomōn (and cognate cases) incentivized proposers of legislation to move toward the preferences of the median member of the jury, thus promoting stability. Second, because the median of the citizenry did not experience dramatic shocks in the course of the fourth century, decisions were likely reasonably predictable and consistent with broadly stable expectations.[9] Third, the procedure also allowed a proposer to move away from the status quo, thus enabling a measure of innovation. Fourth, the model suggests that sub-elite actors were more likely to be the drivers of innovative laws and policies.

The constitution thus shaped policy-making by defining the institutional rules of engagement for actors in the courts. But the fact that the rules incentivized one set of behaviors does not mean that all actors played by the rules. In conclusion, I discuss another, more indirect channel whereby the constitution influenced policy-making. This channel reveals the enduring effect of the consensus on patrios politeia as Solonian legality. In extant law-court speeches, litigants often attribute legislation that supports their proposal or case to an archaic lawgiver, a figure frequently identified with Solon. These strategies, I suggest, reflect an attempt to articulate the conformity of one's position to the principles of the constitution. The evidence thus indicates that the constitution operated on the symbolic as well as the institutional plane to shape actors' behavior toward rule conformity.

3.1. Actors and Preferences

A study of the dynamics of decision-making in the courts must take as its point of departure the identity of actors and their preferences. Classical scholars have traditionally viewed Athenian litigation as a game played by elite litigants and mass jurors. In this section, I formulate three arguments that modify this view.[10]

9. As I explain more fully in the next chapter, the citizen body did not change much in the course of the fourth century. In the years after the civil war, Pericles' citizenship law, originally passed in 451/450, was reaffirmed, which limited citizenship rights to sons and daughters of Athenian parents. Throughout the fourth century, the Athenians were extremely reluctant to extend citizenship to new actors—be they foreign benefactors or noncitizen residents. Limitations on political access were part of a trade-off of inclusion, which ensured a high degree of homogeneity among decision-makers that was critical to political stability (cf. chapter 4; Carugati 2019b).

10. Early challenges to the dichotomy between mass and elite: Hansen (1990b); Johnstone (1999). For Hansen, the composition of the elites changed dramatically between the fifth and the fourth centuries; the *rhētores* constituted only a small percentage of the politically active in

First, litigants did not solely belong to the elite. Second, jury panels were representative of the Athenian population as a whole. Third, litigants and jurors participated in a thick web of social networks, which shaped actors' identities and preferences in ways that were meaningfully pluralistic.

3.1.a. Was Litigation an Exclusively Elite Domain?

The portrayal of Athenian litigation as the domain of elite litigants emerges forcefully from the literary sources, particularly the Attic orators. Accordingly, scholars generally assume that the courts remained primarily, if not exclusively, an elite forum.[11]

This evidence is problematic for two reasons. First, as I discussed above, the corpus of the Attic orators offers only a very small window into the dynamics of decision-making in the courts (0.025%) and the sample is biased in problematic ways. Second, if the Athenians litigated at least two thousand cases a year (Hansen 1999: 186–88), then the elite could not have done all the litigating—the numbers simply don't add up.[12]

A handful of scholars have considered the question of sub-elite participation (as litigants) in the law-courts.[13] Considering Hansen's estimates of the volume of litigation and passages in [Aristotle] discussing deme judges and arbitrators, P. J. Rhodes (1998: 145) concludes that, "in the law-courts as in the Assembly the man who was a mere voter on one day may well be an active participant on another." Following Rhodes, Victor Bers (2009: 7–24) maintains that evidence of sub-elite participation as litigants in the law-courts emerges from various, though perhaps less-than-reliable, sources. First, in courtroom

---

Athens in the period covered by Ober; and finally, the stark dichotomy between *plousioi* (the haves) and *penētes* (the have-nots) overlooks the important role of the hoplite middle class. For Johnstone, mass and elite identities were not given, but constructed and reproduced through the very language of courtroom rhetoric. Law-court interactions are best exemplified as exchanges between individuals whose defining feature is that they are all adult male citizens. On mass vs. elite as an insufficient heuristic to analyze Athenian politics in the archaic period: Kierstead (2013: 75ff.).

11. Of the three components of Ober's tripartite definition of elite (1989a: 11–17), the evidence below tracks wealth and, to some extent, birth, but not education.

12. A conservative estimate of two thousand cases a year would require a minimum number of four thousand elite litigants. However, as we know from later reforms (cf. ch. 4), the Athenian elite class numbered between 1,200 and 2,000 people (cf. Kron's 2011 wealth distribution below).

13. Including Ober himself (1989a: 109), who recognized that ordinary citizens spoke in public forums (i.e., there were no legal restrictions), and did participate on some occasions (Isoc. 12.248).

speeches, the litigants themselves sometimes describe their socioeconomic condition as sub-elite. However, the obvious advantages of doing so in terms of (mass and elite) rhetorical self-presentation suggest that we should beware of any such statements. Second, comedy's frequent references to Athenian litigiousness suggest a more variegated set of actors. As Bers himself notes, however, such evidence is largely inferential. Like Rhodes, Bers relies on Hansen's calculations to drive the point home (2009: 21), but with a proviso: given the high volume of litigation, "it is reasonable to assume that, other things being equal, the greater the proportion of small cases, the greater the number of *idiōtai* [laymen] who appeared in court." In sum, the average Athenian litigated in court with some frequency for Bers, particularly in private, small cases (cf. Lanni 2016: 131–32).

Bers' conclusion prompts the question: were elite litigants exclusively or primarily involved in prominent public cases revolving around major political issues? Hansen's work suggests otherwise (cf., more recently, Lambert 2017). His study of the number of decree-proposers in the Assembly in the period between 355–322 shows in fact that legislation was a common form of political activity not dominated by a small elite. For Hansen (1984: 155), "in addition to the political leaders there was an important group of politically-minded citizens who were active, even as proposers, but only occasionally and not professionally; ... the number of citizens involved in politics as proposers (and not only as voters) was much larger than usually believed, and there was no sharp distinction between the professional, the semi-professional, and the ordinary citizen; ... hundreds of minor and probably also some major political figures are completely unknown to us." Claire Taylor has similarly shown that decree-proposers "were not concentrated in the city area but came from demes throughout Attica. ... If decree proposers came from all corners of Attica and included a large number of citizens, then we might assume that the composition of the Assembly was quite varied. Thus, a wide range of citizens both attended and participated actively in the Assembly, and the Athenian democracy was not merely the concern of a privileged few" (Taylor 2007b: 340).[14] Moreover, Taylor's analysis of prosopographical evidence from a sample of 2,183 citizens reveals that nonurban participation was not limited to decree-proposers, but encompassed all sorts of office-holders, including "*strategoi, tamiai,*

14. C. Taylor discusses and ultimately dismisses the role of migration: if migration surely occurred from the coastal and inland areas to Athens, it is hard to see why it would only concern elite citizens. Conversely, it seems perhaps more likely that poorer, particularly landless, individuals would try their luck in the big city, most notably in search for jobs, including public service. Moreover, as Taylor suggests, "it is very difficult to assess whether this movement was widespread or occasional, [or] whether it was permanent or temporary" (Taylor 2007b: 339; cf. Taylor 2011).

bouleutai . . . archons, phylarchs, hipparchs, dikasts and other (unknown) officials recorded on *pinakia*" (Taylor 2007a: 73). For many of these magistracies, the use of the lot contributed, over time, to reduce the overrepresentation of the city elite in Athenian politics (Taylor 2007a: 88; 2007b: 336–40). As a result, in the fourth century, "non-wealthy citizens played an increasingly active role in democratic politics" (Taylor 2007a: 89).

Hansen's and Taylor's findings focus primarily on the Assembly and magistrates. However, their conclusions have obvious implications for the law-courts as well. As decree-proposers, sub-elite *idiōtai* would have been at risk of graphē paranomōn, and thus would have appeared as litigants in the law courts in major public cases and not only, as Bers suggests, in small private disputes.[15] Similarly, as magistrates of the polis, nonwealthy citizens would have had to undergo accountability procedures (*dokimasia, euthyna*) and risked accusations of misconduct (notably, *eisangelia*) that would have landed them in court as litigants in major public cases (Lanni 2009; 2016).

———

The evidence discussed above does not allow us to conclude that participation was essentially uniform across the mass and elite divide. However, it does suggest that we should temper the picture provided by the orators with the image that emerges from other sources. Accordingly, we should conclude that non-elite actors participated sufficiently frequently in litigation that we should not consider litigation as an exclusively or perhaps even primarily elite domain.

3.1.b. Who Were the Jurors?

At the beginning of every year, six thousand citizens over the age of thirty were selected by lot to serve as jurors in the popular courts. On each day that the courts were in session, jurors would be assigned to jury panels through the complex allotment mechanism known as *klērōtērion*. Panels ranged in size from 201 jurors for small private cases to six thousand jurors for sensational public

15. The argument articulated so far leaves open the possibility that whereas a large percentage of Athenians proposed legislation in the Assembly, sub-elite Athenians only proposed legislation that was unlikely to be important enough to be challenged and end up in the courts. However, in Hansen's list, of those proposers whose names begin with the letter A (which I take to be not correlated with their wealth) only three (or maybe five) out of fifteen can be found in Davies' (1971) account of Athenian propertied families. Moreover, sub-elite proposers are recorded as proposing a number of critical decrees, ranging from domestic to foreign policy (Hansen 1984).

cases.[16] The use of the lot and allotment mechanisms increased the likelihood that jury panels were broadly representative of the population as a whole. According to Hansen, "the 6000 were divided into ten sections each of 600 men, and each section comprised sixty men from each tribe" (Hansen 1999: 183).

Tribe representation, however, tells us little about the sociological composition of Athenian juries. First, the yearly selection occurred among those who had volunteered their name, with no barriers to entry. Second, jurors could iterate their mandate in subsequent years. As a result, representation in the courts was not subject to the strict rules that randomized the selection process in other magistracies and prevented the monopolization of power by any one group, especially over time (Taylor 2007a and b).

Did, then, any one group dominate the courts? Scholars discuss three factors that may have skewed the composition of juries: provenance, age, and wealth.

3.1.B.I. PROVENANCE

In a world of walkers, it seems reasonable to assume that city folks would enjoy greater access, and thus greater representation, due to their physical proximity to the courts. Prosopographical studies of jurors' plaques, however, rule out a city bias. As Hansen remarked, "astonishingly, it turns out that people from the coastal demes (*paralia*) and the inland demes (*mesogeios*) actually prevail over people from the city demes (*asty*)." Migration does not fully account for this result. In fact, Hansen continues, "the geographical spread revealed by the jury plaques is so striking that the growth of the city population cannot be the whole story" (Hansen 1999: 184; cf. Taylor 2007b: 336–37; on *pinakia*: Kroll 1972). City folks, Hansen suggests, did not dominate the courts.

3.1.B.II. AGE

To an extent, the Athenians built an age bias into the composition of the jury. The privilege to sit as a juror in court was reserved for citizens over the age of thirty—a restriction that did not apply, for example, to the Assembly. According to Hansen, about two-thirds of the adult male citizen population was over the age of thirty (Hansen 1999: 89; cf. Akrigg 2011; Hin 2013). Assuming that

16. For most public cases, the normal jury size was 501. Private cases were usually heard by panels of 201 jurors if the sum at issue was less than 1,000 dr., and by 401 jurors if the sum was larger (Hansen 1999: 187).

the fourth-century citizen population numbered thirty thousand, then twenty thousand citizens were, every year, eligible for jury service. Of these, six thousand (30%) were selected as jurors. The numbers thus suggest that, if rotation had regulated the selection of jurors, each adult male citizen (regardless of his socioeconomic status) would have served as a juror once every three years. This, however, was not a rule. Yet, if we recognize that the composition of the jury was skewed toward older folks by design, then assuming that on average older folks would be more resistant to change than their younger counterparts, the question of what mechanisms enabled innovation in law- and policy-making becomes even more pressing.

3.1.B.III. WEALTH

Scholars have variously identified the typical juror as either a poor or a well-off citizen based on the (skewed) evidence of the orators, the (dubious) references in Aristophanes' comedy, or the (subjective) assessments of the consequences of jury pay.[17] I take the absence of a consensus on the issue to suggest, albeit indirectly, the absence of explicit or obvious socioeconomic biases.

When we turn to the evidence for wealth distribution in Athens, the simple dichotomy "poor vs. well-off" may be entirely misleading as a description of the city's socioeconomic makeup. According to Geoffrey Kron's estimates (2011), out of a total male population of ca. 31,000, 300 people (or ca. 1%) belonged to the super-rich (liturgy-paying) class; 1,200 people (or ca. 4%) belonged to the rich (*eisphora*-paying) class; and 5,000 people (or ca. 16%) possessed no landed wealth and owned movable property amounting to ca. 100 dr.[18] Assuming that Kron accepts Davies' (1981) assessment that ca. 9,000 people (or ca. 29%) owned property amounting to at least 2,000 dr., this leaves about 15,500 people (or ca. 50%) owning some amount of wealth between 100 and 2,000 dr. The distribution of wealth—like other proxies for economic development such as income distribution (Ober 2015a: 89–98; 2017), nutrition (Lagia 2015), real wages (Scheidel 2010), and house size (Morris 2004)—suggests that the Athenian "masses" were a rather heterogeneous middle-class. So, I conclude, were Athenian juries.

———

17. For A.H.M. Jones (1957), jurors were middle class; for Markle (1985) and Hansen (1999), jurors were poor; for Todd (1990), jurors were neither poor nor rich, but farmers. For an overview of these positions, see Todd (1990); Hansen (1999: 184–85).

18. I discuss liturgies and the *eisphora* in the next chapter.

In sum, in terms of provenance, the jurors represented a broad section of the population. In terms of wealth, absent strong suggestions that the jurors were either wealthier or poorer than the average Athenian, I rely on the working argument that jury panels were broadly representative of the population as a whole. Finally, in terms of age, we must acknowledge a probable overrepresentation of older Athenians, which was partly by design, due to the Greeks' association of age with wisdom. But are provenance, wealth, and age the only relevant determinants of individual preferences?

3.1.c. Social Networks and Plural Preferences

But all associations (*koinōniai*) are parts as it were of the association of the State. Travellers for instance associate together for some advantage . . . But the political association too, it is believed, was originally formed, and continues to be maintained, for the advantage of its members . . . Thus the other associations aim at some particular advantage; for example sailors combine to seek the profits of seafaring in the way of trade or the like, comrades in arms the gains of warfare . . . and similarly the members of a tribe or deme. And some associations appear to be formed for the sake of pleasure, for example religious guilds and dining clubs, which are unions for sacrifice and social intercourse (Arist. *NE* 1160a9–22; trans. adapted from Rackam 1934).

Athenian litigants and jurors were, for the most part, adult, male citizens. But as the quote above suggests, adult male citizens participated in a thick web of social, economic, and religious associations that thrived at the sub-polis level. These associations bridged social, economic, and even gender cleavages, shaping individuals' identities and preferences in meaningful ways.[19] As a result, the cleavage between mass and elite adult male citizens was an important, but certainly not the only relevant cleavage in Athenian politics and society.

For Paulin Ismard (2010), Athens was a multilayered society featuring many associations that tended for the most part to be open and nonhierarchical (cf. Kierstead 2013). Although Athenian associations did not enjoy juridical status as persons (as, for example, today's American corporations), they were recognized in Athenian law: first, specific legal procedures may have been designed to solve disputes concerning commercial partnerships (*dikai koinōnikai*) and loans (*dikai eranikai*) among members; second, associations may have provided

---

19. On bridging social networks and the "strength of weak ties:" Granovetter (1973); for an application of these concepts to Athenian institutions (particularly the Boulē): Ober (2008: ch. 4).

supporting speakers (*synēgoroi*) when members were summoned to court; finally, associations could own land (Ismard 2010: 146–49; 149–52; 163–79). Most of all, however, Athenian associations shaped citizens' religious and economic life (Ismard 2010: chs. 3 and 4). Ismard's study depicts a world of tensions between the centralized institutions of the polis and decentralized associations, and concludes that, "l'identité politique serait moins le résultat d'une pratique communautaire spécifique que le produit de ces espaces médiateurs où s'échelonnent et se configurent respectivement, dans un va-et-vient constant, les différentes identités dans la cité" (Ismard 2010: 251).[20]

Similarly, Claire Taylor and Kostas Vlassopoulos suggest that the focus on the polis has led scholars to overemphasize the distinction between the citizen club and the outsiders—namely, women, metics (i.e., resident aliens), and slaves—in shaping social identities (Taylor and Vlassopoulos 2015; Vlassopoulos 2007). For the authors, "although distinctions of status, of course, did matter in some important respect, there is a growing awareness that in many other contexts they were irrelevant or secondary. A number of works have already shown that in some arenas of social interaction, for example finance and banking, status distinctions were mostly irrelevant [i.e. E. Cohen (1992)]; similarly, in the case of religious associations that brought together citizens, metics and even slaves, status distinctions seem to be largely secondary" (Taylor and Vlassopoulos 2015: 3; cf. Arnaoutoglou 2003; Gabrielsen 2007; 2016; but note Kierstead 2013: 51–52, suggesting that there is no positive evidence for mixed citizen/noncitizen associations before the year 325). In her contribution to the same volume, Taylor (2015) examines a series of dedications illuminating the life of associations that brought together citizens and noncitizens. In light of this evidence, Taylor persuasively argues for the existence of communities based less on legal status and more on networks of work, residence, and cult that profoundly affected people's identities, as well as their well-being.

———

Adult, male citizens did not exist in a social vacuum. The evidence discussed above suggests that in many forums of Athenian civic life, interactions among the polis' residents did not adhere to rigid distinctions in terms of socioeconomic and legal status. Accordingly, I conclude that the identities and preferences crafted through these interactions were meaningfully pluralistic.

20. "The political identity was less the result of a specific communal practice than the product of mediating spaces where different identities in the city stretched and reconfigured themselves in a constant to and fro movement."

3.2. Modeling Law-Court Interactions

In this section, I present the basic median voter theorem and the two variations suggested by Randall Calvert (1985), which constitute the building blocks of my model.[21] I then provide an account of the benefits and costs that actors faced when entering the Athenian law-courts.

The median voter theorem applies to decision-making under majority rule, and it is based on three main assumptions.[22] First, the range of policy choices can be represented as a single, one-dimensional continuum (i.e., there is only one issue to vote on) and voters face a binary choice (i.e., guns or butter). Second, voters' preferences are single-peaked (i.e., each individual has an ideal outcome and prefers outcomes closer to their ideal to outcomes further away). Third, actors have complete information.

These assumptions fit the dynamics of Athenian litigation better than they fit modern electoral practice. Like contemporary voters, Athenian jurors may hold single-peaked preferences. But whereas democratic politics today rarely involves voting on a single issue for which there are only two options, Athenian litigation did. In fact, in the law-courts, litigants presented opposing arguments to the jury—e.g., convict/do not convict or approve/reject a policy—and the jury voted for one or the other outcome. Moreover, whereas voters in modern, large-scale, representative democracies are hardly fully informed, the costs of gathering relevant information were lower in Athens' smaller-scale, participatory democracy. This, of course, does not mean that Athenian actors were fully informed. In fact, as we will see in the next section, my model assumes that, if jurors have reasonably complete information about the position of the litigants, litigants are uncertain about the precise position of the median juror.[23] The median voter theorem can therefore be profitably employed to study the dynamics of decision-making in the Athenian law-courts.

21. The model draws from my joint work with Barry Weingast and Randall Calvert. Carugati and Weingast (2018) presents a simplified version of the model; Carugati, Calvert, and Weingast (2019) provides a more technical account.

22. For a detailed overview of the origins and development of the median voter theorem: Ansolabehere (2006).

23. The role of uncertainty in the model is limited. To simplify the model, in all the specifications presented below, litigants know where they stand vis-à-vis both the expected median and the status quo. The simplification is consistent with the idea that Athenian citizens knew a great deal about each other's preferences, due to their frequent interactions in the polis' participatory institutions.

3.2.a. The Median Voter Theorem

The basic median voter theorem can be articulated as follows:

Assumption 1: politicians seek to win office over their opponent;

Assumption 2: each voter has an ideal preference over a given policy issue that he or she prefers over all the other alternatives;

Conclusion: competition for office will lead candidates to propose the median voter's ideal policy.

The problem with the median voter theorem, however, as Stephen Ansolabehere (2006: 31) remarks in his overview of the literature, is that its "central prediction ... does not hold. Candidates and parties generally do not converge on the median voter's ideal policy." Many explanations have been offered to account for this divergence, including factors such as "primary elections, incumbency advantages, political parties, and interest group contributions" (Ansolabehere 2006: 35–38). These analyses have led political scientists to modify the assumptions of the basic median voter theorem.

Calvert (1985) proposed to relax the two assumptions concerning actors' full information and the candidates' preferences. In his version, candidates are motivated not only by the desire to win office, but also by policy concerns. Moreover, candidates are unable to predict exactly where the median is located. Calvert concludes that when both assumptions apply, candidates do not converge on the median in equilibrium, but the degree to which candidates diverge from the median depends on the extent to which the assumptions are relaxed.

Like Calvert, I assume that litigants are uncertain about the precise position of the median. And like Calvert, I assume that litigants are driven by policy concerns, as well as by the desire to win.[24] However, in Athens, a successful litigant did not win office. So what was at stake for litigants in the Athenian law-courts? To answer this question, we must analyze the costs and benefits of entering litigation.

3.2.b. Litigants' Preferences: Honor vs. Policy

Elite litigants cared about policy outcomes, but they also cared about honor (Ober 1989a: 124; cf. Finley 1985). "Honor" (*timē*) captures a form of social capital that enables a litigant to solidify his position of leadership to the detriment of his opponent. This is consistent with the view, expressed frequently in the

---

24. In the median voter, winning means maximizing the vote share, which means that each candidate will propose a platform that can win 50% of the votes plus one. Because my model adds a fixed status quo, a litigant can win without maximizing the vote share.

existing scholarship, that the normal mode of interaction between elite litigants was competitive and zero-sum, aimed at maximizing one's political influence to the detriment of the opponent.[25] But members of the elite did not enter politics only to feud with one another. Ober, for example, postulated the existence of different roles for elite speakers—namely, "mouthpiece," "protector," "advisor," and "leader." A mouthpiece of the demos might receive a majority of the votes on occasion, but if his policies prove time and again to be detrimental to the people's interest, his career will be short. Similarly, a leader who is able and willing "to oppose the will of the people in advocating a new and innovative policy" (Ober 1989a: 323) will earn the people's trust, but if the opposition is systematic, the people will soon grow tired—a lesson that Socrates learned all too well.

A successful elite litigant, then, must be careful about how he ranks his preferences for honor and policy. Sometimes, honor and policy might have been aligned—when the politicians' preferred policy happened to be the one with the greater likelihood of winning the demos' approval. But perhaps more often than not, honor and policy were at loggerheads. In these cases, a litigant who cared not only about policy outcomes, but also about honor faced a trade-off.[26] Moreover, the zero-sum, competitive ethos of the elites suggests that, when honor is at stake, a litigant's preference is not merely to get a slim majority of the vote, but to crush his opponent. For these reasons, I operationalize "honor" as a function of the number of votes a litigant receives. In other words, the larger the proportion of the jury that votes in favor of a litigant, the greater the honor.[27] The "policy" parameter, instead, captures the extent to which a litigant cares about "the quality of the policies resulting from [a vote]" (Calvert 1985: 69).

25. Ober stresses repeatedly the competitive nature of the relationship between elite actors (e.g., 1989a: 10, 79, 84–85, 105, 114, 121, 153, 154, 155, 243, 244, 245, 250 (competition as zero-sum), 291, 310, 333, 335). The notion of zero-sum competition among elites emerges even more starkly from David Cohen's model. Cohen argued that the dynamic between elite litigants mimicked a type of feuding behavior that revolved around the pursuit of honor and revenge typical of Mediterranean societies (Cohen 1995). Against Cohen's pessimistic view of Athenian litigation as a zero-sum game among elites, Herman stressed instead the role of cooperative attitudes, such as self-restraint and nonretaliation (Herman 1995; 1996). Christ rejected either extreme and emphasized how Cohen's and Herman's opposing views were the product of the ambivalence the Athenians felt toward litigation (Christ 1998).

26. In the model below, the former scenario occurs when $m^* < L^* < q$, the latter when $L^* < m^* < q$.

27. In a repeat play situation, there are cumulative gains from honor. This emerges clearly from the ancient sources, where important politicians like Demosthenes, Lycurgus, or Eubulus earned and maintained a reputation as good advisors for long periods of time (Ober 1989a).

But what if a litigant was not a member of the Athenian elite? In the hypothetical case of graphē paranomōn that I model below, the protagonist is one Leochares, a shoemaker from the deme of Sphettos—whom we shall call Leo. Leo represents the kind of sub-elite Athenian that might have been involved in policy-making—perhaps not frequently, but occasionally. The relative weight that Leo attributes to honor and policy will differ from that of a career politician, for example the great orator Demosthenes. Demosthenes cares about policy issues. In fact, to a large extent, his reputation as a politician depends on proposing policy that is beneficial to the demos. However, Demosthenes also cares about honor—he cares about winning as a means to increase his political influence and strengthen his position of leadership vis-à-vis his elite opponents. Leo doesn't much care about honor. He is not a career politician and the chances that he might find himself proposing legislation frequently, or ever again, are quite low. I mean, winning would be good—don't get him wrong. But what Leo really cares about is his policy proposal.

But would a sub-elite Athenian ever enter the graphē paranomōn game?

3.2.c. Costs

The graphē paranomōn was not a costless game (Hansen 1974: 28–43, 53; 1999: 206–7).[28] Fines awaited a prosecutor who failed to gather one-fifth of the votes.[29] Fines also awaited a defendant whose proposal was successfully challenged by graphē paranomōn, but only within a year from the original proposal.[30] Fines ranged from relatively small sums (e.g., 25 dr.) to much larger ones (usually in the amount of 1,000 dr., but we also have evidence for higher sums).[31]

28. Some scholars believe that death was a possible punishment. However, in the extant court cases, death is mentioned only twice (Hansen #12; 14) and in both cases it seems more of a rhetorical stunt than a proposed penalty. In Hansen #12, death appears as a punishment for other crimes unrelated to the graphē paranomōn (Dem. 22.69). In Hansen #14, the decree is time-barred by the time it gets to court and therefore the proposer is not liable to be punished at all (Dem. 23.93).

29. Or a prosecutor who dropped the indictment before the issue reached the courts (he would be liable to pay 1,000 dr. and would incur a ban on bringing another graphē paranomōn in the future: Hansen 1999: 206).

30. After a year, a successful graphē paranomōn would only strike down the legislation, without consequences for the original proposer.

31. If unable to pay, the guilty individual was liable to incur temporary disenfranchisement (atimia) until the debt was paid; permanent atimia, instead, awaited the person against whom three judgments were made (Hansen 1999: 207). If a penalty had to be meted out, it would be assessed during a second stage of the trial, which took place in the same day and with the same jury, just after the adjudication phase. In this second phase, the litigants would each propose a

Based on these costs, classical scholarship usually assumes that only the elite had the resources to enter the graphē paranomōn game. Three arguments run counter to this conclusion. First, fines were not always conspicuous (Hyp. 4.18), and they were not always applied. If a defendant's original proposal took place more than a year before the indictment was brought, or if a graphē paranomōn failed and the prosecutor gained more than one-fifth of the votes, none of the litigants was punished.[32] Second, the evidence for sub-elite participation in the extant sources, if meager, exists. In fact, some Athenians that are not in Davies' catalog of Athenian propertied families appeared as litigants in cases of graphē paranomōn (Hansen #19, 20, and 37).[33] Finally, there were also reputational costs involved in the graphē paranomōn game. If pecuniary fines affected sub-elite actors more than elite actors (especially when fines were conspicuous), reputational costs affected elite actors more than sub-elite actors.

3.3. Decision-Making in the Courts

In this section, I provide some details on the Athenian decision-making process, which culminated, but did not entirely take place in the law-courts. I then present the model though a series of steps that include a hypothetical case (b), the modeling assumptions (c), the analysis of the legal process and the equilibrium outcomes (d), and finally the model's implications (e).

3.3.a. The Legislative Process

Athenian policies originated in the Council of Five Hundred. As I mentioned in chapter 1, since its establishment under Cleisthenes (508/507), the Council was a key institution in Athens' democracy. Councilors were selected by lot to serve for a full year. Each Athenian could serve only twice in the course of his lifetime. The Council was thus meaningfully representative of the population

---

penalty and the jury would vote for one or the other proposal. For simplicity, I do not model this second stage here since the proposed penalties were known in advance, probably from the original statement of the charges (Phillips 2013: 40; Lanni 2016: 58; Pl. *Apol.* 28b passim; Dem. 45.46).

32. Of the thirty-eight extant cases collected by Hansen (1974; but see Hansen 1999: 211), twelve went for the prosecution, thirteen for the defense, and twelve are unknown (one was withdrawn). In four of the thirteen cases won by the defense, the prosecution failed to gather one-fifth of the votes.

33. The fines in the first two cases (which might actually be the same case) were conspicuous (ten talents), suggesting that the Athenians did not discriminate based on wealth when it came to punishment.

as a whole, both synchronically and over time (Taylor 2007a; Ober 2008). Since the middle of the fifth century, councilors received compensation for their service (Hansen 1999: 253–55). The Council had a number of duties, of which the most important was to set the agenda for the Assembly ([Arist.] *Ath.Pol.* 44–50; Hansen 1999: 255–65).

There were two ways in which the Council could put items on the Assembly's agenda. The Council could either simply put an item on the agenda that the Assembly must discuss (e.g., state finance) or it could formulate a specific proposal concerning that agenda item (e.g., a recommendation to move funds from one treasury to another). In the former case (an open *probouleuma*), the discussion began with the question "who wishes to speak?" and the Assembly would hear specific proposals from the floor. In the latter case, the Council's proposal would be put to a vote (a concrete *probouleuma*).[34] I model a case in which the Council put on the Assembly's agenda a discussion of policies to raise state revenue without formulating a specific proposal.[35]

Once a proposal is formulated on the floor of the Assembly, anyone can bring a graphē paranomōn.[36] In order to bring a graphē paranomōn, one has to show that the proposal contradicts at least an existing statute. Moreover, one has to show that the proposal is inconvenient (*asymphoron*) to the interests of the Athenians. A graphē paranomōn can be brought before the Assembly has taken a vote on the proposal, after the Assembly's vote, or after the proposal has been approved and implemented. I model a case in which the graphē paranomōn is brought before the Assembly has taken a vote on the proposal.[37] Strategically,

34. For the distinction between (and evidence of) open and concrete *probouleumata*: Rhodes (1972b: 52–81); Hansen (1999: 138–39).

35. Rhodes' (1972a: 78–81) study of the preserved epigraphic evidence suggests that half of the decrees were open and half were concrete *probouleumata*.

36. In the model, I only consider one proposer. In reality, Leo's proposal would have competed with others advanced by fellow citizens on the floor of the Assembly.

37. For simplicity, I assume that the median is the same in the Assembly and in the courts. If this assumption is, on average, accurate (cf. ch. 1), it is important to stress that selection rules allowed for some variation. For this reason, future work will relax this assumption, providing a more accurate sequential game of the entire policy-making process. To speculate: the different composition of the courts and the Assembly suggests that the two medians may in fact vary. But if this were the case, then, the representative nature of the courts yielded less uncertainty about the position of the court median vis-à-vis the Assembly median. This suggests that one of the basic functions of the graphē paranomōn (and cognate cases) was to eliminate some of the uncertainty that policy-makers faced in the Assembly, where the median changed more frequently and where many more policy proposals were discussed.

it is a risky move to expose oneself to the potential costs associated with bringing an indictment before feeling the Assembly's pulse. Nonetheless, we have direct evidence of such a practice (Hansen 1974).[38] Moreover, other considerations may have offset the risk of indicting a proposal immediately after it was presented to the Assembly. An immediate indictment is a powerful signaling device, suggesting that someone feels strongly about the detrimental effect of a proposal—so strongly indeed, that he is willing to forfeit the benefits of the vote.

When an indictment is brought, the matter is transferred from the Assembly to the courts. It is important to stress at this point that not all detrimental proposals were eliminated through the graphē paranomōn. In fact, if someone were to propose an outrageous policy—for example, to raise state revenue by eliminating all compensation for public service—such a policy would be unlikely to end up in court, and more likely to be rejected (shouted down) in the Assembly. The multistep legislative process thus limited the range of proposals that reached the courts. If a proposal reached the court, then in court the individual who proposed the new legislation acted as the defendant, while the individual who brought the indictment acted as the prosecutor. The litigants had equal time to speak. A jury of 501 listened to the litigants' arguments and voted by majority rule, secret ballot, and without deliberation.

3.3.b. A Hypothetical Case: Leo v. Ernie

Leo is a country boy, but has resided in the city for a number of years. He owns a successful workshop, which employs a handful of slaves. Leo does not consider himself a politician, but he knows the ropes around the Agora, the city's central marketplace and political hub. At the venerable age of forty-five, Leo is quite versed in Athenian politics, due to his experience as a juror and as an Assembly-goer. A businessman operating in the Agora, Leo interacts daily with buyers and other sellers. Leo may also be a member of one or more of those associations mentioned by Aristotle and discussed earlier.

In the year 354 business is slow in the Agora. Athens has just lost the Social War. The city needs new revenue. Leo has an idea. He has discussed his idea for some time with his fellow artisans in the Agora (some of whom are metics), with citizen friends, and even with his slave employees. The reactions were, overall, quite favorable and many of those supporting his proposal promised to

38. In the extant evidence (Hansen 1974: 49), four proposals were indicted prior to being passed by the Assembly and ten proposals were indicted after being passed by the Assembly.

help by spreading the word. Some even promised to help Leo defray the cost of litigation were his proposal indicted as unconstitutional.

Leo's idea is as follows:

> suppose that, in the first place, we studied the interests of the resident aliens. For in them we have one of the very best sources of revenue, in my opinion, inasmuch as they are self-supporting and, so far from receiving payment for the many services they render to states, they contribute by paying a special tax. I think that we should study their interests sufficiently, if we relieved them of the duties that seem to impose a certain measure of disability on the resident alien without conferring any benefit on the state . . . since there are many vacant sites for houses within the walls, if the state allowed approved applicants to erect houses on these and granted them the freehold of the land, I think that we should find a larger and better class of persons desiring to live at Athens.[39]

Leo's proposal, then, is to extend land grants to metics. The privilege would increase state revenue in two ways: by expanding Athens' tax base, and by increasing the volume of trade.[40] This latter prospect is quite appealing to Leo the shoemaker and his fellow businessmen.

Leo's proposal is neat, but risky. It provides for an extension of privileges associated with citizenship to noncitizens.[41] And of all privileges, it seeks to extend the one that is most closely associated with the very idea of citizenship

---

39. The passage is a direct citation from Xenophon's pamphlet *Poroi*, dated to the middle of the fourth century (Xen. *Por.* 2.1–7; all translations from Xenophon's *Poroi* are from Marchant (1925), unless otherwise noted). In the *Poroi*, Xenophon listed a series of measures aimed at raising state revenue by boosting indirect taxation in two main areas of the Athenian economy: maritime commerce and silver mining. As such, the proposal I present here ought to be considered as representing ideas that may well have been under the Assembly's consideration. On Xenophon's *Poroi*, see Dillery (1993); Carugati, Ober, and Weingast (2016); and chapter 4.

40. Metics in Athens paid a head tax, the *metoikon*, equivalent to twelve dr. a year. Moreover, metics were in large part involved in commercial activities, particularly around the harbor of Piraeus. More metics in Athens thus meant more money for the state through both direct and indirect taxes. I discuss taxation as it relates to noncitizens and their activities more fully in chapter 4.

41. This scenario must be somewhat similar to the one that saw the establishment of the new commercial cases (dikai emporikai) in the middle of the fourth century, which extended to noncitizens the privilege to participate as litigants in court. On the extension of inclusion through the dikai emporikai: Carugati (2019b). On the dikai emporikai more generally: E. Cohen (1973); Lanni (2006).

in Athens: land ownership. Such a proposal may well be indicted by graphē paranomōn.

Leo arrives early on the day of the Assembly meeting. The agenda: state finances. When the question "who wishes to speak?" is put to the floor, Leo advances his motion. As expected, an old, cranky landowner from the deme of Rhamnous named Eratosthenes, or Ernie, indicts him by graphē paranomōn. Ernie has on his side a law restricting ownership of land to citizens.[42] He further argues that it is utterly against the interests of the Athenian demos to extend privileges associated with citizenship to metics and other foreigners. Indeed, the proposed decree is so iniquitous in Ernie's mind that he brings the indictment even before the Assembly has taken a vote on the proposal. Consideration of Leo's decree in the Assembly is therefore suspended and the case is transferred to the courts.

What kind of considerations weighed on Leo's choice of proposal? And under what conditions will his proposal succeed?

3.3.c. Assumptions

The model is based on the following assumptions:

- (R1) The range of policy choices is represented as a single continuum (x). Because the issue presented here revolves around metic privileges, we might consider the continuum as featuring, on one end, deportation of all metics from Athens and, on the other end, extension of full citizenship to all metics residing in Athens.
- (R2) Ernie, Leo, and all members of the jury have symmetric, single peaked preferences over the set of outcomes.
  - Leo's ideal outcome is L^*.
  - Because Ernie must argue for the status quo, q, his preferences are irrelevant here.[43]
- (R3) Leo faces uncertainty about the exact location of the median juror's ideal outcome, m. For simplicity, I assume that Leo's subjective

---

42. We lack direct evidence for a law that restricted land ownership to citizens. However, the principle seems incontrovertible. As Todd (1993: 243) put it, "the fundamental rule at Athens was that ownership of land . . . was in principle restricted to citizens, and this right was only in exceptional circumstances extended to metics by the special privilege of *enktesis*."

43. More precisely, if Ernie brings a graphē paranomōn, then he must prefer q to L^*. However, Ernie's position is fixed at q, so his precise preferences are irrelevant. Moreover, for a challenge to move forward, Ernie must disagree with Leo on the position of the median.

beliefs about the location of the median are described by a symmetric, unimodal density function (e.g., a bell-shaped curve).[44] Let m* be the expected value of m, according to that distribution.

- (R4) Leo's preferences are represented by a utility function that includes both honor and policy. Honor is a function of the number of votes Leo receives—that is, the more votes Leo earns, the greater the honor. Policy reflects the degree to which Leo cares about the policy that results from the verdict.

3.3.d. The Model

Based on R2, Leo prefers his ideal policy over all other policies, but he also prefers policies closer to his ideal to those further away. Leo's preferences can thus be represented through a utility function, U(x). As indicated in figure 3.1, U(x) is highest at L* (Leo's ideal point).

Based on R3, Leo is uncertain about the median juror's ideal policy. This uncertainty can be represented through a probability density function, f(x), that depicts the likelihood that the median juror is located near any given point along the continuum. In figure 3.2, the expected median of the distribution is located around m*.

Equilibrium outcomes will vary depending on Leo's expectations of the relative position of the median juror and the status quo vis-à-vis his ideal outcome, as well as his preferences for honor and policy.

CASE #1: L* < Q < M*

If Leo believes that the expected median, m*, is located to the right of q, as in figure 3.3, he is not likely to formulate a proposal in the first place because he will lose with any proposal to the left of q.

CASE #2: M* < L* < Q

If Leo believes that the expected median, m*, is located to the left of his ideal point, L*, as in figure 3.4a, he can win by proposing L*. If the expected median, m*, is very far from q, as in figure 3.4b, Ernie will be unlikely to bring a graphē paranomōn in the first place, because the risk of losing would be too high.

---

44. A unimodal density function has one peak (i.e., there is only one area in which the probability that the median is located there is high relative to the probability in other areas).

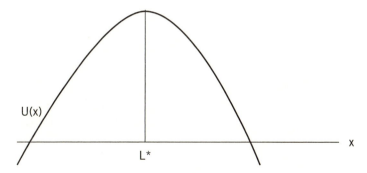

FIGURE 3.1. Leo's utility function U(x)

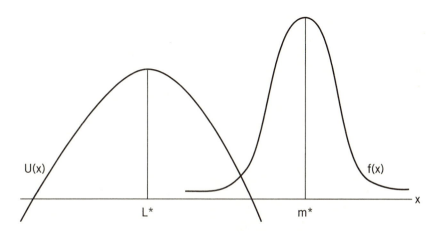

FIGURE 3.2. Probability density function f(x)

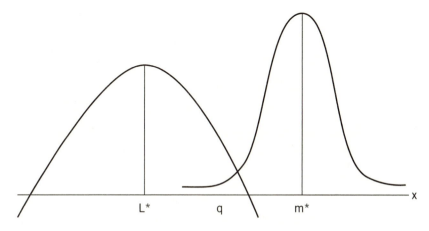

FIGURE 3.3. L* < q < m*—no proposal

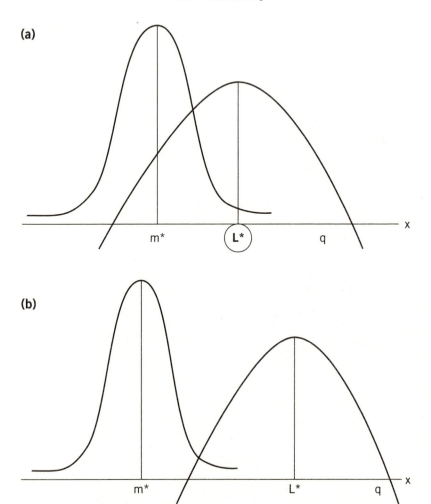

FIGURE 3.4. (a) m* < L* < q—Leo can win with L*,
(b) A large gap between m* and q—no *graphē paranomōn*

CASE #3: L* < M* < Q

If Leo believes that the expected median, m*, is located between his ideal point, L*, and the status quo, then Leo can win with any proposal to the left of q. Where his proposal will fall on the continuum, however, depends on the relative weight that Leo attributes to honor and policy.

Let q' be the reflection of q around m. This means that q' and q are equidistant from m*, but on opposite sides of m*. Hence, a voter whose ideal is m* is indifferent between q' and q. Further, m* prefers all points between q' and q to either q' or q (because these points are closer to m* than either q' or q).[45]

If Leo cares only about policy, then he will try to push his proposal as far away from q (and as close to his ideal) as possible. If Leo cares only about policy, then, his proposal will be slightly to the right of q', as represented in figure 3.5.

If Leo cares only about honor, then his proposal will be somewhere between m* and q—and probably very close to q, as in figure 3.6.

If Leo cares equally about honor and policy, then his proposal will be somewhere between q' and m*, as in figure 3.7.

3.3.e. Implications

In all the specifications presented above, Leo has an incentive to move toward the median. But he can also move away from the status quo. When Leo's ideal point is located between the median and the status quo (case #2), he has strong incentives to propose a new measure because he can win by proposing his ideal point, and establish a new status quo that is closer to the median's preferences than the old status quo (in this case, Leo gets a larger share of the vote *and* his preferred policy). Moreover, when the median is located between Leo's ideal point and the status quo (case #3), Leo has incentives to move closer to the median, and his proposal is likely to fall within a boundary created by the status quo and its reflection around the median.

The model yields two additional results. First, innovation in policy-making was more likely to arise from sub-elite actors. In fact, the extent to which a proposal will depart from the status quo depends on the weight that a proposer gives to honor and policy. Proposers who care a lot about policy and little about honor are the ones with the greater incentives to push new proposals as far away as possible from both the status quo and the median (compare figures 3.5 and 3.6). A sub-elite Athenian like Leo would be more likely to care a great deal about policy and relatively little about honor. Conversely, someone like Demosthenes cared about policy, but also cared about honor. Therefore, Leo would be more likely than Demosthenes to formulate a legislative proposal that departed significantly from the status quo. The model does not suggest that policy innovation always came from sub-elite actors. For example, on a given legislative proposal, Demosthenes himself may decide to forfeit honor to get his proposal passed, albeit the costs of doing so for his position of leadership,

---

45. By the same token, any policy to the left of q' or to the right of q would have a low probability of winning.

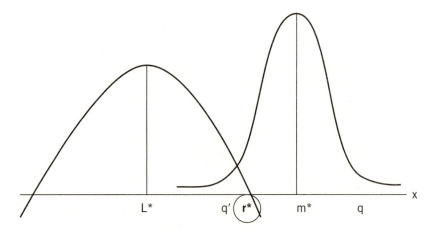

FIGURE 3.5. Leo's equilibrium proposal (r*)—policy

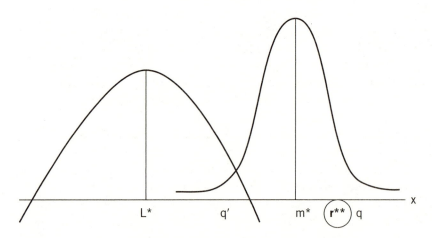

FIGURE 3.6. Leo's equilibrium proposal (r**)—honor

were he to lose, would be high. The model, then, indicates that the design of the law-courts made this forum extremely receptive to diverse sources of expertise and dispersed knowledge.[46]

46. The model thus provides a plausible explanation of how important pieces of legislation whose authors cannot readily be identified as elite (like Nikophōn: Stroud 1974: 163–64), or whose identity is unknown to us (for example, the individual who proposed to establish the dikai emporikai), may have come about. I return to this point in the next chapter.

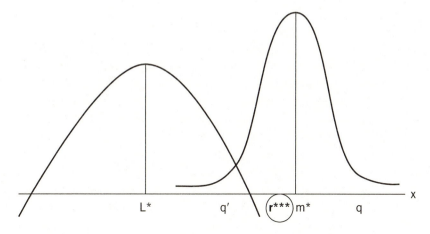

FIGURE 3.7. Leo's equilibrium proposal (r***)—honor and policy

Second, although the case I presented above is a synchronic representation of policy-making in the law-courts, the model also suggests a series of insights about policy change over time. Because juries were large and representative of the population as a whole, and because no significant changes affected the composition of the citizen body in the course of the fourth century, the median juror embodied a relatively stable ordering of preferences over time, as well as normative expectations that were broadly consistent with those of the average or typical member of the Athenian demos.[47]

These features have important implications for the debate on whether the Athenian legal system produced the kind of consistency and predictability that we associate with modern rule-of-law institutions (E. M. Harris 2006a; 2013; contra Lanni 2004; 2009; 2016). For E. M. Harris (2013: 249–50), Athenian courts achieved consistency and predictability in the application of the law through the use of nonbinding precedent, appeals to the intent of the lawgiver, and the use of analogous statutes. In contrast, for Lanni (2009: 709), "individual Athenian court verdicts were . . . the result of many individual jurors' complicated weighing of a variety of factors, both statutory and extra-statutory." Because individual verdicts were ad hoc, Athens' courts did not achieve

47. Simple comparative statics results suggest that, as the size of the jury grows, the variance in the distribution of preferences falls, so that the median in the courts converges on the median of the whole citizenry. This result suggests that changing the size of the jury based on the relevance of the issue was a strategy to increase the likelihood that verdicts would align with community expectations.

predictability and consistency in the application of the law, thus undermining the deterrence effect of statutes.

My account suggests a somewhat different conclusion. To the extent that the median juror embodied a stable ordering of preferences over time, and to the extent that verdicts were broadly consistent with the normative expectations of the median, the Athenians did achieve some form of predictability and consistency, yielding reasonably stable expectations, even if individual verdicts were not, strictly speaking, consistent with one another. Athenian citizens did not model their behavior on previous jury decisions. Instead, they modeled their behavior based in part on statutes, and in part on what they believed the average member of their community would have considered wrongdoing based on his interpretation of those statutes.

3.4. Stability and Innovation between Solon and the Median Juror

The model does not suggest that, because the institutions regulated litigants' behavior as I described, the Athenians always "got it right."[48] Classical scholars have devoted a great deal of attention to the potential pitfalls of the Athenian law-court system. Able speakers could capture the jury through the shrewd use of rhetoric (Ober 1989a). The legal system as a whole could fall in the hands of sycophants who profited from frivolous litigation, threatening to paralyze the legal system (Christ 1998). If the legal system enabled clever leaders and entrepreneurs to guide the demos through the perils of large-scale collective decision-making, what prevented equally clever demagogues and sycophants from hijacking the process?

The evidence suggests that the constitution regulated interactions between litigants and jurors in the courts not only in terms of setting the institutional rules of engagement, but also through discursive strategies that operated on the symbolic plane. In extant courtroom speeches, litigants frequently attribute legislation that supports their proposals to "the lawgiver," a figure often identified with Solon.[49] Classical scholars have often dismissed these appeals. Recognizing that measures attributed to Solon had nothing to do with (what we know

48. I also do not make any claims as to whether the Athenian institutional structure was either unique or more efficient than others.

49. Other founders included Theseus (e.g. Isoc. 10.34 and 12.127ff.; Dem. 59.75; 60.28) and Draco. Only Isocrates in non-law-court speeches discusses Cleisthenes or Pericles: Hansen (1989b: 77–78).

of) the lawgiver's archaic legislation, scholars have stressed the Athenians' lack of legal sophistication (e.g., Ruschenbusch 1966).

Against this tradition, Hansen (1989b) interpreted the fourth-century appeals to Solon as the expression of a commitment to a moderate form of democracy that curtailed the excesses of the fifth-century radical democracy. For Hansen, moreover, the figure of Solon coincided with the notion of the ancestral constitution, and Solon became the constitution's *protos heuretēs*—its original father.[50] Hansen thus stressed the connection between Solon, the ancestral constitution, and the fourth-century constitution, suggesting that the use of the figure of Solon may have replaced the phrase patrios politeia due to the latter concept's association with the late fifth-century experience of oligarchy.[51]

Steven Johnstone (1999: 23–26) suggested instead that the appeals to Solon were a sophisticated form of legal reasoning. Because the texts of the laws have no objective, authoritative meaning, these texts "could support a range of interpretations," but the boundaries of this range, "were themselves open to debate." The appeals to the lawgiver, for Johnstone, defined the limits and the means of legal interpretation: "Not a person, but a trope, 'the lawgiver' created a context for interpretation. . . . The Athenian lawgiver represents not (or not just) the intrusion of the 'extralegal' but an Athenian form of legal reasoning." In particular, appeals to the lawgiver "allowed at least three related interpretive strategies: nonliteral reading, reading in conformity with other laws and reading of laws as fundamentally democratic."

Based on my reconstruction of the role that the notion of patrios politeia played in shaping the fourth-century constitution, I suggest that Hansen's and Johnstone's interpretations are complementary and reveal the elaboration of coordination strategies pioneered during the constitutional debate. By attributing legislation to Solon, Athenian litigants made a case about the conformity of their proposals with constitutional principles. These principles included, for example, the integrity of the corpus of law—that is, what Johnstone terms "reading in conformity with other laws"—and the primary role of law in protecting the democratic constitution from the threats of civil war and oligarchy—that

50. Hansen argues that in the fourth century there are two Solons (or better, two versions of Solonian democracy): one emerging from the orators and [Aristotle]'s *Athenaion Politeia*; the other emerging from Aristotle's *Politics* and from Isocrates' oratory. The former (and most important for Hansen's own purposes) depicts a type of Solonian democracy that curtails the power of the Assembly.

51. Even when referring directly to the ancestral constitution, the Athenians in the fourth century prefer other phrases, like the constitution of the forefathers (*he epi tōn progonōn politeia*), or the ancestral laws (*hoi patrioi nomoi*): Hansen (1989b: 75–76); (1999: 297).

is, what Johnstone terms "reading of laws as fundamentally democratic." But, as Johnstone critically argues, attributing legislation to the lawgiver, often Solon, also enabled litigants to advance new legislation or new readings of existing laws. When new laws or new interpretations of old laws were at stake, then, litigants' appeals to Solon may have encouraged jurors to evaluate such proposals based on their interpretation of "what Solon would have done."

A systematic account of how these appeals operated within each extant speech is beyond the scope of this chapter. The figure of Solon emerges frequently in cases of graphē paranomōn and graphē nomon mē epitēdeion theinai (Dem. 18.6; 20.90, 93–94, 99, 102–4; 22.25, 30; 24.103, 106, 113–15, 142, 148, 211–12; Aesch. 3. 175, 257), where the speakers invite the jurors to evaluate the pros and cons of proposed legislation through the eyes of Solon. In some of these cases, the connection between appeals to Solon and fourth-century constitutional principles is clear. For example, Demosthenes 20 (esp. 93–94, 99) attributes to the archaic lawgiver the very process of fourth-century nomothesia, and charges Leptines, his opponent, with undermining through his proposal Solon's effort to protect citizens' property rights (20. 102–3).[52] But these strategies can also be observed in other public cases, as well as in private cases.[53] Some of these appeals dealt with novel interpretations of existing statutes (e.g., Lyc. 1 and Lys. 31), others did not. Because in most cases we do not know how the jurors ultimately voted, we cannot reach robust conclusions concerning the relevance of the appeals to Solon in terms of outcomes.[54] My hypothesis is that the appeals to Solon reduced the range of possible interpretations by providing a benchmark against which jurors could evaluate proposals. This increased the likelihood that proposals would conform to the expectations of

---

52. In another important passage, Demosthenes (24.148) attributes to Solon the authority of the courts (defined as kuriōtaton, i.e., most powerful) to punish wrongdoers. Other passages define the tenets of citizen morality according to Solon (e.g., Dem. 22.30; 24.103).

53. References to Solon cover the entire period of the orators, from the immediate aftermath of the civil war and the ratification of the amnesty (e.g., in Andoc. 1), down to the period after Chaeronea and before the Lamian War (e.g., in Hyp. 3), and they span private (e.g., Dem. 43) as well as public (e.g., Aesch. 1) cases. Out of twenty-seven orations referring to Solon, the "lawgiver," or the "legislator" in cases litigated before the popular courts, nineteen explicitly refer to Solon. Orations containing these references are: Aesch. 1 and 3; Andoc. 1; Dem. 18, 19, 20, 22, 23, 24, 26, 36, 40, 42, 43, 44, 47, 57, 58; Hyp. 3; Is. 2 and 11; Isoc. 17 and 20; Lyc. 1; Lys. 10, 11 and 30. Of these, Dem 23, 47 and 58; Is. 2 and 11; Isoc. 20, Lyc. 1 (referring, however, to the legislators of the past, the archaioi nomothetai, at 1.64); and Lys 11 do not explicitly mention Solon.

54. Of the roughly one hundred extant law-court orations, we know the outcome of thirty-four trials.

the median. By the same token, as long as the jurors collectively interpreted a proposal as consistent with the spirit, if not the letter, of the laws of Solon, there was room for innovation in law- and policy-making. As a result, as long as proposals lay "between Solon and the median juror" change was possible and leadership rewarded.

3.5. Conclusion

In this chapter, I presented a model of decision-making in the Athenian law-courts. Drawing from epigraphic and prosopographical studies of political participation, and from analyses of sub-polis associations and social networks, I suggested that we should move beyond the dichotomy between mass and elite as the sole interpretive heuristic of political and legal relations in fourth-century Athens. In particular, we must come to terms with a much more variegated and dynamic set of compromises, whose solution was not so much a winner-takes-all model (i.e., the ideological hegemony of the masses over feuding elites), but an ongoing process of negotiation among citizens with meaningfully pluralistic preferences.

In the courts, litigants' and jurors' pluralistic preferences shaped law and policy in ways that were not deferential to the preferences of one group to the detriment of another. Instead, litigants' weighing of both social and policy considerations meant that they had an incentive to propose legislation that was sensitive to the preferences of the median, without necessarily converging on the median's ideal. The courts thus created a space for cooperation that fostered innovation in law- and policy-making without loss of political stability.

The model that I discussed in this chapter is an abstract representation of law-court dynamics. Accordingly, one may reasonably ask whether Athenian law- and policy-making in the fourth century evolved as the model suggests. In the next chapter, I examine whether the historical evidence for fiscal and economic policy is consistent with the model's predictions.

4

The Institutional
Foundations of Prosperity

THE MODEL that I presented in the last chapter suggested that the procedures regulating law- and policy-making in the courts fostered innovation without loss of political stability. Is the evidence consistent with the model's predictions? In this chapter, I focus on the evolution of fiscal and economic policy for two reasons. First, these areas are well documented in the sources and the object of much attention among scholars.[1] Second, and perhaps more importantly, fiscal and economic policy was critical to the stability of the constitutional pact. As I argued in previous chapters, fear of expropriation rocked the fifth-century democracy. The loss of the empire upended Athens' economy. In the fourth century, Athens had to find new ways to generate revenues in the absence of an imperial structure and without jeopardizing the social order.

In the fourth century, as in the fifth, the demand for revenues was driven largely by warfare and the increasing costs that military expenditures imposed on states (Morris 2010; Pyzyk forthcoming).[2] As Pritchard (2015) documents, war-related expenditures in Athens were conspicuous and exceeded the expenditures for democracy and festivals—the other two areas of major state spending.[3] In the

1. Economic analyses: Lyttkens (1991; 2010; 2013); Ober (2015b;) Kyriazis (2009); Halkos and Kyriazis (2010); Bitros and Karayannis (2010); Pitsoulis (2011); Tridimas (2011; 2012; 2014; 2015; 2016; 2017); Karayannis and Hatzis (2012); Kyriazis and Economou (2013). Athenian fiscal policy and institutions: E. Cohen (1992); Gabrielsen (1994; 2013); Ober (2010; 2015a and 2015b); Rhodes (2013); Pritchard (2015). On the development of fiscal expertise as a *techne*: Pyzyk (forthcoming).

2. Increased spending was due to the development of war machines (e.g., catapult and siege engines), and to "larger and more sophisticated navies, stronger and more extensive fortifications, and increasingly specialized and professional soldiers" (Pyzyk forthcoming: 5).

3. Pritchard's (2015: 49, 89, 97, 111) estimates suggest that, in the 420s, Athens spent 1,485 T/yr on warfare and 257 T/yr on democracy and festivals; in the 370s, the city spent 522 T/yr

fifth century, as in the fourth, "war made states," to cite the famous dictum associated with Charles Tilly's theory of state formation. In what follows, I assume, without arguing the point, that warfare was one of the drivers, if not *the* driver of Athens' institutional development. But my analysis focuses less on the demand side and more on the supply side. In other words, I ask: how did fiscal and economic policy evolve in the fourth century in response to the demands of warfare (and other expenditures)?[4] To answer this question, we need to analyze Athens' sources of revenue in the post-imperial period.

Classical scholars often emphasize the extraordinary burden borne by the Athenian elite in matters of taxation and public finance (Lyttkens 1991; Tridimas 2015; Pyzyk working paper). Seeking to explain how such a system may have endured over time, scholars suggest that there existed a balance of interests between masses and elites that enabled the masses to extract an extraordinary amount of wealth from the elite without driving them into revolt (Ober 1989a; Gabrielsen 1994). The traditional justification for the resilience of the pact—the ideological hegemony of the masses over the elites—does some work in explaining the policy bargains that emerge from the evidence. For example, it justifies reforms such as the extension of pay for the Assembly or the reform of the Theoric fund, whereby financial surpluses previously earmarked for war were subsequently directed toward festivals and infrastructure projects. A prior question, however, arises: where did the Athenians find the money to extend welfare spending?

As we will see in the course of the chapter, the elite did contribute a great deal to the polis' coffers. But the evidence suggests that fiscal policy in the fourth century evolved to regulate, rather than increase, elite contributions. Moreover, elite contributions alone cannot account for Athens' remarkable economic performance. New revenue, generated through new economic policies, filled the gap between existing revenues and increased spending.[5]

---

on war and 198 T/yr on democracy and festivals; in the 330s, the city spent 228 T/yr on democracy and festivals (Pritchard does not offer estimates for war expenditures after the 360s). Ober's numbers differ (2015a: 245; 2015b: 499), but war remains the single most burdensome item throughout the classical period (cf. van Wees 2000: 81; Pritchard 2010: 125–26; Gabrielsen 2013).

4. In Carugati and Pyzyk (working paper), we discuss how war drove Athens, Sparta, and Macedon down different paths to state formation in the fourth century.

5. Two factors in the post-conflict period deserve some attention: demography and the cessation of conflict. Demography clearly matters, but it is unclear how. After the Peloponnesian War, the number of adult, free, male citizens dropped from a total of forty to sixty thousand people in the 430s to perhaps as low as fifteen to twenty-five thousand people in the immediate aftermath of Athens' defeat. Population is usually estimated at thirty thousand people in the mid- and late fourth century. We are much less well informed about fluctuations in the numbers

In the fourth century, fiscal reforms proceeded with an eye to the constitutional bargain, and therefore to the issue of political stability. At various stages in the fourth century, the burden on the elites was regulated through measures that enabled the rich to share responsibilities and risks, and that progressively shifted the bulk of payments on the super-rich through the institution of a system of progressive taxation. To say that fiscal reforms sought to regulate the burden on the elite is not to say that the burden was ever light. To clarify this point, it is useful to think about the counterfactual. At various stages, the demos could have passed legislation to increase the burden of taxation on the wealthy, either engaging in forms of expropriation and redistribution typical of other city-states, or, less overtly, by passing measures to counter the phenomenon of the *aphanēs* (lit. invisible, concealed) economy (E. Cohen 1992). This would have been particularly tempting, we may surmise, after major military defeats. But drastic measures could prove counterproductive. Overtaxed elites were at risk of falling out of the elite class, thus lowering contributions in the long run.[6] Most threateningly, though, overtaxed elites could decide, as

---

of other categories of Athenian residents (women, children, slaves, metics, and foreigners), but scholars agree that the total population of Attica dropped from 350,000 people to 250,000 people from the mid-fifth to the mid-fourth century (Hansen 1986; 1988; 2006b; Strauss 1987a; Morris 2009b). While the evidence for a sharp population decline is beyond doubt, problems remain in how to interpret the relationship between demographic decline and economic growth. A smaller citizen population meant a decline in productive inputs, particularly given that the most affected age group was males of military age (the evidence for a decline in the number of noncitizens also suggests that noncitizens did not, or perhaps did not fully, compensate for the decline in citizen numbers). At the same time, a smaller population is at least part of the explanation for a possible increase in per capita consumption growth in the fourth century. The second factor to consider is the possibility that the cessation of conflict yielded a large peace dividend. However, while we cannot assess economic growth in the post-conflict period (a point to which I return below), the peace dividend, if it existed, may have depended more on the restoration of normal economic activity, and less on curtailing war expenditures. In fact, Athens was already at war in 395, a mere eight years after the end of the civil war, and expenditures on security-related items—i.e., rebuilding the navy and walls—were conspicuous. Here, I assume, without arguing the point, that the cessation of conflict favored some level of economic recovery in the immediate aftermath of the civil war. However, the peace dividend alone cannot account for Athens' prosperity, particularly in the second half of the fourth century.

6. Certainly, the Athenians could always redefine the level of income that defined membership to the elite. But more generally, the risk was that the elite would spend more time and effort hiding wealth rather than creating wealth, or might even chose an exit option. On Athenian elites seeking to hide their wealth: (E. Cohen 1992; cf. Lyttkens 1991;).

they had done after the disaster in Sicily, that it was time to overthrow the democracy.

In the context of massive expenditures and with an elite class already stretched thin, the options were limited. But the point I wish to make is that there is no historical teleology in the fact that the Athenians did figure out ways to pay their bills without imperial revenues, without curtailing military expenditures, and without driving taxpayers into revolt. How they did so changed throughout the fourth century, but especially as the century progressed, public spending and social order demands put a premium on innovative thinking in matters of fiscal and economic policy.

In the first half of the fourth century, the Athenians deployed a mix of market incentives and various forms of rent extraction from other constituencies beyond the elite. Market incentives aimed at lowering transaction costs in the marketplace (for example, the law that established coin-testers in the Agora and Piraeus markets: Stroud 1974; Ober 2008), as well as ensuring the credibility of the state's commitment to its benefactors (Engen 2010). Rent extraction included imposing taxes on the dependencies of Lemnos, Imbros, and Scyros (for example, through the grain-tax law: Stroud 1998), as well as taxes on former allies and other Greek states.

The defeat in the Social War (from 357 to 355) ruled out once and for all the coercion option, exposing the polis to a new wave of constitutional and financial instability. Unable to restore the empire, or impose taxes on other cities, the Athenians could have turned to the elite and increased the already burdensome level of taxation. But they didn't. They turned instead toward their domestic resources—first and foremost, the Laurion silver mines and the harbor of Piraeus—and began to intensify their exploitation. To do so, the polis had to provide incentives to those actors that were primarily involved in such exploitation. The Athenians thus began to gradually extend forms of institutional access to previously excluded actors, including categories of foreign merchants, metics, and even slaves. Access encompassed a number of institutions in the realms of society (e.g., the right to form associations), the economy (e.g., tax exemptions, or the right to own land), and the law (e.g., litigation rights through the dikai emporikai).[7] The Athenians did not extend access to these institutions to all noncitizens. Instead, they targeted only specific categories of economically productive actors. Moreover, none of these actors obtained

---

7. Prejudices against noncitizens certainly continued to exist (see e.g., Hyp. 3), but the breadth of these forms of inclusion—from the polis' central institutions to decentralized associations—suggests that changes were ongoing at the local as well as the national level. Social norms may have evolved accordingly (Lanni 2016).

access to political institutions. In fact, the right to participate in the decision-making process remained restricted to adult male citizens.[8]

This arrangement raises a series of questions. If noncitizens were so critical to Athens' prosperity, why didn't the Athenians extend the full franchise to them?[9] Or, conversely, why didn't noncitizens demand to be included in the citizen body? And finally, how did the Athenians manage to make their commitment not to renege on inclusion credible?

I argue that the tradeoff between political rights and other forms of institutional access was sustainable because it was incentive-compatible for all actors involved. By limiting the franchise, the Athenians maintained a high degree of cultural and ideological homogeneity among decision-makers that was a key to stability in a political system where decisions were made, collectively, by the people. Those citizens who had hammered out the consensus on Solonian legality in the late fifth century shared a great deal with those citizens who proposed and evaluated legislative changes in the fourth century. Limitations on the franchise meant that throughout the fourth century, no radical shifts occurred in the preferences of the median. Reforms, then, were by design protecting a median that meaningfully represented, both synchronically and over time, the expectations of the average Athenian.[10] By limiting access to political

8. The extension of Athenian citizenship to noncitizens (individuals as well as groups) as reward for military participation and other forms of assistance to the polis was indubitably rare, but it was not unheard of. In 411, citizenship was bestowed on the assassins of Phrynichus, one of the ringleaders of the regime of the Four Hundred (Sinclair 1991: 25; Carawan 2013; Shear 2011). In 406, the Athenians may have extended citizenship to slaves and metics, though the evidence is contested (Sinclair 1991: 27). Finally, only two years before the ratification of the amnesty, the Samians received Athenian citizenship as a reward for their help in the war against Sparta (cf. section 4.1.c). In the aftermath of the civil war, Athens' disastrous demographics might have called for an extension of citizenship to those noncitizens who risked their lives to rid Athens of the tyrants. Instead, Pericles' citizenship law was reenacted ([Arist]. *Ath.Pol.* 42.1), restricting citizenship to sons and daughters of Athenian parents. Similarly, the practice whereby freedmen acquired metic status rather than citizenship upon manumission remained in place throughout the fourth century and beyond (M. J. Osborne 1981). According to Carawan (2013: 255), concerns with citizen status, "haunted the Athenians down to the year 346, when they launched a systematic review of deme rosters."

9. A comparison with another high-performing ancient society—Rome—may suggest that this was a policy mistake. By limiting access to political institutions, Athens deprived itself of the human and social capital that drove Rome's imperial expansion across the Mediterranean. This is an interesting, but so far untested hypothesis.

10. A modicum of continuity was further ensured by the structure of the law-courts, which fostered gradual legislative change. For Lanni (2016: 153), "the incremental nature of court cases made it easier for litigants and jurors to critically examine norms that might be in flux and to

rights, the Athenians thus ensured that legislative change remained in the hands, and in the interests, of Solon's heirs. Moreover, the trade-off was particularly beneficial to those that had the most to lose: the Athenian elite. If the elites disproportionately contributed to the material well-being of the state, they were also the principal recipients of the gains from increased economic activity— for example, as investors in maritime commerce and as owners of manufacturing workshops. Moreover, taxpayers in Athens accumulated social capital, and public spending was the primary vehicle to a successful political career. So the elite had both material and social-capital incentives to stick to the trade-off.[11]

Noncitizens, for their part, did not obtain political rights, but they did not end up empty-handed either. The problem, however, was one of commitment. By denying noncitizens the franchise, the Athenians de facto excluded them from the decision-making process. As a result, a rational noncitizen may fear that privileges that were extended one day could be revoked the next day. However, under the new constitutional system, reneging on promises that the Athenians made through legislation was difficult. Moreover, as we will see, the Athenians in the fourth century made a great effort to signal to noncitizens their commitment to promises made. Noncitizens could take the offer, leave, or fight for political inclusion. Fighting clearly involved costs, and leaving would have required finding a new place to do business. Two factors may have also helped tip the balance in favor of taking the offer. First, exercising citizenship in the polis' demanding participatory democracy entailed a shift in the allocation of one's time and resources that not everyone may have been willing or able to afford.[12] Second, the Athenians implemented a system of targeted inclusion

---

slowly change the law case by case ... in the modern context, scholars have shown that 'norm entrepreneurs' ... are more successful when they proceed slowly, using 'gentle nudges' ... rather than risking a backlash by getting too far ahead of popular sentiment." Lanni's account centers on the law-courts as the loci of dispute resolution, but her conclusions apply equally to the process of decision-making. On the role of institutional adaptation for the stability of the fourth-century democracy: Rhodes (2010). For Rhodes (2011: 29), appeals to the past in the fourth century helped to create an atmosphere in which Athens' government could be modified without a revolution.

11. These reasons go some way in explaining why, for example, the Athenians did not try to extend the tax base to raise revenue. The masses did not stand to gain as much from taxation. In addition, although some categories of resident were taxed directly (e.g., metics), taxing the entire population would have required the creation of a stronger bureaucracy and entirely new institutions to assess individual wealth and collect contributions.

12. This emerges most obviously in the case of metics, who had already made the choice to forfeit political rights in their own country to conduct their business activities in Athens. Aristotle (*Pol.* 1275a14–19; trans. Everson 1996) equates their condition to that of "children

that operated almost at the individual level. In other words, inclusion was not extended to broad categories, such as all metics, or all foreigners, or even all merchants. Instead complex regulations defined who had access, and who didn't. This approach may have hindered collective action, thus lowering the probability that noncitizens would unite to demand political inclusion (cf. Carugati 2019b).[13]

The evidence suggest that the tradeoff worked. After the Social War, and increasingly after the defeat in the Battle of Chaeronea at the hands of Philip of Macedon (in the year 338), Athens' prosperity soared. Measured in talents per year, Athenian growth in the 320s did not significantly lag compared to the growth-rate of the imperial period.[14] Even if the evidence does not allow us to assess directly the impact of these changes on individual or group welfare, the fact that slaves were among the recipients of some of these forms of institutional access, and the fact that Athens in the fourth century was a democracy with low levels of inequality, suggest that at least part of the polis' prosperity was broadly shared across the population and did not end up solely in the pockets of the elite.

Before I continue, two caveats are in order. First, the model I presented in the previous chapter focuses on law- and policy-making in the courts. If it is beyond doubt that not every piece of fourth-century legislation passed through the courts, still a good deal did. In particular, a number of important fiscal reforms that I discuss in this chapter were introduced through the procedure of nomothesia—for example, the laws of Periandros and Demosthenes (in the years 358/357 and 340, respectively). Moreover, some controversial proposals concerning matters of fiscal and economic policy were indicted as illegal through the graphē paranomōn and the graphē nomon mē epitēdeion theinai, as it happened to both Leptines' (Dem. 20) and Demosthenes' (Dem. 18.102–3) proposals. Some of these reforms were clearly the product of Athens' most brilliant politicians. However, it is possible that some sub-elite entrepreneurs were responsible for reforms whose authors have fallen out of the historical record—for example, the proposer of the reform that established the dikai emporikai.

---

who are too young to be on the register, or to old men who have been relieved from state duties."

13. By the same token, as I show later in the context of the dikai emporikai, this approach was extremely costly for the Athenian state, who had to carefully police the boundaries of inclusion.

14. Burke (1984; 2010; cf. Plut. *Mor.* 842F): 1,200 T/yr under Lycurgus, compared to 1,000 T/yr under the fifth-century empire (Xen. *Anab.* 7.1.27). In Ober's (2015a: 245; 215b: 499) estimates, state income under the empire (1,300 T in 435, and 1,600 T in 425) compares well with state income under Lycurgus (1,350 in the 330s).

Second, my analysis of Athenian fiscal and economic policy does not aim at fully accounting for Athens' post-imperial growth. Athens was not the only Greek polis that experienced economic growth, and exogenous factors not part of this analysis played a conspicuous role in the development of Hellas as a whole (Ober 2015a). Instead, my analysis provides an explanation for Athens' growth that focuses primarily on institutional change, and that considers the issue of political stability as a critical component of any explanation of Athenian growth.

For clarity, I divide my analysis in this chapter in three phases. First, I analyze Athenian policy in the period between the end of the civil war in 403 and the Social War in 357–355. I then focus on the period between the Social War and the Battle of Chaeronea in the year 338. Finally, I turn to the period between Chaeronea and Athens' defeat at the hands of the Macedonians in the Lamian War of the year 322.

4.1. After the Civil War

When the civil war drew to a close, Athens' coffers were empty and the polis had long run out of reserve funds. Yet, conspicuous disbursements loomed large. First, in order to defend herself, Athens had to rebuild its walls and ships, in addition to Piraeus' shipsheds, destroyed by the Thirty Tyrants (Isoc. 7.66; Garland 1987: 96; cf. chapter 5). Second, the Athenians had to repay the debt that the Thirty had incurred with Sparta ([Arist]. *Ath.Pol.* 40.3). It is therefore surprising to learn that, soon after the restoration of democracy, the Athenians introduced pay for the Assembly. Set at three obols per participant, this reform added approximately twenty talents per year to Athens' expenditures.[15] Based on Pritchard's (2015) estimates, the introduction of pay for the Assembly added approximately 25% to the total cost of democracy (estimated at ninety-eight talents in the 370s). The pressure of these disbursements on the polis' already fragile financial situation must have been heavy. Where did the money come from?

In this section, I reconstruct the evolution of the system of taxation in the first half of the fourth century. I then place that reconstruction within Athens' broader foreign and economic policy goals. The evidence suggests that fiscal reforms sought to incentivize tax compliance by enabling the elite to share fiscal responsibilities, and do so with an eye to regulating the burden on those

---

15. Three obols, ca. six thousand participants, meeting forty times a year. Later in the fourth century, pay for the Assembly increased to one dr., and one dr. and three obols (i.e., 1 ½ dr.) for the *ekklēsia kyria* (lit. principal Assembly, which took place once every prytany, or ten times a year), bringing total costs to forty-five talents a year (Pritchard 2015: 60–63).

among the elites whose fortunes could not keep up with state demands. At the same time, Athens sought to extract rents from abroad, develop market incentives aimed at lowering transaction costs, and strengthen the credibility of the state's commitments to make the polis a more attractive trade center.

4.1.a. Fiscal Policy Reforms

The system of taxation in Athens required the elite—those with assets worth three to four talents or more (Davies 1971)—to contribute to the polis' fiscal needs. Obligations included regular outlays—such as financing festivals (*chorēgia*) and equipping warships (*triērarchia*)—and extraordinary expenditures—namely, the military head-tax (*eisphora*).

In the first half of the fourth century, the fiscal burden on the elite was quite heavy. Between the years 403 and 378, in addition to the regular liturgies, the Athenians levied between seven and nine military head-taxes (*eisphorai*) to repay the loan from Sparta and later to finance the war with Thebes (Brun 1983: 26–28; Frazer 2009: 272). Between the years 378/377 and 356/355, they levied additional military head-taxes for a total sum of 300 T (an average of 13.6 T/yr: Dem. 22. 44; Gabrielsen 2013: 342).

In the same period, however, the Athenians were also busy in the domain of fiscal policy reforms.[16] Between the years 403 and 378/377, we have evidence for three major innovations. First, a law that regulated the allocation of resources to various boards of magistrates (the *merismos*, Rhodes 1972b; Faraguna 1992). Second, an "obligation for each free man (metics as well as citizens) to register a self-assessment (*timēma*) of his property" (Davies 2004: 506). Third, the introduction of a new system to finance the military head-tax whereby one hundred groups of wealthy citizens shared the obligation to pay the tax (groups were known as *symmoriai* and were each composed of twelve to fifteen members).[17]

16. As discussed in chapter 2, fiscal reforms had already begun in the era of the constitutional debate. In response to the oligarchic governments' abolition of state pay, the first restored democracy reinstated pay for office, introduced the *diobelia*, and levied two *eisphorai*, probably in an attempt to repay the debt to Athena (cf. Blamire 2001: 117–18). At the same time, the fiscal burden on the elites was regulated by the introduction, in 406/405, of the *syntriērarchia* and *synchorēgia* (Gabrielsen 1994; Wilson 2000: 265, suggesting that the *synchorēgia* was no longer used after the year 406/405). These measures allowed the wealthy to join forces in order to discharge onerous liturgies in the dramatic period between the Battles of Arginusae and Aegospotami.

17. In the same year or shortly afterwards, the Athenians also introduced the *proeisphora*, a system whereby the three wealthiest members of each group would advance the sum to the state and then collect the dues from other members (Christ 2007: 55).

The *symmoriai* system for the military head-tax introduced in Athens the principle of progressive taxation. Each group of one hundred wealthy citizens was responsible for one hundredth of the total sum requested by the Assembly. But, as Christ (2007: 63–64) argues, "within each group, individuals paid shares of the group's liability in proportion to their level of wealth, as determined on the basis of their current declarations of their assets (*timēmata*)." The *symmoriai* system and the self-assessment thus enabled the state, which did not know and had no means to estimate individuals' wealth, to tax the elite by creating incentives for the members of each group to scrutinize and police one another.

In the year immediately before the Social War (in 358/357), the practice of enabling the elite to pool resources when discharging burdensome taxes was extended to the trierarchy (the obligation to finance a warship for a year). Through Periandros' law, the number of individuals liable to pay the tax was formally set at 1,200. The 1,200 were divided in twenty groups of sixty members each. The naval records suggest that the reform enabled the Athenians to overcome difficulties in equipping warships (Gabrielsen 1994: 193). Interestingly, the principle of progressive taxation was not immediately extended to the trierarchy. In fact, until Demosthenes' reform in the year 340 (on which more later), each group member paid the same amount.

4.1.b. Athenian Foreign Policy: Rent Extraction or Market Incentives?

According to Pritchard (2015), war, democracy, and festivals cost Athens approximately 720 T/yr in the 370s (cf. 665 T/yr for Ober 2015a). As burdensome as Athens' taxes were for those who discharged them, the proceeds were likely insufficient to cover the polis' needs in the post-war period.

In the early fourth century, additional financial help came, perhaps most unexpectedly, from Persia. The Persians had perfected the tactic initially recommended by the Athenian rogue-general Alcibiades during the final phase of the Peloponnesian War. Intent on getting recalled from exile, Alcibiades had promised to the Athenians the financial support of Persia. To persuade the Persian satrap Tissaphernes to switch his allegiance from Sparta to Athens, Alcibiades suggested that if Tissaphernes were to support a number of Greeks poleis simultaneously, he could weaken them by playing them against one another (Thuc. 8.46.1–2). During the Peloponnesian War, Tissaphernes did not heed Alcibiades' advice, and Persian support of Sparta contributed not in small part to Sparta's victory. But now that Sparta was at the helm of Greece, the Persians turned to financing Athens, Thebes, and Corinth against Sparta. The influx of Persian money into Greece that sparked the Corinthian War (from 395 to 386) allowed Athens to rebuild the Long Walls and the fleet, and to regain control of the grain-rich islands of Lemnos, Imbros, and Scyros (Strauss 1987a).

In addition to the money from Persia, the Athenians also sought to increase the fiscal pressure on other Greek cities. In the 390s, Thrasybulus conducted a series of campaigns in the North Aegean, imposing a tax on the Hellespont (*dekatē*) and taxes on other cities (Xen. *Hell.* 4.8.26–30; Burke 2010). In the early 370s, Athens established the naval league known as the Second Athenian Confederacy. Created as a defensive alliance against Spartan hegemony to ensure the integrity of member poleis' autonomy and territory, the confederacy showed an eerie similarity with the early Delian League—the anti-Persian alliance that later morphed into the fifth-century Athenian empire (cf. chapter 1). Instead of the tribute (*phoros*), the allies now paid contributions (*syntaxeis*), and decisions were made by an assembly (*synedrion*) in which Athens had conspicuous but not sole power. However, as Athens' aggressiveness toward the allies increased in the 360s, the most powerful among them showed that they had learned the lesson from the fifth century. Chios, Cos, and Rhodes (and perhaps Byzantium) revolted in the year 357. After the conflict, known as the Social War, the confederacy was no more.

Scholars have long debated whether Athens' foreign policy in the first half of the fourth century was aimed at rebuilding the empire (Cargill 1981; Harding 1995; contra Cawkwell 1981; Badian 1995). Cutting across the debates' opposing arguments, Edmund Burke (2010: 406–8) suggested that imperial (or imperial-like) aspirations were not an end in itself, but a means to an end: economic recovery. In particular, for Burke, Thrasybulus' campaigns and the Second Athenian Confederacy reflected Athenian concerns with protecting Aegean trade routes and boosting the role of Piraeus as the ultimate destination of trade.

Epigraphic documents dated to the mid-370s indicate that the Athenians promoted both rent extraction and market incentives in this period. The grain-tax law makes clear that, as late as 374/373, the Athenians still considered rent extraction a perfectly viable tool to secure critical revenues (or, more directly, the items to be obtained through such revenues).[18] The law imposed a tax (*dodēkatē*) on grain grown on Lemnos, Imbros, and Scyros, and another tax (*pentēkostē*) to be collected also in grain from "ships entering the Piraeus" or for "grain sold in a special grain market" (Frazer 2009: 285). The taxes, previously collected in cash, sought to ensure that "there may be grain for the people (demos) in the public domain" (Agora I 7557; Stroud 1998).

---

18. On whether the *syntaxeis* from the confederacy belong to the same category: Cawkwell (1973;) Hornblower (1983); contra Cargill (1981).

The Athenians also sought to incentivize trade. In the year 375/374, the law on silver coinage introduced the figure of the coin-tester (*dokimastēs*) in the Athenian marketplace. As Ober (2008: 222) argued, the law "sought to facilitate market exchanges by using government institutions to lower transaction costs." It did so by providing two expert public slaves (one in the Agora and one in Piraeus) to evaluate the coins used in the markets and by establishing criteria for "good" and "bad" coins. The former included state-issued original "owls," as well as "foreign silver coins that possess . . . two bona fides characteristics . . . : the public stamp and . . . the right silver content." Original owls were accepted, and good fakes were returned to owners at no cost. All the other bad coins were confiscated.

The coexistence of these two strategies emerges perhaps most clearly in the decree regulating the trade of Cean ruddle (Rhodes and Osborne 2003: 204–9). In the mid-fourth century (the decree cannot be dated more precisely, but it must belong to the period before the Social War), Athens established a monopoly in the ruddle trade with three cities on the island of Ceos (Carthaea, Coresia, and Iulis), an ally of Athens in the Second Athenian Confederacy. As Rhodes and Osborne (2003: 207) suggest, the document reveals that "the major Athenian concerns were: that particular vessels be identified as the only ones in which ruddle is to be exported; that prosecution of offenders be encouraged by the offering of rewards to prosecutors [including, most notably, freedom for slaves]; and that agreement be secured to accept future Athenian decisions related to the security of the ruddle trade." The puzzling aspect of the decree is that it appears thoroughly unclear how "the agreement to export ruddle only to Athens and in specified vessels could be presented as in the Cean interest, except as a way of avoiding even more direct interference" (ibid. 208) The decree thus confirms the persistence of a logic of imperial-like rent extraction in Athenian foreign policy in the first half of the fourth century. However, compared with the fifth century, the focus of Athens' hegemonic concerns may have shifted from securing monetary contributions (i.e., the tribute), to regulating and controlling access to markets in the Aegean.

The fact that rent extraction and market incentives coexisted in early fourth-century Athenian policy may mean that Athens consciously chose to pursue both strategies, or that the preferred strategy—rebuilding the empire—simply turned out not to be an option. In the absence of a proper imperial structure, the exploitation of others—such as Athens' dependencies of Lemnos, Imbros, and Scyros—likely returned dividends that were insufficient to cover Athens' needs. But if rent extraction was limited, market incentives alone insufficient, and elite taxation constrained to preserve the social order, it was imperative to find new solutions to increase revenues. The evidence suggests that soon after the civil war, the Athenians turned toward their noncitizens and began to honor them for actions performed in the interests of the state.

4.1.c. Credible Commitment: The Issue of Noncitizens

The last five years of the fifth century changed Athens' position vis-à-vis the rest of the Greek world dramatically. The loss in the Peloponnesian War meant a new, much weakened geopolitical role. The Thirty Tyrants inflicted another blow to Athens' reputation by harassing the people of Piraeus—e.g., the metics that suffered expropriations and persecutions during the tyrants' bloody reign (Xen. *Hell.* 2.3.21). As the city sought to lay the foundations for economic recovery, the Athenians had to regain a whole lot of people's trust.

The reestablished democracy moved fast to signal to noncitizens that a) there was a new, legitimate government in town; b) support for such a government earned praise and privileges; and c) the new government could credibly commit to enforcing the privileges it bestowed on its friends, at home and abroad. These signals emerge most clearly in the publication and prominent display in the Agora and on the Acropolis of a series of documents. These included inscriptions honoring the loyal Samians and the men who fought for the democracy against the tyrants, as well as a series of proxeny decrees,[19] which were reinscribed after being destroyed by the Thirty.[20] A parallel development was the trend, documented by Darel Tai Engen (2010), to increasingly bestow honors on noncitizens not solely for military or political purposes (as it had been the practice in the fifth century), but also for trade-related services. In what follows, I discuss the inscribed documents and then turn to Engen's findings.

---

19. *Proxenia* expressed a formal relationship of friendship between a polis and a noncitizen honorand (*proxenos*). According to Mack (2015: 1–3), "this relationship was based on the gratitude of the polis for the intermediary services the *proxenos* performed for its citizens within its own political community, services which facilitated their access to local civic institutions and networks there." Greek *proxenia* was a hallowed social institution that "reflected and facilitated the full range of . . . inter-polis interaction, public and private, from diplomatic negotiations to economic transactions and inter-city pilgrimage." On the proxeny decrees destroyed by the Thirty: cf. chapter 5.

20. Other documents include the revised laws of the polis; the accounts of the sale of the property of the Thirty; honors for Euagoras of Cypriot Salamis and the Athenian general Conon; and Theozotides' decree honoring the orphans of those Athenians who died in battle: Shear (2011: ch. 8).

4.1.C.I. THE LOYAL SAMIANS

Samos had served as Athens' primary naval base in the Aegean from the year 412 until Athens' defeat in the Peloponnesian War. Supporting Athens earned the Samians the ire of the Spartan commander Lysander who, after the war, established a government of ten men there, before returning to Sparta (Xen. *Hell.* 2.3.6–7). For their enduring support, the Athenians honored the Samians with citizenship (Rhodes and Osborne 2003: 12–17).[21] The decree was originally passed in the year 405/404, but it was subsequently destroyed by the Thirty. In the year 403/402, the new democracy reinscribed the decree and prominently displayed it on the Acropolis (Shear 2011: 231). The democracy's effort to reinscribe honorary decrees that the Thirty's isolationist government had destroyed indicates an attempt to mark a break with the recent oligarchic past and to restore alliances with the city's friends and benefactors.

4.1.C.II. THE PROXENY DECREES

Target of the same fury, a series of proxeny decrees were also destroyed by the Thirty.[22] As Shear (2011: 176) suggests, proxeny decrees "attest to a relationship both between the city and the honorands and between Athens and the honorands' cities. Removing the *stēlai* [stones] visibly breaks these bonds which the documents had created and signals that no such relationship exists between the honorands and their cities and the Thirty and oligarchic Athens." In restoring and prominently displaying the inscribed stones in public places, then, the new democracy signaled to her *proxenoi* Athens' renewed commitment to honoring privileges and immunities that the demos had previously granted.[23]

---

21. For the Samians, as for other benefactors that received citizenship for actions performed in the interest of the Athenians, this privilege was purely honorific. The Samians would not exercise the political rights associated with Athenian citizenship and therefore did not cause significant shifts in the median.

22. Fragments of at least six decrees reinscribed between 399/398 and 386/385 are extant. For a full analysis: Shear (2011: 231; 235–36; 246–47).

23. Notably, the trend continued in the period after the Social War, when a man named Leptines carried a proposal to revoke immunities from public service granted by the demos in the past and to make them illegal in the future (Dem. 20). The proposal was successfully challenged through the procedure of graphē nomon mē epitēdeion theinai on the grounds that it contradicted an existing law ("all rewards granted by the people shall be valid," Dem. 20.96; trans. Vince 1926) and on the grounds that reneging on privileges previously granted was detrimental to Athens' reputation, at home and abroad (Dem. 20.120, 124, passim). Indeed, reneging on one's promises was the mark of a tyrant or an oligarch (Dem. 20.15–17). This case must

4.1.C.III. THE MEN FROM PHYLE

Like the decree for the loyal Samians, the proxeny decrees honored foreign benefactors. But in the aftermath of the civil war, the Athenians also bestowed privileges on noncitizen residents who fought for democracy against the tyrants. The
debates that took place in Athens over how to properly recognize these men's
service are preserved in the literary sources ([Arist.] *Ath.Pol.* 40.2; Aesch. 3.187–
90) and emerge in a highly fragmentary state from the epigraphic record.
Scholars are extremely divided on the interpretation of critical elements of two
important honorary decrees, including the identity of the recipients and the
types of honors bestowed on them.[24] But for the purposes of my reconstruction one point is clear: whether they were metics, slaves, or more generally foreigners, and whether they received citizenship, freedom from slavery, or the
right to own land, the decrees show that noncitizens who fought for the democracy against the tyrants received significant privileges.

4.1.C.IV. HONORS FOR TRADE-RELATED SERVICES

The beneficiaries of honors and privileges discussed above were noncitizen
populations and individuals that had either helped Athens militarily or were
part of an established interstate civic network (*proxenia*). In the fourth century,
Athens continued to honor those who helped the city in war, and *proxenia* remained a bastion of Greek interstate relations long after the classical period.
But in the course of the fourth century, the list of people that Athens deemed
worthy of honor expanded to include new actors.[25]

   According to Engen (2010), beginning in the last decade of the fifth century,
and increasingly in the fourth century, the Athenians began to bestow honors
on noncitizens for actions that were neither military nor civic/political in nature. Despite the partial nature of the sources, Engen's study of thirty-four
inscriptions persuasively argues for a shift in attitudes in the course of the
fourth century, when the Athenians began to praise noncitizens for what he
terms "trade-related services." Engen (2010: 78–100) distinguishes five categories of trade-related services: "gifts of imported goods (or the money to buy
those goods) free of charge;" "shipments of goods;" "sale of imported goods at

---

have signaled to noncitizens who had received privileges in exchange for their contribution to
the Athenian economy that those privileges would not be revoked.

   24. SEG 28 45: Meritt (1933); Raubitschek (1941); Krentz (1982); M. C. Taylor (2002). IG
II2 10: Wilhelm (1922); Krentz (1980; 1986); M. J. Osborne (1981); Whitehead (1984); Harding
(1987). I discuss the debates surrounding these inscriptions in Carugati (2015).

   25. A similar development is the practice of supplication to the Assembly, which seems to
have conferred honors on noncitizens (Gottesman 2014).

reduced prices;" "import of goods;" and "miscellaneous trade-related services." Honorands included men of various ethnicities (i.e., both Greeks and
non-Greeks), legal statuses (both metics and foreigners), and socioeconomic
condition (including common, moderately wealthy, and wealthy professional
traders, in addition to foreign potentates). Forms of praise included honors—
defined as "items whose value as symbols of honor... outweigh" their functional
value (2010: 140 and ch. 7)—and privileges—defined as items that "entailed
functional benefits far in excess of honor" (2010: 182 and ch. 8).

Based on this taxonomy, Engen argues that, in the fourth century, the Athenians bestowed honors on foreigners to incentivize them to trade in, or bring
gifts (of foodstuff, especially grain) to, Athens. Such a shift was brought about
by Athens' need to secure the grain (and timber) supply and encourage trade
after the collapse of the empire. But in the course of the fourth century there
was also an evolution in the types of actions and individuals that the Athenians
honored. For Engen (2010: 220), "the general trend appears to be that with
each shock that threatened the city's revenues and food supply—in particular,
its defeats in Sicily, in the Social War and at [Chaeronea]—Athens expanded
the range of trade-related services and statuses of men that it would deem
worthy of honor." In other words, whereas in the last decade of the fifth century it was mostly foreign potentates that received honors for "gifts of imported
goods free of charge," by the end of the fourth century the Athenians honored
"a motley crew of men of varying ethnicities and legal and socioeconomic statuses" (Engen 2010: 104) for much less conspicuous trade-related services.

———

In the aftermath of the civil war, the Athenians passed a series of fiscal reforms
aimed at regulating the fiscal burden on the elite. To increase revenue, the polis
employed a mix of rent extraction—such as taxing other poleis—and market
incentives—e.g., lowering transaction costs in the market and bestowing honors and privileges on traders. The paucity of the evidence makes it extremely
hard to quantify the impact of such measures on Athenian public finances. Unlike for later periods, we lack any information that would enable us to assess
levels of economic growth, much less the pace of Athens' recovery. The first
figures we find in the sources date to the period after the Social War and they
do not paint an optimistic picture.

4.2. After the Social War (357–355)

There was a time not long ago when the revenue of your state did not exceed a
hundred and thirty talents.

—[DEM.] 10.37; TRANS. VINCE 1926

> Nay, we shall see our city enjoying twice the revenues which she now receives, and thronged with merchants and foreigners and resident aliens, by whom she is now deserted.
>
> —ISOC. 8.21; TRANS. NORLIN 1980

After the defeat in the Social War, both the polis' stability and its finances came under intense pressure. Institutional reforms were prominent on the agenda. First, the powers of the Council of the Areopagus were extended: the Council came to supervise sanctuaries, act as a court of first instance for a newly introduced criminal procedure (*apophasis*), and intervene in elections (Hansen 1999: 291).[26] Second, the *apophasis* was introduced to prosecute people charged with treason, attempts to overthrow the democracy, and corruption. Third, the Athenians introduced a comprehensive annual review of legislation to be performed on the eleventh day of each first prytany (Dem. 24. 20–23; Canevaro 2013b; contra Hansen 2016). These reforms suggest that concerns with the stability of the constitution, and with the integrity of the law code on which the constitution rested, were of paramount importance in this period.

The city's finances were another area of concern. From [Demosthenes] (quoted in the epigraph) we learn that, after the Social War, Athenian public revenues did not exceed 130 T. In response, the Athenians implemented a series of reforms aimed at curtailing unnecessary expenditures. Domestically, Athens passed reforms that limited expenditures associated with running the democracy, including a reduction in the number of Assembly meetings and the transfer of some trials from the Assembly to the popular courts (e.g., *eisangeliai*).[27] In the sphere of foreign policy, the city sought to reduce military expenditures (Burke 1984: 113).[28] Symbolic of this new course of action was the introduction or the reform of the Theoric fund, whereby surplus money previously

26. The reforms followed a trend that had begun with the restoration of democracy in 403, when the Areopagus acquired the power to supervise the administration of the laws by the magistrates (Hansen 1999: 290; cf. ch. 2)

27. Hansen (1999: 159) calculates that "it cost a whole talent . . . to try an *eisangelia* in the Assembly [where the participant numbered in the thousands], whereas it cost only 250 drachmas . . . for a jury panel of 501."

28. The evidence however suggests that Athenian spending on the military increased from 130 T in the aftermath of the Social War to 200 T in the 340s and to 400 T in the 330s (Ober 2015a: 245; 2015b: 499). Under Eubulus (ca. 355–342), the Athenians built new dockyards (Din. 1.96), and expanded the fleet (Dem. 14.13; IG II2 1613, line 302; cf. Amit 1965: 26). Scholars debate whether these projects indicate a new phase of Athenian militarism, or if they instead benefited trade by expanding the polis' capacity to fight piracy in the Aegean (Burke 1984: 115–16; 2010: 413; Gabrielsen 2013).

directed toward financing military campaigns was now earmarked to finance social goods like festivals, public buildings, and roads (Hansen 1999: 98, 263–64; Rhodes 1981).[29]

With an account as low as 130 T, however, the question was not so much how to save money, but how to generate new streams of revenue. The evidence for this period suggests a new round of fiscal policy reforms. These included the reminting program of the year 353, the introduction in the year 347/346 of an annual military head-tax of ten talents, and Demosthenes' reform of the trierarchy in the year 340. In addition to these measures, the Athenians turned to their endowments—most notably, the Laurion silver mines and the harbor of Piraeus—and began to intensify their exploitation. To do so required extending critical forms of institutional access to key categories of noncitizens.

4.2.a. Fiscal Policy between the Social War and Chaeronea

As they had done after the civil war, so after the Social War, the Athenians sought to regulate elite disbursements. Beginning in the year 347/346 (and until the Macedonian conquest), the state transformed the once-ad-hoc, burdensome emergency war-tax (which in the year 428 extracted from the elite 200 T all at once) into an annual contribution of ten talents (Gabrielsen 2013: 334).[30] As it had been since the reforms of the year 378/377, those who paid the military head-tax continued to be divided into one hundred groups and within each group, members paid in proportion to their wealth. But now the principle of progressive taxation was extended to the trierarchy. As I mentioned earlier, Periandros' law of the year 358/357 had distributed the task of financing Athens' warships among twenty groups of elites, each made up of sixty members. From the year 358/357 to 340, the burden of taxation under Periandros' system was shared equally among individuals (Gabrielsen 1994). But in the year 340, Demosthenes proposed a modification of Periandros' law according to which the financial burden was now to become proportional to an individual's economic standing. As a result, "the wealthiest citizens among the Twelve Hundred—those commonly referred to as the Three Hundred—were made to pay more that their less wealthy colleagues" (Gabrielsen 1994: 225). The reform seems to have been successful. In Demosthenes' own words (18.107–8; trans. Vince 1926),[31]

29. Like the introduction of pay for the Assembly in the early fourth century, the reform of the Theoric fund overwhelmingly benefited the masses, although not necessarily to the detriment of the elite.

30. The Assembly could still impose additional wartime levies (Christ 2007: 53; Brun 1983: 54–55).

31. Epigraphic evidence confirms Demosthenes' claims: Gabrielsen (1994: 210).

during the whole war, while the squadrons were organized under my regulations, no trierarch made petition as aggrieved, or appeared as a suppliant in the dockyard temple, or was imprisoned by the Admiralty, and no ship was either abandoned at sea and lost to the state, or left in harbor as unseaworthy. Such incidents were frequent under the old regulations, because the public services fell upon poor men, and impossible demands were often made. I transferred the naval obligations from needy to well-to-do people, and so the duty was always discharged.

In this period, new forms of taxation were also devised. In 353, the Athenian state recalled all the tetradrachms (four-drachmas coins) in circulation in order to mint what numismatists refer to as the "PI-style tetradrachms." The new coins were not pretty. As Kroll puts it (2011: 232), "apart from their unremitting monotony, certainly the most conspicuous characteristic of the pi tetradrachms is their hasty, slapdash minting on irregularly shaped flans." Yet, the ugly coins served their purpose. For Kroll (2011: 237), the reminting program yielded between 3% and 5% "of all wealth held in larger denomination cash in Attica." Moreover, "since the program taxed the rich and people of ordinary means progressively, each person in proportion to his assets in cash, one can understand why the program would have been politically attractive to democratic lawmakers" (2011: 249).[32] Finally, the tax fell on citizens and noncitizens alike, whoever happened to have tetradrachms in their pockets.

How should we evaluate the reminting program? The program seems to fall squarely within the category of ad hoc, temporary, cunning-verging-on-fraudulent measures that, according to Paul Millett, Greek states devised to raise money in an emergency, particularly in the aftermath of war.[33] Offering a more nuanced interpretation, Kroll (2011: 249) suggests that the reminting program was indeed "an exceptional scheme, belonging to an exceptional

32. Even more so if, as Kroll argues, the reminting focused particularly on tetradrachms—that is, larger denominations that were more likely to be owned in larger quantities by wealthier people. Kroll's discussion of smaller denominations: (2011: 246–48).

33. For Paul Millett (1991), Greek fiscal policy in the fourth century evolved through an ad hoc, haphazard process of reforms whose lack of direction was due to the absence of a flexible system of taxation and reliable sources of revenue. Millett found support for his analysis in book 2 of [Aristotle]'s *Oeconomica*, where the author relates a series of anecdotes about how Greek rulers deployed a mix of cunning and deception to raise revenues. Pyzyk (forthcoming) offers a compelling argument to rehabilitate *Oeconomica* book 2 as a product of Greek intellectual attitudes to public economics. In particular, Pyzyk interprets the episodes focused on the cunnings of tyrants (especially Dionysius) not as recommendations, but as cautionary tales, and views the later anecdotes as instantiations of Greek expertise being transferred to Near East kingdoms.

historical moment when Athens was struggling to make ends meet." But instead of being the product of fraudulent emergency circumstances, for Kroll the program fits more broadly within a time-period "when a kind of political leadership was coming to the fore that placed a premium on creative economic and fiscal thinking." Embodied most famously by the figures of Eubulus and Lycurgus, creative thinking in fiscal and economic policy was especially prominent in the years after the Social War. Such thinking focused on extracting elite contributions, as well as on boosting indirect taxation accruing to the state through the exploitation of Athens' major resources—the Laurion mines and the harbor of Piraeus.

4.2.b. The Laurion Silver Mines

In the Laurion area, in the southeast region of Attica, the abundant mineral resources below the ground belonged to the state, the land above to private citizens. The state rented out mining rights to private individuals who would then assume all costs and risks related to the extraction (and processing) of raw materials.[34] In addition to the leasing costs, according to van Alfen (2011: 16), "various fixed and recurring fees appear to have been associated with the leases including state taxes and rents paid to land owners; it is also possible that the state took some additional proportion of the silver produced by the leases, although there is no evidence for this practice or the amount." In the fifth century, lessees were predominantly citizens, and mine workers overwhelmingly slaves.

In the last decade of the fifth century (from 412 to 403), the mines were shut down due to the Spartan occupation of military strongholds in the Attic countryside. We do not know precisely when mining resumed. The debate hinges on the interpretation of a passage in Xenophon's *Poroi* (4.28),

> Then why, it may be asked, are fewer new cuttings made (*kainotomousin*) nowadays than formerly? Simply because those interested in the mines are poorer. For operations have only lately (*neosti*) been resumed.

Van Alfen (2000: 21) interprets the passage to mean that the first half of the fourth century was a "period of near inactivity of the mines." In contrast, for Kroll (2011: 241), at the time of Xenophon's writing, it was new cuttings that had been made (*kainotonousin*) only lately (*neosti*), not *mining altogether*.

---

34. At the height of their productivity in the fifth century, the mines yielded between 700 and 1,000 T a year to investors (van Alfen 2011: 17; cf. Conophagos 1980; Flament 2007).

Regardless of which side of the debate we choose, in the second half of the fourth century the Athenians were discussing new strategies to exploit the mines.[35] Xenophon's modest proposal revolved around a simple idea: more workers in the mines equal more profits. Hence, he suggested (4.11),

> we need not hesitate to bring as much labour as we can get into the mines and carry on work in them, feeling confident that the ore will never give out and that silver will never lose its value.

There are two problems with Xenophon's suggestion. First, increasing mining productivity was not just a matter of increasing labor inputs. Xenophon seems to suggest that, despite the fact that the mines have been exploited for many generations, most of the silver is still in the ground (4.2–3). But, as the evidence of the *Poletai* leases testifies, extracting it was far from an easy or risk-free enterprise (Crosby 1950; 1957; Langdon 1991).[36] The existence of filled-up and abandoned mines (*palaia anasaxima*) indicates that mining was not just a matter of digging a hole in the ground. As Hopper (1953: 202) maintains, "the reasons for such surrender may be various: the chief would probably be a failure to make a *sufficient* profit in comparison with other forms of activity, or a failure to find sufficiently rich ore." Mining entailed conspicuous risks and a good dose of luck.

But there is another problem with Xenophon's proposal. The workers he had in mind—public slaves—came with costs attached, which Xenophon largely fails to spell out (perhaps because he assumed that his average reader would be familiar with them). Analyses of slavery suggest that large number of slaves (in Xenophon's own estimates, "three for every citizen," 4.17) entail high policing costs, particularly if the slaves are employed in what Stefano Fenoaltea (1984) has termed "effort-intensive activities" like mining.[37] Moreover, public

---

35. The trend may have begun earlier: van Liefferinge et al. (2014) discuss expansion of mining activity in the Thorikos area around 370, and document differences in water technology between Thorikos and the Sureza Valley.

36. The *Poletai* were a board of magistrates selected by lot whose task was to oversee leases of public and sacred land, as well as mine leases. They also auctioned the right to collect taxes and sold confiscated property (Hansen 1999: 401)

37. According to Fenoaltea, effort-intensive activities such as mine-working or cotton-picking involve high policing costs and a pain-system of incentives, whereas care-intensive activities such as vine and olive arboriculture (or the higher-order numeracy and literacy positions in the administration of Athenian law and finance) involve low policing costs and a reward-system of incentives. For an adaptation and application of Fenoaltea's model to the Greco-Roman world: Scheidel (2008).

slaves in the mines would have raised all sorts of liability issues. If state-owned slaves were hired out to private mine lessees, who bore the policing costs? The state? The individuals? Or both? Xenophon is silent on this point and there are no direct comparisons from other areas of Athenian public life. Therefore, we are left to speculate. The common Athenian practice of appointing a superintendent of public slaves (*epistatēs tōn dēmosiōn*) to oversee activities may suggest that the state could have rented out slaves and superintendents as a package.[38] But this would have raised the problem of how to structure the personal relationship of a public slave to a private master. More likely, the *epistatēs* was the private master's trustworthy fellow, in which case it remains unclear how the complex process of defining liabilities would have worked.[39] Finally, the average lifespan of a mineworker, at Laurion as elsewhere, tended to be exceptionally short, probably as short as one year, which would have made purchasing public slaves a short-term investment requiring frequent additional influxes of capital.[40] Once these costs are factored in, one is left wondering if the ratio of benefits to costs would still have been positive.

These limitations notwithstanding, Xenophon's proposal for a fuller exploitation of the silver mines makes for an excellent counterfactual. In the fourth century, the Athenian state faced two options in terms of labor investments. First, a coercion option that required conspicuous sunk costs to secure a volume of unfree labor that would generate rents for the state. The second option was to invest in free labor to expand the volume of revenues generated through economic activity.[41] When it came to the exploitation of the mines, Xenophon recommended the former route. The polis, instead, chose a mix of the two.[42]

38. See IG II2 834 on the Eleusinian workers: Jacob (1928).

39. On the complexities of legal liabilities arising from marriages involving privately owned slaves in Gortyn (and other comparative cases): D. Lewis (2013). The Gortyn code suggests that the Athenians could have developed rules to deal with liabilities involving public slaves in the mines. But we have no evidence that they ever did.

40. Studying the mines of Laurion in Attica and Rio Tinto in Spain, Humphrey (2006: 108) suggests that the "life expectancy for miners was less than a year."

41. Xenophon's *Poroi* is all the more compelling because Xenophon himself lays out both strategies in his recommendations for the mines and the harbor of Piraeus.

42. The capital-intensive reforms that I discuss below existed alongside the coercion-intensive system of exploitation of slave workers. My emphasis is on the capital-intensive aspects because this is where meaningful institutional reforms occurred. The practice of using slave workers in the mines did not change between the fifth and the fourth centuries. If anything, the high levels of exploitation of Laurion in the fifth century suggest that more slaves were

In the fifth as in the fourth century, the exploitation of the Laurion mines relied on large numbers of slave miners, whose condition does not seem to have improved over time. Reforms concentrated instead on incentivizing free private individuals, citizens as well as non-citizens, to become involved in the exploitation of the mines by reducing the risks that firsthand exploitation entailed, and by keeping transaction costs to a minimum. These measures included the extension of leases to noncitizens (Xen. *Por.* 4.12); the option to pool resources by spreading risk over a number of lessees (ibid. 4.32); and the use of a flexible system regulating mine leases.[43] Hopper's analysis (1953: 203) reveals the following structure: "where expenditure is considerable and/or results uncertain . . . , there should prevail a small payment . . . and long lease. If a successful strike is made and the lease is renewed or taken over immediately by another . . . , the price may fairly be higher or at any rate subject to competitive bidding, and the period of guaranteed tenure shorter." The Athenian state thus sought to intervene in regulating mining enterprises. The solution was a compromise between private and public interests whereby the polis incentivized private individuals to take up the risks associated with mining, while sharing the profits (Burke 1984; 1992; Faraguna 1992; 2003; contra van Alfen 2011: 20, for whom the public interest was dominant).[44]

But the mines were not the only resource that Athens could count on.

4.2.c. The Harbor of Piraeus

As Isocrates observes in the passage quoted in the epigraph to this section, in the aftermath of the Social War, "merchants and foreigners and resident aliens" had deserted Athens and its markets. These people were a vital asset for Athens' harbor. Metics and foreigners were workers on the docks, rowers on the ships, and investors in maritime commerce. As an added bonus, metics and foreigners paid a good deal of taxes to do their business in Athens—most notably the metic tax, the tax on foreigners trading in the Agora (Dem. 57.34) or entering Piraeus ([Xen.] *Ath.Pol.*1.17), and the tax on goods sold in the Agora (Pollux. *Onom.* 7.17, with Burke 1984: 114). Unlike more public slaves in the mines, more

---

exploited in the fifth century compared to the fourth century. I return to the coexistence of capital- and coercion-intensive paths to growth in fourth-century Athenian economic policy in the conclusion to this chapter.

43. On whether mine lessees were given exemption from liturgies: Hopper (1953); Burke (1984); Faraguna (1992, discussing the evidence of [Dem.] 42. 17–18).

44. In a recent contribution, Shipton (2016) analyzes mining leases from 367/366 and 342/339, showing that the number of wealthy investors declined between the two periods, but the number of total investors increased.

metics and foreigners in Piraeus could really boost state revenue—with little overhead.

The critical reform targeting these categories was passed sometime between the years 355 and 347, when Athens established new tribunals for the resolution of contractual disputes: the so-called dikai emporikai. The dikai emporikai were established to resolve "commercial maritime cases involving a written contract providing for trade to or from the port of Athens" (Cohen 1973: 99; Dem. 32.1).[45] The extension of access was not granted broadly to 'slaves' or 'metics.' Instead, regardless of their identity and social status, only those actors that had a claim as stated in the law could access the new tribunals. The costs of such a complex method to identify who could and who could not access the institution emerge clearly from the extant evidence: of the five extant court speeches in dikai emporikai, four are paragraphai—that is, counter-indictments where the defendant claims that the plaintiff does not have a written contract and cannot therefore access the court.[46]

The dikai emporikai differed from established Athenian practice in the popular courts in three critical respects (Cohen 1973).[47] First, they extended to noncitizens—including foreigners, metics, and perhaps even slaves— the privilege to defend oneself in court.[48] Second, the dikai emporikai entailed

45. Scholars have debated their specific purpose: Lanni (2006) and Isager and Hansen (1975) argue that the dikai emporikai established legal privileges aimed at attracting merchants to Piraeus and Athens. Their view superseded E. Cohen's (1973), who argued that the new tribunals were established to secure the grain supply.

46. The only genuine dike emporike is Dem. 56. Of the four paragraphai, two state that the dispute is not admissible as a dike emporike because there is no written contract (Dem. 32 and 33); while the other two look like delay tactics (Dem. 34 and 35).

47. The limited evidence at our disposal does not allow us to reach robust conclusions concerning some key features of the dikai emporikai. As to the identity of the jurors who heard the cases, Cohen argues that "specially chosen judges sat in the commercial courts . . . selected from those conversant with commercial matters" (1973: 93), but Lanni argues instead that these cases were heard by "ordinary jurors in the popular courts" (2006: 153). As to the relationship between the dikai emporikai and the larger Athenian legal system, Todd suggests that the dikai emporikai reveal a measure of structural informality in the legal system whose application is so limited that it cannot be generalized to other areas of Athenian law (Todd 1994). For Cohen, the dikai emporikai embody instead a mature transition from status to contract that emerges not only in the creation of these tribunals, but more generally from Athenian attitudes to economic transactions in the fourth century—attitudes that emerge most clearly in the banking realm (Cohen 1992; 1994). I discuss the debates surrounding the dikai emporikai more fully in Carugati (2015) and Carugati (2019b).

48. The issue of whether slaves were allowed to litigate is debated: Lampis (Dem. 34) was the only slave in an extant dikē emporike. He participated in the arbitration, but was not at the trial.

expedited procedures to resolve a dispute. We do not know how long it took for an average litigant to get his day in court. But we do know that there existed in Athens a category of cases, known as *dikai emmenoi* (i.e., monthly suits), that may have featured more expedited procedures.[49] The dikai emporikai fell within this category of monthly suits. Third, the dikai emporikai featured special measures for enforcing judgments, including post-trial detention and pre-trial bail. In Athens, enforcement was generally highly decentralized. Private individuals were responsible for executing court judgments, and the state played a very limited role in enforcing judicial decisions (Lanni, 2006, 2016). In the dikai emporikai the state played a somewhat greater role. But such role should not be overestimated. In fact, many steps in the process of enforcing judicial decisions still had to be carried out by private individuals.[50]

———

In the aftermath of the defeat in the Social War, another wave of fiscal policy reforms further regulated elite disbursements. No longer able to exploit foreign cities, the Athenians responded by promoting policies that incentivized individuals to exploit the Laurion silver mines and the harbor of Piraeus. How successful were these policies?

For Crosby (1950), during the peak years of exploitation of Laurion in the late 340s, the mines yielded 160 T/yr.[51] As to the dikai emporikai, we can only speculate. In theory, if more access incentivized more people to trade in Athens, then the Athenian state would benefit in two separate ways. First, more people increased the volume of trade, which meant an increase in indirect taxes on cargoes moving in and out of Piraeus. Second, more people increased the volume of direct taxes on trade. Precise numbers, however, are hard to come by. My estimates of the proceeds of the 2% tax (which I discuss in appendix B)

49. The meaning of *emmenoi* (monthly) is disputed: for Harrison (1955: 16) "monthly" means that adjudication must occur within thirty days. For E. Cohen (1973: 12–36), "monthly" means that complaints are accepted at monthly intervals.

50. As Cohen (1973: 77) suggests based on the evidence of Demosthenes (21.176), "if he [i.e., the plaintiff] were unable to lead his convicted opponent to jail immediately, he might attempt arrest at a later time. The state's role was only to give its sanction to the arrest and provide the prison."

51. Crosby's estimate has attracted remarkably few critics over time, and is cited in both Hopper (1953: 239) and Burke (1984: 113–14; 2010: 396). Crosby's number only takes into account leasing revenues, not minting fees. Ober provides some guesstimates, suggesting that minting fees added another 100 T in this period (Ober 2015a: 245; 2015b: 499). If Ober is right, then the contribution of the mines to annual state revenue rises to 260 T.

based on Amemiya's (2007) calculations of the volume of imports and exports suggest that revenues from that tax yielded 110 T/yr in the mid-fourth century. This a remarkable increase compared to forty to forty-six talents in the early fourth century, although we should keep in mind that the early fourth-century numbers reflect a period when Athenian trade was at an all-time low after the Peloponnesian War.

Demosthenes (10.38; cf. Ephorus *FGrHist.* 115F 166) suggests that Athenian state income in the 340s was 400 T/yr. If 160 T/yr came from the mines, then we must account for an increase of about 110 T from the post-Social War low of 130 T (Burke 1984). The fact that this assessment coincides with my estimate of the 2% tax should not be taken at face value. Given the margin of error, we are on safer ground simply concluding, with Burke (1984: 117), that is it probable that the bulk of the increase in state revenue derived from trade. Establishing a link between revenue from trade and the introduction of the dikai emporikai, however, remains a goal well beyond the evidence at our disposal.

4.3. After Chaeronea (338)

Athens' defeat in the Battle of Chaeronea against Philip of Macedon was another severe blow to the stability of the polis. In its aftermath, the Athenians were concerned with the possibility that the democracy could be overthrown. Reforms centered once again on the powers of the Areopagus, but the evidence reveals the profound ambivalence that the Athenians felt toward the Council in the delicate years after Chaeronea. On the one hand, the Areopagus acquired the power to judge citizens for any offense independently of the Assembly and the courts (Din. 1.62) and to execute defectors on its own authority (Lyc. 1.52; Aeschin. 3.252).[52] On the other hand, a new law against tyranny, dated to the year 336, that ensured immunity for tyrant-killers (Rhodes and Osborne 2003: 388–92; Teegarden 2014) explicitly limited the Council's powers in the event of a coup. The law reads: "it shall not be permitted to any of the councilors of the Council of the Areopagus, if the demos or the democracy at Athens is overthrown, to go up to the Areopagus or to sit together in the meeting or to deliberate about anything at all" (trans. Teegarden 2014: 87). It is significant that such specification was absent from a similar anti-tyranny measure

---

52. The fact that the Areopagus acquired these powers does not mean that the popular courts lost their ability to judge wrongdoers. Instead, prosecutors could choose whether to lay a complaint before the popular courts or before the Areopagus (Hansen 1999: 292).

that the Athenians passed in 410 when democracy was restored after the reigns of the Four Hundred and Five Thousand.[53]

But, once again, political stability and the balance of institutional power was not the only concern for the polis. In fact, Philip and the weather combined to threaten Athens' life line: the food supply (Faraguna 1992: 248). Already in the year 340, Philip had intercepted 230 grain ships bound to Athens, showing that he had both the power and the willingness to interfere in the polis' shipments. The threat was magnified in the 330s and 320s when Athens, like the rest of Greece and parts of the eastern Mediterranean, suffered protracted drought conditions.

It is therefore remarkable that, in this period, Athens experienced its most dynamic period of economic growth. According to Plutarch (*Mor.* 842F), under the statesmen Lycurgus (338–326), state revenues ballooned to 1,200 T/yr (cf. Faraguna 1992: 171). The new wealth was used, among other things, to finance a massive building program. As Faraguna suggests (2003: 123), "most of the building activity . . . was concentrated on the principal loci of communal participation. The Pnyx, where the Athenian Assembly met, was remodeled, the theater of Dionysius and the Panathenaic stadium were completed, and there was extensive building activity in the Agora and in some of the major sanctuaries both in the city and in the countryside." Like the introduction of pay for the Assembly and the reform of the Theoric fund, Lycurgus' building program overwhelmingly benefited the masses (who received both jobs and festival subsidies). However, as it had been for Pericles' building program in the fifth century, so this new phase of construction also signaled to the rest of Hellas that, even after Philip's blow, Athens was alive, rich, and powerful. Boosting Athens' reputation was not just for the benefit of the masses.

Compared to the preceding periods, evidence for reforms of the system of taxation are largely absent for the Lycurgan period. Under the rules established in the years 378/377 and 340, wealthy citizens continued to disburse the naval and military head-tax, each in proportion to their wealth. The amount for the military head-tax continued to be set at ten talents per year. So the bulk of

53. The decree of Demophantus, which prohibited all magistrates from exercising their functions during a coup: Teegarden 2012; 2014: 15–56; 88–89. I do not delve here into the debate concerning the reasons why the Athenians singled out the Areopagus. Teegarden's (2014: 99–105) interpretation of the Areopagus as a signaling institution is interesting, but somewhat overstretched. He argues that the Athenians looked to whether the Areopagus was meeting or not in order to decide whether the democracy was being overthrown. A more straightforward interpretation suggests that the Areopagus' increasing power was perceived as a potential threat to democracy (Wallace 1989).

Athens' prosperity in this period was not generated through an increase in the contribution of the elite by means of reforms of the tax code.

For Michele Faraguna (1992; 2003: 121), the high volume of revenues of the Lycurgan era was a function of "careful supervision over activity in the Laurion silver mines, large-scale sales of uncultivated or abandoned public land, the systematic leasing of sacred properties, the thorough inventorying of the riches and precious offerings stored in the temples." Moreover, Faraguna continues, "Lykurgos was successful in securing the financial support of a number of well-to-do Athenians and metics, who made substantial private donations to the state." Burke (1984; 2010: 395) agrees with Faraguna, adding that, above all, "Piraeus revenues were the key." In order to determine the relative contribution of these measures to state revenue, we must analyze each item in turn.

4.3.a. The Laurion Mines and Public and Sacred Lands

As argued earlier, the mines had been a conspicuous source of state revenue in the fifth century. After the Social War, the potential of the mines was once again fully exploited. The trend continued into the Lycurgan period, although it is unclear whether the mines' productivity slowed down after the year 330 (Faraguna 1992: 322; contra Burke 2010: 396). For the purposes of this account, I assume that the mines would have contributed the same amount throughout the Lycurgan period and assess this amount, with Crosby, at 160 T/yr.

The sale of public lands may have yielded between 200 and 300 T (D. Lewis 1973; Faraguna 1992: 325), but it was a one-time phenomenon or possibly occurred on two separate occasions (Faraguna 1992: 325; contra Lambert 1997: 213–19; cf. Burke 2010: 396).[54] Taking the higher number (300 T) and dividing it by the twelve years of the Lycurgan administration, the sale of public lands yielded an annual return of twenty-five talents per year. As to the leases of sacred property, Nikolaos Papazarkadas suggests that sacred rentals in the age of Lycurgus would have amounted to around eighteen talents per year (1.5% of annual state income, Papazarkadas 2011: 94).

---

54. Faraguna links the sale of public lands with the grain crisis, suggesting that even if these plots were marginal lands, the rise in the price of grain may have turned even marginal lands into relatively productive investments. Yet, the sale would have done little to ease Athens' grain shortages. In fact, the Athenians in this period were busy securing trade routes where the Macedonian presence was limited, particularly those connecting the polis with the West (on which more below).

4.3.b. The Contribution of the Elite

The Athenian elite's contribution was far from negligible. In addition to the regular military head-tax of ten talents per year, the elite performed the regular liturgies. Ober (2015a: 245; 2015b: 499) estimates festival costs at 150 T/yr for the 330s.[55] Estimating annual outlays connected with the navy requires a series of steps. There are two numbers for the costs of a trierarchy in the ancient sources: 5,142 dr. in Lysias (21.2) and 6,000 dr. in Demosthenes (21.155). Gabrielsen (1994: 216) suggests that "to be on the safe side . . . the average cost for an entire trierarchy" should be set at "6,000 to 7,000 drachmas." I take the middle-range number of 6,000 dr. (equal to one talent). The number of ships fluctuated greatly in the fourth century, from twelve in the immediate aftermath of the Peloponnesian War to 420 ships in the year 325 (Garland 1987: 97–98).[56] But Gabrielsen (1994: 216) assumes an annual number of sixty trierarchies. If correct, this assumption yields sixty talents per year.[57]

The contribution of the elite in this period was not limited to regular outlays. As Faraguna suggests, one of the hallmarks of the Lycurgan period was the reliance on private donations, which may have yielded up to 650 T.[58] Lycurgus' reach into the elite's pockets was deep. Private donors included citizens as well as metics, but in many cases, the phenomenon seems to have involved citizens serving as magistrates who carried out civic duties with private riches—and received honors in return (Faraguna 1992: 387–90; Fawcett 2016: 159). Together with the (meager) evidence for sumptuary legislation, these measures indicate an attempt, on the part of Lycurgus, to channel the elite's ostentatious display of wealth toward civic ends. The role of private munificence, therefore, should not be underestimated. Six hundred and fifty talents is a lofty sum, but if we

55. I use Ober's higher estimate here to account more fully for total state revenue. Pritchard (2015: 49) instead estimates total festival liturgy costs at one hundred talents per year.

56. Athens had about 100 ships in the 370s—a contingent that steadily grew until 325, when Athens is recorded to have 420 ships (cf. appendix B).

57. Gabrielsen's number is consistent with Pritchard's (2015: 109). But an average of sixty trierarchies a year seems like an absolute minimum. Pyzyk (working paper) suggests that the absolute ceiling for the average yearly contribution of a liturgist amounted to ca. 2,625 dr., yielding a total contribution of 525 T/yr (assuming a pool of 1,200 liturgists). These numbers could sustain a year in which all of the 420 ships were deployed (420 T) and festival liturgies were discharged (at Pritchard's rate of 100 T). Pyzyk models the period before the introduction of the trierarchic *symmoriai*, but the reform should not affect total costs. Ober (2015a: 245; 2015b: 499) estimates total costs of war in the 330s at 400 T/yr.

58. The evidence is from [Plut.] *Mor.* 852 B; but [Plut.] *Mor.* 841 D assesses it at 250 T; cf. Faraguna (1992: 381–82).

divide it by the twelve years of the Lycurgan administration, the resulting contribution is a little over fifty-four talents per year.

To sum up, the total contribution of the elite to Athenian public finances under Lycurgus was ca. 274 T/yr. If the numbers presented above are broadly correct, then we must conclude that the Athenian elite footed a considerable amount of Athens' bills in the Lycurgan period. Yet, their contribution to Athens' total revenues per annum actually declined compared to previous periods: from 59–67% after the Social War, to 19–21% in the 340s, to 18.7% under Lycurgus (Gabrielsen 1994: 216).

4.3.c. The Contribution of Piraeus

As Burke suggests, an important source of revenue in this period was the harbor of Piraeus. According to my estimates (cf. appendix B), Piraeus' 2% tax yielded ca. 110 T/yr in the 340s. But under Lycurgus, the Athenian state devised a series of additional measures to increase the volume of trade and attract merchants. These measures included revitalizing the harbor's infrastructure, ensuring the safety of cargoes against the threat of piracy, and bestowing honors and privileges on noncitizens.

First, then, the city's walls were repaired, the infrastructure of Piraeus was expanded, and the fleet was further enlarged to secure maritime trade routes and the safe anchoring of Athenian and foreign ships. For Burke (2010: 397), "these initiatives, combined with the enforced peace after Chaeronea, made it possible for Piraeus to become the principal trading center of the Aegean, the great entrepôt among Greek poleis."

Moreover, in the year 325/324, the Athenian Assembly authorized a major military expedition to the Adriatic to set up a naval station (Rhodes and Osborne 2003: 512–26). As Ober (2008: 124–33) documented, the inscription bearing the decree offers invaluable information concerning the coordinated work of Athenian public institutions in the late fourth century. At the same time, the decree explicitly refers to the purpose of the expedition. The naval base is to be established, most notably, "in order that the demos may for all future time have its own commerce and transport in grain, and that the establishment of their own naval station may result in a guard against the Thyrrenians [i.e., Etruscan pirates]" (trans. Ober 2008). The establishment of the naval station, therefore, aimed at lowering the transaction costs related to the shipment of grain.

Further, the Athenians increasingly courted maritime traders by extending substantial privileges to noncitizens. Fourteen of the thirty-four grants of honor and privileges in Engen's study date to the period between 337 and 323 (2010: 225–29). Of the twelve known beneficiaries, two are foreign potentates, six are wealthy professional traders, and four are common professional traders. Two of the common professional traders received minor honors, such as commendations and an inscribed stone. The other two received exceptionally high honors, such as gold crowns, *proxenia*, honors for benefactions (*euergesia*), the right to own land (*enktēsis*), the right to dine in the Prytaneion (*xenia*), and theater seats.[59]

Finally, after extending access to legal institutions through the dikai emporikai, the Athenians further extended access to noncitizens in the realm of civic associations. In the year 333/332, Cyzicene metics obtained the right to establish private organizations on Attic soil in the form of a land grant that enabled the construction of a sanctuary to Cyprian Aphrodite. The decree further reveals that the Cyzicene metics were not the first to obtain such a privilege. In fact, their grant was modeled on a previous land grant that enabled Egyptian metics to build a sanctuary to Isis (Rhodes and Osborne 2003: 462–66; Ober 2008: 252; 2015a: 247).

It is impossible to estimate the impact of these measures on Athenian finances. Based on the yield of the 2% tax in Thrace, Burke speculates that the 2% tax in Athens would have yielded 200–300 T/yr or more under Lycurgus (Burke 2010: 397). But the number cannot be taken at face value. Moreover, the 2% tax was only one of many taxes connected with Athens' harbor. However, of the taxes mentioned above—i.e., the metic tax, the tax on foreigners trading in the Agora or entering Piraeus, and the tax on goods sold in the Agora—we can relatively accurately estimate only the annual yield accruing from the metic tax (yielding around twenty-five talents per year: Ober 2015b: 507).

———

A complete account of Athenian public revenues under Lycurgus is beyond the available evidence. The Athenian state levied numerous other taxes, from taxes on silver (van Alfen 2011), to taxes on prostitutes (which yielded a whopping fifteen talents per year: Lyttkens 2013: 107; Ober 2015b: 508; cf. Gabrielsen 2013; Fawcett 2016). However, more often than not, estimating annual yields is an arduous if not impossible task.[60] Yet, even if we cannot precisely estimate the contribution of each stream to total annual revenues, we can still draw some conclusions about Athens' performance on the eve of the Macedonian conquest. If in the 330s Athens experienced its most dynamic period of growth, it

59. As Engen repeatedly points out, such largesse was in part due to the food shortages of the 330s, which made the import of grain to Athens a matter of survival. At the same time, the honors that the Athenians lavished on foreigners and metics under Lycurgus are but an upsurge in a trend that characterized Athenian policy throughout the fourth century.

60. Taking the higher estimate for Piraeus' contribution (i.e., 300 T), my reconstruction of Lycurgan public revenue accounts for about 68% of total state income (817 out of 1,200 T/yr).

was due in part to the contribution of the elite (ca. 23%) and in part to the efforts devoted to the exploitation of the city's resources, particularly Laurion and Piraeus (ca. 30–38%).

4.4. Conclusion

Throughout the fourth century, the Athenians sought to square the conflicting demands of economic growth and social order. Prominent on the agenda was the need to regulate elite contributions to extract as much as possible from Athens' wealthy citizens without driving them into revolt. Equally prominent were expenditures that benefited the Athenian masses, such as the introduction of pay for the Assembly, the reform of the Theoric fund, and finally Lycurgus' building program. The question is how this delicate bargain was kept in place throughout a century punctuated by military defeats and fiscal crises.

Bargaining in the shadow of the constitution raised the cost of reneging and helped maintain social order. Proposing policies that sought to vastly increase the contribution of the elite to Athenian public finances or that diverted the proceeds of the polis' prosperity away from the masses meant sowing the seed of civil war, oligarchy, and, ultimately, tyranny. Faced with limited options to increase revenues, the Athenians extended forms of institutional access to key categories of noncitizen actors in order to incentivize their economic activity. These actors included foreigners, metics, and even slaves. Access encompassed a number of institutions in the realms of society, the economy, and the law.

In the course of the fourth century, Athens progressively abandoned imperialistic attitudes to boosting her economy. After the loss of the empire, the fifth-century economy of coercion was progressively superseded by an economy that we might reasonably describe as increasingly moving toward open access (Carugati, Ober, and Weingast 2019). The extension of meaningful forms of institutional access, however, was not universal, but gradual and highly instrumental. First, political access was never extended. Second, if some categories of noncitizens benefited from important forms of access, many others continued to be brutally exploited. The point is best exemplified in the policies that regulated one of Athens' most lucrative resources: the Laurion silver mines. If, as I argued above, reforms of mining leases incentivized free actors to become involved in mining, mining itself depended on a large population of slave laborers whose condition did not improve over the course of the fourth century.

Athens' trade-off of inclusion entailed a bargain enshrined in and protected by the constitution. It is beyond doubt that such a bargain fell short of universal inclusion motivated by a normative commitment to inalienable human rights. Nevertheless, the bargain benefited many by fostering both political stability and economic development.

5

The Paths Not Taken

IN THE previous chapters, I argued that Athens' stability and prosperity in the fourth century rested on the establishment of a new self-enforcing constitution. The constitution imposed a series of constraints on decision-making, fostering political stability without curbing growth-enhancing policy innovation. But how do we know that it was, in fact, the constitution, and not some other variable, that determined the outcome?

As I argued in the introduction, neither geography nor culture alone can account for Athens' fourth-century development. But what about other institutional variables? The limited nature of the evidence concerning the institutional histories of other Greek poleis precludes a systematic comparative investigation. In this chapter, therefore, I collect the available comparative and counterfactual evidence that suggests that, in the absence of the constitution, Athens' development would have lagged in the fourth century.

First, I use comparative evidence from two other high-performing ancient states: the Greek polis of Syracuse in Sicily during the classical period and late republican Rome. I show that Rome and Syracuse experienced crises similar to that of Athens, but responded in different ways. By "similar crisis," I mean a crisis that involved civil conflict (which I define below). In Syracuse, recurring violence yielded frequent constitutional transitions and a boom and bust cycle where productivity gains were eroded in the long run. In Rome, civil conflict generated unsustainable growth gains for the masses and was followed by a permanent transition to authoritarianism, which yielded political stability, but also a probable decline in prosperity and an increase in inequality.

Second, I provide a counterfactual reconstruction of Athens' developmental potential under an oligarchy. I identify the commercial port of Piraeus as central to Athenian economic prosperity. Piraeus was also central to Athens' grain supply, and therefore to both the size and well-being of Attica's population. I show that had Athens been ruled by an oligarchy, Piraeus' potential would not have been fully tapped. I conclude that, under an oligarchic government,

Athens would have survived, but with a smaller population and a slower growth rate.

5.1. Prosperity and Civil Conflict: A Comparative Study

The ancient sources regarded civil conflict as a powerful threat to the very existence of the political community.[1] But evidence from Syracuse and Rome contradicts this view. Throughout the classical period (fifth–fourth centuries), Syracuse achieved high levels of prosperity despite regular outbreaks of internal violence. The same picture emerges from the archaeology and history of Roman Italy during the late Republic (first century). Under what conditions did economic growth occur in the presence of civil conflict in Syracuse and Rome? Were those conditions present in Athens?

The comparative nature of the investigation requires that I define at the outset the terms of my inquiry, beginning with the definition of civil conflict. Although similar in many respects, the Greek word *stasis* encompasses a broader set of phenomena than the English words "civil war." Greek historians define stasis in various ways. Some deny that stasis necessarily involved violence (e.g., van Wees 2007: 8–11; Berger 1992: 12, 88). Others emphasize instead the role of violence as a definitional requirement (e.g., Lintott 1982: 34; Arcenas 2018).[2] Another issue concerns the degree to which the Greek word stasis

---

1. Thuc. 3.69–85; Pl. *Resp.* 8; Arist. *Pol.* 5; Xen. *Hell.* 2. Cf. Luc. *Phar.* 1.71–76. On archaic attitudes to *stasis*: van Wees (2007). On civil conflict in Rome: Lintott (1971). Analyses of classical attitudes to stasis: Ober (2002); D. Cohen (1995: ch. 2); Kalimtzis (2000). On the resilience of the polis as a political unit: Mackil (2004); contra Runciman (1990).

2. For Arcenas, stasis is more likely to have been a high-frequency, low-intensity phenomenon, than a predictor of the "death of the polis." Those ancient sources that describe stasis as a major threat do so because 1) being members of the elite, they were more likely to be personally threatened by stasis and suffer exile; 2) stasis tended to generate cycles of instability that were difficult to stop. Arcenas also hypothesizes, although this point must await further study, that as a high-frequency, low-intensity phenomenon, stasis may have been ultimately beneficial to the Greek economy. First, the higher likelihood that stasis would affect agricultural inputs incentivized people to take up activities in other, growth-enhancing sectors of the economy—most notably trade. Moreover, stasis created incentives for people to strengthen relationships with individuals and communities outside of their mother polis, in case exile forced them to relocate elsewhere. These connections fostered the diffusion of knowledge across political units, contributing to the cycle of competition, specialization, and exchange that Ober (2015a) identifies as critical to Hellas' growth. In terms of both intensity and frequency, civil conflict in Athens is an outlier in Arcenas' dataset.

overlaps with the Latin phrase *bellum civile*.[3] For the purposes of this chapter, I sidestep these debates. Instead, I define my unit of analysis as a *violent clash between domestic actors,* and I refer to this phenomenon throughout the chapter with the words "civil conflict."

The ancient sources provide little guidance into an investigation of the economic impact of civil conflict, devoting substantially more attention to the investigation of its causes.[4] Classical scholarship has largely followed the ancient sources in privileging the investigation of the sociopolitical causes of civil conflict over its economic consequences.[5] Similarly, economists and political scientists who study civil conflict today overwhelmingly focus on causes— particularly, on ethnicity as a driver of conflict (Easterly and Levine 1997; Collier and Hoeffler 1998; Fearon and Laitin 2003; cf. Ray and Esteban 2017). Some research exists on the consequences of civil conflict and particularly on the impact of conflict on economic structures and performance (e.g., Collier 1999; 2000; Imai and Weinstein 2000; Murdoch and Sandler 2002; 2004; Kang and Meernik 2005). However, the available models and theories present major difficulties when applied directly to the ancient world because we lack relevant data (for example, concerning the number of casualties), which makes it difficult to categorize ancient civil conflicts according to modern definitions (see e.g., the Correlates of War dataset; Fearon and Laitin 2003; cf. chapter 2).

This literature nonetheless offers an important starting point in the observation that the impact of civil conflict on growth operates through two primary mechanisms. First, the impact of conflict on the factors of production, including land, labor, and capital. Second, the impact of conflict on political structures and how (and whether) they change in response to the conflict. In this section, I analyze how these mechanisms operated in Syracuse and Rome. The evidence suggests that, in Syracuse, the impact of conflict on growth varied depending on the economic conditions that pertained before the conflict.

3. On the difference between Greek stasis and Roman *bellum civile*: Armitage (2017: 38–45). Kalimtzis (2000) offers a diachronic development of the concept of stasis in classical Greece.

4. Many Greek and Roman authors stressed the failings of human psychology, although socioeconomic considerations also played a role in their reflections (e.g., Arist. *Pol.* 1266a-7a; Sall. *Cat.* 37.7ff. and *Jug.* 41.7–8).

5. For Gehrke (1985), as for Berger (1992), the experience of civil conflict was rooted in the sociopolitical structure of the polis (hence, its sheer frequency). The aim of civil conflict was the acquisition of political power through the control of the city's decision-making institutions. Other scholars emphasize socioeconomic motives and foreign policy intervention as genuine causes or catalysts of civil conflict in Greece and Rome. On socioeconomic causes: Fuks (1984, drawing heavily from Aristotle and Isocrates); Lintott (1999). On social causes: de Ste. Croix (1981). On foreign policy reason: Gehrke (1985); Ruschenbusch (1978); cf. Riess (2012); Lintott (1982).

Moreover, civil conflict tended to generate cycles of violence that culminated in constitutional transitions. In Rome, civil conflict may have contributed to an increase in growth gains for the sub-elite population, but the increase could not be sustained in the long run due to both economic and political processes.

Before I continue, a series of caveats deserves attention. First, I discuss the available evidence concerning economic growth according to two measures: aggregate growth and per capita growth. Second, since economic growth (either aggregate or per capita) per se tells us little about well-being, I also discuss measures of inequality whenever possible. Third, the evidence for Rome and for Syracuse varies dramatically. Whereas, for Rome, efforts to quantify the conspicuous material remains abound, there is little quantitative evidence available for Syracuse. While I purport to analyze the available quantitative and qualitative evidence for both case studies, my account of Syracuse must necessarily rely more on the literary sources. I acknowledge their potential bias, particularly when compared to the biases that I detect in the Roman literary sources, and I seek to support the ancient sources' conclusions with independent evidence whenever possible.

5.1.a. Syracuse (Fifth–Fourth Centuries)

In the classical period, Syracuse experienced a time of efflorescence, with concomitant increases in economic growth and population (De Angelis 2016: ch. 4; on efflorescences: Goldstone 2002). The city's fertile land and reliable rainfall made it a primary grain exporter (ibid. 226–29).[6] For Ober (2008: 47), Syracuse ranked third (after Athens and Sparta) among Greek poleis in an aggregate measure of prominence based on territory size, fame, international activity, and public buildings. For Morris (2004: 711; 2005: 3, 16; 2009b: 115), Syracuse was highly populated and urbanized.

Prosperity in Syracuse occurred in the context of recurrent civil conflict. The extant evidence suggests that fifteen civil conflicts exploded in Syracuse in the period between the years 485 and 317.[7] Moreover, civil conflict tended to

---

6. De Angelis (2016) paints a variegated and highly dynamic picture of the Sicilian economy in general and of Syracuse in particular. His account seeks to move beyond the picture of Sicily's economy as based solely on agriculture. But the island's agricultural resources are not to be underestimated: De Angelis (2000; 2006; 2010); Morris (2005: 17–18). On Syracuse's resources in comparative perspective: Morris (2009b: 159).

7. My reconstruction of the Syracusan civil conflicts relies on Berger (1992: 34–53; cf. Lintott 1982: 185–221). In the period under investigation here (485–317), Berger records eighteen instances of stasis. Note, however, that Berger defines stasis as "not necessarily violent" (1992: 12, 88) and in fact some of these uprisings did not involve any form of violence (notably, in 454/453, 412, and 396). Based on the definition of civil conflict offered above, these nonviolent

coincide with constitutional transitions from tyranny to democracy and vice-versa. Did Syracuse fare well under the tyrants or under a democracy? And can we assess, even if we cannot precisely quantify, Syracuse's economic performance over the long run?

According to Ian Morris, Syracuse was extremely prosperous under the tyrants Gelon, Hiero, and Thrasybulus (485–466) and later under Dionysius I (405–367). The city's prosperity was the result of the tyrants' ability to "generate tremendous power through direct taxes on their own subjects, expropriations from the aristocracy, population relocations, the hiring of temporary mercenary forces and dynastic marriages" (Morris 2009: 163).[8] Moreover, as Shlomo Berger suggests, under the tyrants Syracuse did not experience outbursts of civil violence.[9]

How did Syracuse fare when it was ruled by democracies?[10] According to the historian Diodorus Siculus (11.68.5–6, trans. Oldfather 1989), under the fifth-century democracy Syracuse "increased greatly in prosperity."[11] But once again, prosperity coincided with a long period of peace.[12]

---

confrontations are excised from my analysis, which focuses therefore only on fifteen episodes of civil conflict. A final caveat: in Berger's study, the narrative of the episodes (which occupies pages 34 to 53) differs from the summary results he presents on page 117–18. The civil conflicts that match my definition occur in 485 (Gelon's coming to power, labeled by Berger as occurring in 491); in 467 (the removal of Thrasybulus); in 466 (the revolt of mercenaries); in 408/407 (Hermocrates' attempted coup); in 406 (Dionysius' coup); two episodes in 405 and again in 404 (against Dionysius' tyranny); in 357 (Dion's coup); in 355 (the complex episode featuring Dionysius, Dion, and Heracleides); in 354 (the conflict leading to Dion's murder); in 353 (the revolt against Callippus); in 352 (the conflict between Dionysius and Hicetas); in 343 (the conflict between Timoleon, Hicetas, and Dionysius); and finally in 317 (Agathocles' coup).

8. For an account of how the tyrants built Syracuse into an imperial city, and Sicily into Syracuse's imperial network: Morris (2009: 161ff.).

9. The only episode of civil conflict that Berger records between 485 and 466 and between 405 and 357 is a nonviolent attempt to revolt against Dionysius I in 396 (Berger 1992: 44). Because the revolt in question, as far as we know, was confined to a (nonauthentic) speech in the Assembly, it does not fall into the category of civil conflict as defined above.

10. In his reconstruction of the political history of Syracuse between the years 465–317, Lintott (1982) is very cautious when it comes to defining Syracuse as a democracy (similar caution is applied to other cities in Sicily: Asheri 1980; De Angelis 2016: 193–94). He seems willing to use this term only for the period between the reforms of Diocles in 412 and the coup of Dionysius in 405. On whether Syracuse's institutions can be properly called democratic: Arist. *Pol.* 1304a27; Rutter (2000); E. W. Robinson (2004; 2011: 67–92); Morris (2009b).

11. All translations from Diodorus Siculus are from Oldfather (1989), unless otherwise noted.

12. Berger's study (1992: 38–39) confirms Diodorus' observation: between 466 and 412, no civil conflicts were fought. The constitutional transition that consolidated the Syracusan

The Syracusans, having liberated their native city in this manner [i.e. having overthrown the tyrant Thrasybulus in the year 466], gave permission to the mercenaries to withdraw from Syracuse, and they liberated the other cities, which were either in the hands of tyrants or had garrisons, and re-established democracies in them. From this time the city enjoyed peace and increased greatly in prosperity, and it maintained its democracy for almost sixty years, until the tyranny which was established by Dionysius [in the year 405].

In sum, under both tyrannical and democratic governments Syracuse experienced peace and prosperity. When did civil conflict occur? And did it have an impact on Syracuse's prosperity?

Berger suggests that ten of the fifteen instances of internal conflict throughout the classical period occurred during constitutional transitions (*metabolai*). Between the years 412 and 396, when democracy in Syracuse began to collapse and was eventually replaced by tyranny, the Syracusans experienced five episodes of conflict. Similarly, between the years 357 and 343, in the aftermath of the reign of Dionysius II, when tyranny yielded once again to democracy, Syracuse experienced another five episodes of conflict. In order to understand the relationship between civil conflict and prosperity in Syracuse, we need to take a closer look at these periods, beginning with the turmoil of the late fifth century.

5.1.A.I. CIVIL CONFLICT IN THE LATE FIFTH CENTURY

To put pressure on Diodorus' testimony, we may ask: if the Syracusan democracy was so stable and effective in fostering peace and economic prosperity, why was it eventually overthrown and replaced by tyranny? Ancient sources and modern commentators provide two different, yet interrelated answers to this question.

For Andrew Lintott (1982: 193; cf. E. W. Robinson 2011: 67ff.), democratic prosperity in Syracuse had peculiarly inegalitarian features, even after the reforms of Diocles in the year 412.[13] With these reforms, "the political position of the poor became stronger [but] this does not seem to have been matched by their social and economic conditions." In particular, for Lintott, the Syracusan

---

democracy in 412 took place in the Assembly and did not involve any fighting (Berger 1992: 39–40).

13. For De Angelis (2016: 284) increased prosperity translated in "material well-being for a wide range of social groups." Compared to the tyrannical period, more people may have benefited of the fruits of prosperity, particularly via access to land (2016: 302). De Angelis, however, does not contradict Lintott's account of relative overall inequality based on the role of powerful elite clans (ch. 3).

democracy failed to solve the problems of land redistribution and citizen enrollment.[14]

The ancient sources stress a set of related foreign policy constraints. After the victory over the Athenians in the year 413, an exhausted Syracuse had to ward off another powerful threat: that of the Carthaginians in the year 409. The double success over Athens and Carthage, however, proved insufficient to preserve democratic stability. Under the pressure of war, the democratic leadership fell apart, and Dionysius I imposed himself as sole ruler. Diodorus suggests that the success of Dionysius' coup was due to his ability to take advantage of the Carthaginian threat to stir up enmities and mutual distrust between *the people and the generals* (13.92.2) and between *the citizens and the former exiles* (13.92.7). The genius of Dionysius, then, lay in his ability to exploit the socioeconomic clefts that Lintott emphasized (cf. De Angelis 2016: 213).

Although the evidence is admittedly limited, the unequal distribution of resources, paired with weak leadership, may have undermined the stability of the Syracusan democracy in two ways. First, inequality fostered instability, as increases in the political power of the masses did not yield proportional increases in their economic power. Second, instability fostered constitutional change when the pressure of external war destabilized weak political institutions.

Once Dionysius was firmly in power, his enlightened tyranny brought to Syracuse unprecedented levels of fame and prosperity. As with Gelon and Hiero, so with Dionysius, Syracusan prosperity relied on predatory means, such as the imposition of direct taxes, expropriations of the aristocracy, population relocation, and the hiring of temporary mercenary forces. But Dionysius' strategy to quash the lingering elite opposition by seeking the support of the people meant that more of the spoils ended up in the hands of the lower strata of society (De Angelis 2016: 213ff.). At the same time, the limited impact of external war and civil conflict on economic structures allowed the tyrant to inherit much of the prosperity accumulated in previous periods.[15]

14. Land redistribution, in particular, seems to have constituted a recurring problem throughout the history of the polis in the fifth and fourth centuries (Plut. *Dio*. 48.3). Enrollment demands turned violent as soon as democracy was established, when mercenaries enfranchised under the tyrants subsequently lost rights of active political participation and revolted (Diod. 11.72–73 and 76).

15. The experience of conflict, both external and internal, did not erode previously accumulated economic resources. According to Lintott (1982: 193), in the (largely naval) battles fought against Athens (415–413) and Carthage (412–404), "the countryside had not been seriously devastated. . . . There was a plethora of cheap slaves arising from the prisoners of war . . . and a fair amount of booty besides. In the short term, there may have been a post-war boom in

5.1.A.II. CIVIL CONFLICT IN THE MID-FOURTH CENTURY

Things turned out differently when a new cycle of civil conflicts broke out in the middle of the fourth century. The Golden Age of Syracuse under Dionysius I was followed by a period of mismanagement and rapid decline under his son, Dionysius II (367–357). When Dionysius II was ousted, infighting among his would-be successors plunged Syracuse into a new cycle of civil violence. Instability lasted for over two decades and seriously threatened the prosperity that the Sicilian polis had enjoyed for more than a century (Westlake 1994).[16] When the democratic leader Timoleon finally managed to restore stability to the polis around the year 343, Syracuse was on its knees. According to Plutarch (*Tim.* 22.3–4; trans. Perrin 1918;[17] cf. Diod. 16.65.9):[18]

> The city which he [i.e., Timoleon] had taken had not citizens enough, since some had perished in their wars and seditions, while others had gone into exile from tyrannical governments. Indeed, for lack of population the market place of Syracuse had produced such a quantity of dense herbage that horses were pastured in it, while their grooms lay down in the grass; and the other cities, with almost no exceptions, were full of deer and wild swine, while in their suburbs and around their walls those who had leisure for it went hunting, and not one of those who were established in fortresses and strongholds would hearken to any summons, or come down into the city, but fear and hatred kept all away from market place and civic life and public speaking, which had produced the most of their tyrants.

To overcome the crisis, Timoleon had to jumpstart the process of recovery by bringing to the city a new inflow of colonists from the Greek mainland (Plut. *Tim.* 23; Diod. 16.82.5–7).

Political reforms in this period provide some important similarities with the Athenian case, even if the limited nature of the evidence precludes robust conclusions. According to Diodorus (16.82.6), "Timoleon revised the existing laws

---

manufacture and trade, but little change in agriculture." Similarly, the civil conflicts that exploded when Dionysius I came to power affected the city and its hinterland only in a minor way, if at all (Berger 1992: 39–44).

16. On democracy under Dion: E. W. Robinson (2011: 89–91).

17. All translations of Plutarch's *Timoleon* are from Perrin (1918), unless otherwise noted.

18. De Angelis (2016: 303; cf. Vandermersch 1994) argues that we should beware of the bleak picture painted by Plutarch and Diodorus because these sources are biased against tyranny: such a dismal situation, De Angelis suggests, could not have been resolved quickly and by a single individual. I take this caution seriously, but nothing in De Angelis' account suggests that (or how) we should substantially modify the picture of mid-century economic crisis in Syracuse.

of Syracuse, which Diocles had composed;" he also "built the courts of justice (*ta dikastēria*)" (Plut. *Tim.* 22.2). The emphasis on laws and courts reminds us of the new democracy's work at Athens. One may even push the analogy further, highlighting the role of the "laws of Diocles," which, like the "laws of Solon," provided a shared past for the Syracusans on which they could collectively build their new *politeia*.[19] But the analogy stops here. The evidence in fact suggests that Timoleon may have modified the original democratic constitution by adding some oligarchic features (Diod. 16.82.6; Talbert 1974: 133; E. W. Robinson 2011: 91–92). The fact that Timoleon could modify the constitution so easily suggests that his role was perhaps closer to a third-party enforcer than a reformer, and that the constitution was therefore far from being self-enforcing.

Nonetheless, Timoleon's constitution did return a measure of economic prosperity to Syracuse.[20] According to Diodorus (16.83), peace was, once again, the key to economic flourishing, enabling the Syracusans to fully exploit the conspicuous potential of their abundant and fertile land.

> So, having established peaceful conditions everywhere throughout Sicily, he [i.e. Timoleon] caused the cities to experience a vast growth of prosperity. For many years, because of domestic troubles and border wars, and still more because of the numbers of tyrants who kept constantly appearing, the cities had become destitute of inhabitants and the open country had become a wilderness for lack of cultivation, producing no useful crops. But now new settlers streamed into the land in great numbers, and as a long period of peace set in, the fields were reclaimed for cultivation and bore abundant crops of all sorts. These the Siceliot Greeks sold to merchants at good prices and rapidly increased their wealth.

Once again, however, prosperity did not last for long. In the year 317, Syracuse fell again prey to civil conflict and tyranny.

———

19. For a discussion of the meaning of the phrase "laws of Diocles," see Talbert (1974: 134–36). For a more comprehensive account of Timoleon's constitutional reforms: Talbert (1974); E. W. Robinson (2011).

20. In the absence of reliable quantitative data, the question of whether Syracuse's late fourth-century growth was comparable to that achieved under the fifth-century democracy or under Dionysius I must remain unanswered. However, both Morris (2009b: 159–63) and De Angelis (2016: ch. 4) seem to suggest that Syracuse's prosperity was greater under the tyrants than under the democratic governments (even in the fifth century).

The evidence discussed above allows us to make a series of observations. First, in the classical period, Syracuse's economy grew remarkably in the aggregate, particularly during periods of peace, under both tyrannical and democratic governments. Per capita growth is harder to estimate, largely because we lack reliable numbers to assess how the population may have fluctuated throughout the tumultuous classical period. Inequality seems to have remained high, both under the tyrants and under the democratic governments. Second, the impact of conflict on growth varied depending on the circumstances that pertained before the conflict. In the late fifth century, recovery under Dionysius was rapid due to both available resources (which the violence of the late fifth century failed to exhaust), and Dionysius' ability to exploit what Morris terms "tyrannical means of wealth production," such as population relocations, the imposition of taxes, expropriations of the aristocracy, and so on. Conversely, in the mid-fourth century, when a decade of mismanagement and instability under Dionysius II and his successors had eroded Syracuse's resources, a new cycle of civil conflict seriously threatened the city's prosperity. Third, when civil conflict broke out in Syracuse, in the years 412–396 and 357–343, it tended to lead to cycles of violence, culminating in constitutional change. If tyranny proved, overall, short-lived in Syracuse, democracy suffered from major design defects that made it profoundly unstable.

5.1.b. Rome (First Century)

From the Social War of the years 91–88 to the dawn of the Principate in the year 27, Rome was ravaged by eleven civil conflicts.[21] Did Rome experience economic growth in this period?[22]

For long, the prevailing model of the Roman economy in the period of the late Republic posited, "a causal connection between imperial conquest, a vast enrichment of the Roman elite, a rapid increase in the number of urban and rural

---

21. The conflicts that fall under my definition include the Social War (91–88); Sulla's two civil conflicts (88–87 and 82–81); the Sertorian War in Spain (83–72); Lepidus' rebellion in Italy (78–77); Catiline's conspiracy (63); the civil conflict between Caesar and Pompey (49–45); the civil conflict between Caesarians and Republicans (44–42); the Sicilian revolt (44–36); the Perusine War (41–40); and the civil conflict between Octavian and Antony (32–30). I limit myself to listing these disturbances, but do not delve into issues of periodization (i.e., whether two or more of these conflicts could be grouped together). On the impact of civil conflict on the fall of the Republic: Flower (2010).

22. The bibliography on the issue is vast. For the purposes of this section, I do not rehearse the primitivist vs. modernist debate. Nor do I discuss the relationship of that debate with Moses Finley's influential model (Finley 1973b; Morris 1999: ix–xxiii).

slaves, the gradual proletarianization of an ever-growing proportion of the Italian peasantry and a numerical decline of the free peasantry" (Hin 2013: 20; cf. De Ligt and Northwood 2008. See also Hopkins: 1978; Brunt: 1987[1971]). More recently, evidence drawn largely from nonliterary sources has contributed to put pressure on this view. In what follows, I discuss the model of decline and then turn to the new growth model of the Roman economy.

5.1.B.I. THE MODEL OF DECLINE

According to Brunt (1987[1971]), contrary to the early days of Roman expansion—when war may have helped alleviate the so-called struggle of the orders between patricians and plebeians—in the long run, the expansion deepened the cleft between classes, as the rich squandered the newly available wealth in luxury consumption, in addition to investing it in land (largely seized from the lower classes) and slaves (which put small peasants out of work). While senators grew fat with booty, allowances, and exactions, the knights (*Equites*) benefited from contracts for public works, army supplies, and provincial taxes.

If capital inflow from the provinces landed largely in the pockets of the rich, the resources of Italy offered a meager alternative to the poor. Erdkamp (1998) analyzed the impact of violence on the civilian food supply via two mechanisms: the impact of warfare on agricultural products and on the process of production. He suggested that, first, Roman armies caused a great deal of damage, contributing to the recurrence of food crises.[23] Second, violence disrupted production and trade (the latter compounded by the phenomenon of piracy at least down to 66–65), and siphoned off resources from the civilian population toward the soldiers. Finally, the economic malaise arising from the disruption of agricultural production and food provision caused the dislocation of many sectors of the economy.

But forced conscription also had demographic consequences. In the course of the first century, hundreds of thousand of peasants abandoned their fields to join the army.[24] The impact of conflict on demography increased over time as a consequence of military reforms. The property qualification for military service continued to shrink from the Hannibalic War onward, until the reforms of Marius in 107 swung the doors of the army open to the poorest strata of the population (*capitecensi*). Military service may have offered a real alternative to

23. On the destruction of Italian land during civil conflicts: Brunt (1972); Nicolet (1994). On food crises: Garnsey (1988: 172ff.; 198ff.); Brunt (1972: 27).

24. For Brunt (1972: 15; 1987[1971]), in the decade beginning with the Social War, a number of Italians ranging between 250,000 and 300,000 took up arms. From 78 to 49, the number decreased to somewhere between 60,000 and 150,000, only to spike again between 49 and 27 (150,000 to 200,000).

the number of dispossessed small peasants that were flocking to Rome in this period. However, as Brunt argued (1972: 15), the idea that the lower classes welcomed this option is a myth. First, conscription continued to be enforced, especially during the civil conflicts. Second, the benefits that common soldiers received for their service—in terms of both stipends and looting—paled compared to the resources that ended up in the hands of the generals and the upper echelons of the army. Third, as free Italian peasants joined the army, their richer neighbors seized their small properties and aggregated them in larger estates (*latifundia*), where they employed the massive number of slaves that were pouring into Rome as a result of foreign conquests.

5.1.B.II. THE GROWTH MODEL

The traditional view of concomitant economic and demographic decline among the free peasantry in the period of the late Republic has now been challenged. The challenge has its roots in a methodological sea change that, beginning in the 1980s and taking up speed in the 90s, pushed scholars towards archaeological, epigraphic, numismatic, and papyrological evidence. Over the last three decades, a remarkable number of proxies for Roman economic growth have emerged: shipwrecks, lead and copper pollution, animal bones, levels of urbanization, and technological and institutional innovation (Parker 1992; Kylander et al. 2005; Jongman 2007; Temin 2006; Schneider 2007; Frier and Kehoe 2007; cf. Scheidel 2009; Hin 2013: 46ff.; Kay 2014: 274ff.). These proxies are problematic, both independently and as a group (Scheidel 2009; Temin 2013: part 3). But the picture they provide is remarkably consistent. As Rome came to control much of the known world, the size of the Roman economy grew dramatically, with increases in productivity gains from more land, more labor (slaves), and more capital (Kay 2014: 279ff.).

The critical questions that grip current debates are whether we can speak of real or intensive economic growth in the Roman economy, what was its tempo and magnitude, and how the fruits of the increased prosperity were distributed across the population. For the purposes of my investigation, the most interesting aspect of the debate on Roman economic growth is "the growing appreciation, if not a consensus . . . that the major period of growth in the Roman economy was in the [war-ridden] second to first centuries BC, with only limited growth during the [peaceful] Principate" (Kay 2014; cf. Bang 2009).[25] Scholars are thus beginning to turn their attention from the empire to the late Republic.

---

25. A crucial question here is when exactly did growth plateau and inequality rise. The lack of fine-grained proxies makes it hard to reach bulletproof conclusions. Here, I just want to note that the question is an open one. Economic historians employing different proxies reach

Scheidel's (2007) model of real income growth in the years between 300 and 30 is of particular value in that it focuses specifically on the impact of conflict on the well-being of sub-elite Romans.[26] Scheidel identifies military attrition, emigration, and urbanization as responsible for depressing the reproductive capacity of free Italians.[27] A demographic downturn among the population of free Italians was paired with the massive redistributions of financial resources from Roman elites and provincial subjects to the Italian sub-elite population. These two dynamics interact in the model to yield a rise in real income.

Redistribution took various forms. First, the abolition of the head tax (*tributum*) in 167 and of Italian harbor dues in 61.[28] Second, the removal of intracommunal tributes extracted from the Italian allies upon enfranchisement in the 80s. Third, the conversion of common land (*ager publicus*) into privately owned land (in the 130s and 120s and later in the 50s). As a result of these and other reforms, the contribution of the Italian population to the Roman state shrunk considerably over time. In addition, public works and grain subsidies— not to mention the doles that punctuated the last decades of the Republic— benefited the lower strata of the urban (and to some extent rural) population. Finally, beginning at least with Sulla, military service became an increasingly lucrative business. As both the numbers of conflicts and the autonomy of military commanders grew exponentially, profits reached unforeseen levels and trickle-down effects accordingly multiplied.

Trickle-down effects were not the only cause of potential increases in sub-elite real income. First, "the net benefits of these disbursements [i.e., to the soldiers] were greatly enhanced by the way in which the necessary funds were obtained by the Roman warlords: by seizing sequestered wealth in the form of

---

different results. For Scheidel (2007), real income growth began to decline sharply (and inequality rose) soon after Augustus came to power. For Morris (2013), energy capture peaked in the first century CE, suggesting that political transformations had little impact on overall economic performance. For the purposes of this account, I follow Scheidel's account of a rapid decline in real under Augustus, but I accept the possibility (with Morris) that aggregate growth (proxied by energy capture) may have continued to rise in the first century CE. Still, it seems beyond doubt that if aggregate growth rose in the first two centuries of the empire, so did inequality (Scheidel 2007).

26. Other models focus on the imperial period: Hopkins (1980); Goldsmith (1984); Temin (2006; 2013); Maddison (2007); Scheidel and Friesen (2009). Scheidel's (2007) conclusions are supported in Geraghty (2007) and Kay (2014) (who focuses on elite actors). On sub-elite actors in the last century of the Republic and under the empire: Mayer (2012).

27. There is an ongoing debate over demographic trends in Roman Italy from 100 onward: Turchin and Scheidel (2009), contra Hin (2013).

28. For an account of how the abolition of the tributum was made possible by imperial wealth, and its negative impact on the masses' bargaining power, see Tan (2017).

state reserves and temple treasures; by confiscating the assets of some members of the Roman elite and imposing extraordinary taxes on the others; and, above all, by extorting funds from provincial communities" (ibid. 332). Second, ordinary citizens suffered relatively little loss of property in this period—mostly, in the form of partial expropriation of a number of cities by Sulla and Octavian. Finally, the impact of warfare on the physical capital of Italy greatly declined over the course of the last two centuries of the Republic, as civil conflicts were increasingly fought outside the Boot.

In sum, demographic decline, war-led redistribution policies, and the externalization of the direct and indirect cost of civil conflict "greatly boosted the economic benefits that accrued to the general population of Italy" (ibid. 333). Civil conflict, it turns out, may have been good for Rome, and particularly for the masses. But not for long. If conflict (that is, both external war and civil conflict) was initially a motor of real income growth and declining inequality, these conditions could not be sustained in the aftermath of conflict. In fact, the increase in sub-elite real income was an epiphenomenon that depended on factors related to the experience of conflict, such as forcible redistributions. The paradoxical result, was that "however much the literati celebrated the peace, stability and security established by the new monarchy, these conditions were not necessarily conducive to the well-being of ordinary Italians" (ibid. 342). Peace favored large-scale acquisition of real estate and the development, in the provinces, of export businesses on the part of the elites. Peace also caused labor prices to fall due to population growth and the thickening of labor markets as a consequence of reduced mobility and attrition.

Political factors likely compounded these economic processes. Augustus *could* have passed reforms to ameliorate the socioeconomic condition of the masses, in line with the processes that the civil conflicts of the late Republic had birthed. Or he could have chosen to entrench the position of the elites, distributing privileges to violence-endowed actors in a way that would have made it easier to control them and establish himself more firmly in power. Augustus, unmistakably, chose the latter option. After decades of turmoil, destabilizing violence was a much more dangerous prospect than low(er) growth, especially if the structure of the empire could still—and amply—provide for the powerful rich. The well-being of the masses had almost never been a political conundrum for the Roman leadership. Even if recent developments had unearthed a different path, Augustus had almost no reasons to explore it further. The new constitutional structure proved very effective in managing the threat of recurring violence and in restoring stability after decades of unrest. That the solution may have proven detrimental to the many was, in all probability, not something that would keep the *Princeps* up at night.

In reviewing recent contributions to the debate on Roman economic growth, it was not my goal to provide an exhaustive summary of the literature, much less to make a substantive contribution. Instead, the analysis above was meant to answer a specific question: if we assume, as most Roman historians nowadays do, that Rome's economy grew in the last two centuries of the Republic (both in aggregate and per capita terms), what was the impact of civil conflict on growth? Scheidel's model provocatively suggests that civil conflict increased real income growth, but only in the short run.

From the evidence discussed above, three conclusions may be drawn. First, Rome was able to externalize the cost of civil conflict by exporting it outside of Italy, thus minimizing the impact of armed conflict on Italy's territory and resources. Second, the economy could count on the huge imperial network that Rome controlled, which emerged largely unscathed from the struggles. Third, the economic effects of external wars and civil conflicts interacted in the history of the late Republic to generate increased but unsustainable real income growth for the Italian population—an increase which may have come to a halt with the advent of Augustus' rule.

5.1.c. Conclusion

The histories of classical Syracuse and late republican Rome suggest that civil conflict per se does not necessarily hinder economic growth. But why didn't Syracuse—with her grain and her weak neighbors—outperform Athens, especially after Athens lost the empire? And why were growth gains likely eroded with the advent of Augustus, despite the presence and (marginal) expansion of Rome's huge empire?

The political economy literature suggests that, to analyze the impact of civil conflict on growth, we must pay attention not only to the impact of conflict on the factors of production, but also to the impact of conflict on political structures. The comparative analysis of civil conflict in Syracuse and Rome yields two main results. First, Syracuse's and Rome's ability to weather periods of civil conflict depended to a large extent on the availability of human, physical, and financial capital. Second, both in Syracuse and in Rome, civil conflict may have negatively affected growth in a long-term perspective via the erosion of growth-enhancing political institutions. In Syracuse, frequent regime changes, weak democracies and democratic leaders, and the recurring experience of tyranny may have meant that growth gains were captured by a small fraction of the population. In Rome, the experience of violence paradoxically led to a temporary rise in real incomes, which was not sustained after the transition to authoritarian rule.

While both Syracuse and Rome proved remarkably successful in dealing with the problem of violence and the recurrent experience of civil conflict, they both did so in ways that confined them to what political scientists Douglass North, John Wallis, and Barry Weingast (2009) term the "natural state equilibrium"—an equilibrium characterized by low growth captured by a small fraction of the population. In this framework, Syracuse embodies the model of the boom-and-bust natural state, where sharp rises in prosperity and equally sharp downturns led to low growth in the long run (cf. Morris 2009b). Rome, instead, is the prototype of the mature natural state—the wealthiest form of natural state.

In conclusion, I return to the question that motivated this section: were the conditions that enabled Syracuse and Rome to prosper despite outbreaks of civil conflict present in Athens? The answer is a resounding no. In Athens, the loss of an imperial network such as the one that funded the Roman civil conflict, the lack of alternative and readily available sources of revenue—which may have sustained Syracuse's recovery after the civil conflicts of the late fifth century— and the destructive impact of violence on the polis' territory and depressed economy rendered the civil conflict of the year 404/403 a powerful threat to the polis' growth potential, if not to its very existence. Had the civil conflict led to a cycle of instability, as in Syracuse in the mid-fourth century, Athens would have likely experienced no significant growth in the subsequent period. Returning stability to the polis after the late fifth-century crisis was key to Athenian recovery, but the fact that Athens did not establish growth-inhibiting political institutions may have been equally crucial. In the next section, I further elaborate on this point.

5.2. Resources, Regime, and Growth: Athens and Piraeus

Athens did well in the fourth century. As noted in previous chapters, the polis' prosperity in this period matched the levels reached during the heyday of empire. Would Athens have done equally well under a different constitutional arrangement?

To answer this question, we must begin by identifying the constitutional options at Athens' disposal. First, because kingship and tyranny had disappeared from the mainland by the end of the sixth century, it is unlikely that forms of sole rulership would have emerged in fourth-century Athens.[29] Second, because

29. Kings disappeared after the collapse of Mycenean civilization in the twelfth century (on Mycenean kingship: Renfrew 1985; on Dark Age kingship: Mazarakis-Ainian 1997), and tyrants disappeared by the end of the sixth century (cf. ch. 1). An obvious exception is the Spartan double kingship, which was however, by definition, not sole rulership. Simonton (2017: 3–9)

the democrats had prevailed over the supporters of the Thirty in the civil war, they could have pushed for a more "radical" form of democracy—for example, they could have restored, unchanged, the structure of the fifth-century democracy. But if the Athenians had simply reestablished the previous structure, I suggest, it is unlikely that Athens could have prospered in the fourth century. The Sicilian expedition triggered a profound loss of trust toward the democracy among both masses and elites (as I showed in chapter 2). After the persecutions of the Thirty, Athens also lost the goodwill of the noncitizen population (as I showed in chapter 4). Unable to credibly commit to policies that protected the rights of elites as well as noncitizens, Athens would have lacked both political stability and economic resources (perhaps, under these conditions Athens would have looked a lot like Syracuse, but without Syracuse's natural advantage in land).

But let us consider for a moment the possibility that the oligarchs had won the civil conflict of the year 404/403. What would Athens' growth potential have been under an oligarchy? There is no reason to believe that regime type per se determines the possibility or even the rate of growth. During the approximately five hundred years of Greek efflorescence (800 to 300) a number of poleis were ruled by autocratic (i.e., oligarchic) governments. Although we lack robust data, it seems clear that both oligarchic and democratic poleis grew during this period (Ober 2008: 47).[30]

To structure the analysis, I turn to the vast literature in political economy that seeks to assess the relationship between democracy and growth. Early approaches, stimulated by the so-called second wave of democratization after World War II, found a positive impact of economic growth on democracy. In particular, modernization theorists (Lipset 1959; Huntington 1968) argued that democracy is more sustainable when economic growth enables the creation of a strong middle class. The last two decades have seen a burst of empirical

---

distinguishes between *oligarchia* as a classical phenomenon and archaic elite-led regimes. In the course of the classical period, and particularly from the fourth-century onward, democracy becomes predominant (Teegarden 2014: 2, 223).

30. Simonton's (2017) excellent study of oligarchy does not cover economic structures, but see Salmon (1984) on Corinth. A separate but important question concerns the differential impact of growth on the population's welfare, which, almost by definition, would have been greater in democracies than in oligarchies. Oligarchies were more prone to concentrate wealth in the hands of a few leading individuals or families (as in Rome or tyrannical Syracuse). Democracies tended to distribute the proceeds of growth more broadly across the population (as in democratic Syracuse and Athens). The argument that I develop in this section, however, does not engage with these important questions of redistribution and citizen welfare.

work, spurred by Przeworski et al.'s (2000) finding that modernization, as measured by wealth, has no impact on a country's probability of democratizing.
Critical to this new generation of studies is the sister question: does democracy cause economic growth? Until the mid-2000s, the consensus view was
that democracy has a negative or no impact on growth (Barro 1997; for an
overview of the literature: Gerring et al. 2005). But in recent years, a series of
important studies has sought to show instead that democracy positively affects growth (e.g., Acemoglu et al. 2014). However, taken as a whole, the literature has reached no consensus (Knutsen 2012).

This literature nonetheless provides two useful guidelines for the present
investigation. First, assessing the relationship between democracy and growth
requires identifying the channels through which democracy (or some aspects
thereof) affects growth. Critical variables include institutions protecting property rights, investment, (a degree of) state autonomy, and checks on predatory
behavior (Przeworski and Limongi 1993), but also institutions fostering political stability (Feng 2003) and the accumulation of human capital (Tavares and
Wacziarg 2001; Baum and Lake 2003; Doucouliagos and Ulubaşoğlu 2008).
Throughout this book, I showed that the new Athenian constitution paid a
great deal of attention to these institutions.

The second insight, which I exploit in this section, comes from a spinoff of
the research on democracy and growth: the so-called "resource curse" literature. This literature developed from the observation that countries with conspicuous natural resources—especially oil—fail to grow more rapidly than
those without such resources (Sachs and Warner 1995; 2001). The literature later
morphed into the empirical assessment of whether natural resource wealth fuels
authoritarianism (Ross 2001; 2015; contra Haber and Menaldo 2011). For the
purposes of this section, I draw on the literature's basic intuition—which was
perhaps first articulated by the Greek historian Herodotus (9.122.3–4): the relationship between regime type and economic development must take into
account exogenous constraints on growth and, particularly, the sources of a
country's prosperity.

To understand the relationship between regime and growth in fourth-
century Athens, then, we must begin by assessing the potential sources of
Athens' prosperity. A comparison with the fifth century helps identify the available options. As I mentioned in chapter 1, in the fifth century Athens could
count on the revenue accruing from the empire (both tribute and rents), indirect taxes from Piraeus and the proceeds of the exploitation of the Laurion
silver mines. After Athens' defeat in the Peloponnesian War, revenues from the
empire were no longer an option. The mines at Laurion took a hit during
the last phase of the Peloponnesian War, when they were shut down due to

the Spartan occupation of military strongholds in Attica. However, as I documented in chapter 4, the mines probably resumed operations soon after the civil conflict (Kroll 2011: 240–41). If the mines contributed to the Athenian economy under the democracy, there is no reason to doubt that they would have contributed to Athens' economy under an oligarchy.[31]

What about Piraeus? In the fifth century, Piraeus was critical to the Athenian economy. The harbor not only generated substantial revenues from indirect taxes on trade, but it was also central to Athens' grain supply. Given Attica's limited carrying capacity, imports of grain were necessary to feed the population.[32] Without Piraeus, importing grain into Athens would have been either exceedingly costly, if done via land, or much costlier if Athens had relied on the harbor of Phaleron (which could not be easily protected), as the city had done in the archaic period before the population boomed (see appendix A).

Because Piraeus played such a prominent role in the fifth-century economy, previous scholarship has variously attributed Athens' recovery from the late fifth-century crisis to the mere existence of Piraeus. Robert Garland (1987) emphasized the contribution of the harbor to the polis' naval supremacy in the fifth century, both as a military base and as a commercial center. Garland then simply assumed that Piraeus continued to contribute to Athens' success in the fourth century, as it did in the fifth. Moshe Amit (1965) has put forth a more compelling version of this type of path-dependent explanation. In the absence of "definite evidence on the factors which permitted the continuation of [Athenian] prosperity," Amit suggests that Piraeus fostered prosperity through four mechanisms (1965: 140). First, the construction, in the fifth century, of the material basis of trade, such as installations of the harbor and the Emporium. Second, the prosperity of the city and its role in attracting rich foreigners. Third, the successful crippling of Athens' competitors. Fourth, Athenian reputation, or what may be termed the owl-effect—i.e., the notion that Piraeus, like the popular Athenian coinage, was something that traders grew accustomed to and were unwilling to change.[33] In assessing the role of Piraeus in the recovery of Athens, therefore, a story can be told that explains the prominence of Piraeus

31. I return to this point in the conclusion to this section, where I try to quantify the potential contribution of the silver mines to a counterfactual oligarchic Athens.

32. For Garnsey (1988: 104), "Attica was capable of feeding 120,000–150,000 people." In the classical period, Athens may have seen such low population levels only in the immediate aftermath of the Peloponnesian War. For Garnsey (ibid. ch. 7), permanent grain imports were not necessary until well into the fifth century. For Morris (2005: 13), permanent imports were necessary by 500, but local production remained more important until the Peloponnesian War. By the mid-fourth century, as Demosthenes (20.31–32) suggests, imports probably mattered more than local production.

33. I will come back to these four mechanisms in the conclusion to this section.

in the fourth century as a mere extension of its prominence in the fifth, and that interprets Athens' fast recovery from the sociopolitical and economic crisis of the late fifth century simply as a function of the success of Piraeus in the fifth century.

But Piraeus, like Athens, suffered conspicuous losses in the last decade of the fifth century. First, Piraeus' rise in the fifth century depended at least in part on the economy of coercion that revolved around the Athenian empire. An inscription dated to ca. the year 430 granting the people of Methone in Macedonia the right to import grain from Byzantium suggests that, at the height of the Athenian empire, Athens' allies were *required* to sail to Piraeus or to other Athenian depots in the Aegean in order to buy grain as well as, presumably, other commodities (Garland 1987: 87; Amit 1965: 133; cf. Panagos 1968). When Athens lost the Peloponnesian War, the empire ceased to exist and with it, the structure of coercion that had made Piraeus the primary Aegean entrepôt. Second, in the late fifth century, the infrastructure of the harbor was severely damaged. The terms of the peace treaty deprived the harbor of its walls and ships. Moreover, the Thirty further damaged the infrastructure of the port by auctioning off for destruction its costly shipsheds, and by persecuting and killing Piraeus' manpower, especially foreigners and metics. Third, the civil conflict—which was fought primarily *in* Piraeus—would have provided a strong incentive for those lucky to escape the Thirty's persecutions to relocate elsewhere. It is unlikely that traders would have kept coming to Piraeus in the fourth century by choice if the harbor had provided no facilities, or if they thought that they would be cheated, robbed, or killed. As a result, we cannot simply assume that Piraeus' contribution to Athens' economy would have carried over, unaffected, from the fifth to the fourth century.

In this section, I take stock of path-dependent arguments. I show that Piraeus enjoyed a favorable geographic location, but that geography per se cannot explain Piraeus' success in the fifth century or at any point thereafter.[34] In fact, if Piraeus benefited from its natural endowments, the harbor's development and subsequent fortunes depended on conspicuous infrastructural investments. Moreover, critical to the harbor's success was the type of management it was subject to. I then show that, had Athens been ruled by an oligarchy, Piraeus' potential would not have been fully tapped. I conclude by comparing Athens' growth under the democracy with a counterfactual reconstruction of Athens' growth under an oligarchic government. The comparison reveals that had Athens been ruled by an oligarchy, growth would have been significantly slower.

34. In sections 5.2.a and 5.2.b, I summarize the conclusions of two extensive investigations into Piraeus' geography and long-term history. I report the full analyses in two appendixes at the end of the book.

5.2.a. Piraeus' Geography

Ancient commentators repeatedly point out that Piraeus enjoyed an exceptionally privileged geographic location in the Aegean (Thuc. 1.93.3; Isoc. 15.307; Plut. *Them*. 19.2). Their remarks find support in geomorphologic, oceanographic, and meteorological evidence. But geography alone cannot explain Piraeus' success for two reasons. First, Piraeus lacked an obvious natural advantage vis-à-vis its rivals—namely, the ports of Aegina, Megara, and Corinth. Second, until the 490s, Piraeus was an insalubrious marsh. Therefore, geography may have been a necessary, but not a sufficient condition for Piraeus' success during the classical period.[35]

5.2.A.I. AEGEAN NAVIGATION

In order to identify favorable conditions for navigation in the Aegean, I draw on Jamie Morton's (2001) study of the role of the physical environment in ancient Greek seafaring.

As shown in figure 5.1, the interaction of geomorphologic, oceanographic, and meteorological factors created a highly fragmented coastline that presented ancient mariners with many obstacles to navigation. The analysis identifies the Euboian Sound and the Saronic Gulf as sweet spots of Aegean navigation, confirming the existence of a strong link between a city-state's maritime proficiency and its geographic location. In fact, first- and second-generation Greek maritime powers—namely, Chalcis and Eretria (perhaps even Lefkandi), as well as Athens, Aegina, Megara, and Corinth—were all located in these sweet spots.

5.2.A.II. PIRAEUS' RIVALS

Did Piraeus enjoy a natural advantage over the harbors of Athens' sixth-century Saronic rivals, Aegina, Corinth, and Megara? For the purposes of this investigation, I define a good harbor as a harbor that is 1) easy to reach and 2) easy to defend. A comparative analysis of the early development of these cities' ports reveals that Piraeus may have enjoyed a small advantage over Corinth and Aegina, but not over Megara.

A tiny island with a barren territory, Aegina took advantage very early on of her privileged position in the middle of the Saronic Gulf. However, the early

---

35. In this section, I maintain the transliteration of Greek places as they appear in the references I use in appendix A.

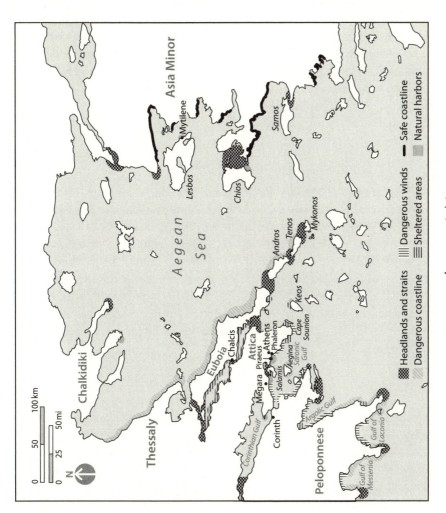

FIGURE 5.1. Aegean constraints.

association of the island with piracy, her rugged coastline, and the dangers to navigation associated with it, suggest that Aegina's advantage may have depended on privileging defense over accessibility, and predation over trade. Corinth is located in a favorable position between the Corinthian and the Saronic Gulfs. However, the geography of the region and the location of the city's harbors suggest that the polis may have had easier access to the former than to the latter. Like Corinth, Megara was one of the first Greek poleis to send out colonies, particularly in the Propontis and in Sicily. Like Corinth, Megara enjoyed a strategic position between the Peloponnese and the rest of mainland Greece, and between the Corinthian and the Saronic Gulfs. Unlike Corinth, however, Megara was better situated on the shores of the Saronic Gulf. There, the harbors of Nisaia and Minoa, protected by the island of Salamis, enjoyed a particularly favorable (that is, both easily defensible and easily accessible) position.

5.2.A.III. PIRAEUS' LATE DEVELOPMENT

Was Piraeus critical to Athens' success in the fight against Megara for Saronic supremacy? When Athens crushed Megara in the archaic period, Piraeus was an insalubrious marsh. Down to the 490s, Athens made do with another port: the beach landing of Phaleron, located just southeast of Piraeus. Until then, the fact that Piraeus was located further away from Athens than Phaleron, and the fact that the area around Piraeus was not fit for construction may have deterred the Athenians from developing it. It was probably only when Athens' population began to swell and the city became a major market that needed constant food imports that Piraeus' advantages began to outweigh its shortcomings.[36]

––––––

The four major maritime powers of the sixth century were all located around the coasts of the Saronic Gulf. The gulf provided not only Athens, but also its rivals, with the minimal conditions for maritime development—that is, a safe environment for navigation. If Piraeus' location may have enjoyed some advantage over the harbors of Athens' Saronic rivals (particularly Corinth and Aegina), its development as a port entailed conspicuous investments, as the area was semi-detached from the mainland. By the time Cimon "dumped vast

36. By the same token, Piraeus was a much better location to construct facilities necessary for a substantial navy than the long beach of Phaleron.

quantities of rubble and heavy stones into the swamps" (Plut. *Cim.* 13.7; trans. Perrin 1914), Athens had already defeated the only competitor endowed with similar natural advantages: Megara.

Piraeus, then, was not as remarkable in its natural endowments as the ancient Athenian sources would have us believe. Yet, it is indisputable that Athens' expansion in the fifth century depended in part on Piraeus—a Piraeus that was solidly connected to the mainland, walled, and endowed with state-of-the-art commercial and military facilities.[37] The role of human agency rather than, or at least in addition to, geography per se informed Piraeus' early successes as well as, as we will see, its subsequent fortunes.[38]

5.2.b. Piraeus' History

The combination of favorable geography and state-of-the-art infrastructure gave Piraeus an edge over its competitors in the fifth century. But was this sufficient to ensure Piraeus' success beyond the fifth century? In this section, I turn to an investigation of Athens' and Piraeus' long-term history, from the early fifth century to the twentieth century CE. I show that, throughout this period, the prominence of Piraeus closely mirrored that of Athens: when Athens flourished, so did Piraeus; when the city declined, Piraeus followed suit.[39] I then zoom in on the Macedonian takeover of Piraeus to show that the harbor's success critically depended on the type of management it was subject to.

37. Including, most notably, the Long Walls, built and later extended by Themistocles and Pericles.

38. Had there not been a potentially great harbor in Piraeus, we might counterfactually speculate, Athens would have made do with Phaleron in the fifth century (and the fact that Athens extended the Long Walls to include Phaleron suggests that it remained a more important location than we usually assume). Probably, though, using Phaleron instead of Piraeus would have created a bottleneck for Athenian growth.

39. The analysis relies on highly heterogeneous sources. For the classical period we can quantify both Athens' and Piraeus' performance. For Athens' performance, I rely on Ober's proxies for Athenian state capacity as measured by aggregate military activity, public building, and domestic programs (2008: ch. 2). For Piraeus' performance, I collected proxies based on the definition of "good harbor" provided above. These include: 1) population (both citizens and metics); 2) security (walls); 3) capacity (warships); and 4) volume of trade (import taxes). For the subsequent periods, quantifiable evidence is much harder to come by. I therefore largely employ qualitative evidence to investigate the performance of Athens and Piraeus during their post-classical history.

5.2.B.I. PIRAEUS' LONG-TERM HISTORY

In the classical period, Athens and Piraeus followed broadly similar paths. Their prosperity peaked in the 430s and declined throughout the rest of the fifth century, until Athens' defeat in the Peloponnesian War. The process of recovery proceeded steadily throughout the first half of the fourth century, peaking again in the 330s. After the classical period, both Piraeus and Athens suffered a steady decline. In Hellenistic and Roman times such decline was punctuated by temporary and ephemeral revivals. After the fourth century CE, Athens and Piraeus almost completely disappear from the records, only to resurface in the early nineteenth century when Greece gained independence from Ottoman rule. After independence, when Athens was made capital of the new Greek state, Piraeus became once again one of the principal seaports of the Mediterranean.

The evidence thus suggests that the close relationship between Athens and Piraeus in the classical period was not an accident of history, but an instance of an otherwise consistent pattern. In the absence of (or in the context of a limited role played by) Athens, Piraeus became irrelevant. Conversely, in times of prosperity for the polis, the harbor flourished. The inability of Piraeus to outlast, or to significantly diverge in its path from Athens prompts another question: could Piraeus have prospered under the control of other poleis? To answer this question, I explore the events surrounding the Macedonian takeover of Athens and Piraeus.

5.2.B.II. PIRAEUS UNDER MACEDON

In the summer of the year 322, Athens was defeated in the Battles of Amorgos and Crannon. The polis' unconditional surrender led to the establishment of a Macedonian garrison in Piraeus and to the replacement of the democracy with an oligarchy in which the franchise was limited to nine thousand citizens. The Macedonian conquest of Athens did not mean outright occupation. Instead, according to Garland (1987: 45; cf. Amit 1965: 141–44), Macedon "found it both militarily convenient and politically expedient to control Athens . . . by installing a garrison on Mounichia Hill [that is, in Piraeus]." But under Macedonian control, Piraeus was transformed from the hub of Aegean commerce into a center for shipbuilding and a naval base. The Macedonians therefore did not destroy Piraeus' walls and fleet, as the Spartans had done at the end of the Peloponnesian War. Instead, they exploited the infrastructure of Piraeus for their own needs. As a result, throughout the Hellenistic period, Piraeus remained active as a port, but its lack of independence, paired with its role as a naval base rather than as a commercial center, contributed to the harbor's decline.[40] As Piraeus progressively fell into obscurity, Rhodes rose to become the primary commercial hub in the Aegean.

The Macedonian takeover of Piraeus thus suggests that the critical variable determining Piraeus' prosperity or decline was not the harbor's mere survival, but the type of management it was subject to.

————

The evidence discussed so far yields two results. First, explanations of Athens' post-war recovery that center around the role of Piraeus must move beyond path-dependent arguments, as there was nothing intrinsic to Piraeus that would have guaranteed its success in the fourth century. Second, Piraeus could have contributed to Athenian prosperity in the aftermath of war only if Athens' government had been willing and able to a) invest in the reconstruction of Piraeus' infrastructure, and b) devise a new, post-imperial commercial strategy to incentivize, rather than coerce, merchants to trade in Piraeus. Could an oligarchic government have performed these tasks?

5.2.c. Is the Oligarchic Ship Seaworthy?

The relationship between Athens' oligarchs (and oligarchic sympathizers) with Piraeus and the sea was choppy. Antidemocratic writers frequently expressed uneasiness, if not open hostility, toward the harbor and its people.

Traditionally, the sea was closely connected with Athens' democracy. The Old Oligarch (1.2) captures the essence of this connection sharply, if caustically.

> In the first place, I maintain, it is only just that the poorer classes and the people of Athens should be better off than the men of birth and wealth, seeing that it is the people who man the fleet, and put around the city her girdle of power. The steersman, the boatswain, the commandant, the lookout-man at the prow, the shipwright—these are the ones who engird the city with power rather than her heavy infantry and men of birth and quality. This being the case, it seems only just that offices of state should be thrown open to everyone both in the ballot and the show of hands, and that the right of speech should belong to anyone who likes, without restriction.

40. Another important factor, but one harder to measure, is the profound geopolitical shift brought about by Alexander's conquests. I discuss this shift in appendix B.

The key to understanding Athens' democracy, the Old Oligarch tells us, is the navy. If sailors protect the city, then "it is only just" that they should govern it. As Gary Cox, Douglass North, and Barry Weingast (2012) will put it over two thousand years later, a stable polity distributes political and economic power proportionally to actors endowed with violence potential. The oddity, in Athens, is that violence potential was distributed among the many, rather than the few.

Plato's opinions on the matter are less nuanced. In the *Laws* (705a; trans. Cooper 1997) he demurs,

> for a country to have the sea nearby is pleasant enough for the purpose of everyday life, but in fact it is a "salty-sharp and bitter neighbor" in more senses than one. It fills the land with wholesaling and retailing, breeds shifty and deceitful habits in a man's soul, and makes the citizens distrustful and hostile.

The sea, for Plato, corrupts. For this reason, the ideal city should be built eighty stadia from the sea (Pl. *Laws* 704b)—a distance that is roughly double as that between Athens and Piraeus (von Reden 1995: 27).

Reiterating the connection between the power of the people and Athens' navy, Plutarch tells a story that powerfully captures oligarchic hostility towards the sea (*Them.* 19. 2–4; trans. adapted from Perrin 1914).

> Themistocles equipped the Piraeus, because he had noticed the favorable shape of its harbors, and wished to attach the whole city to the sea . . . And so it was that he increased the privileges of the common people as against the nobles, and filled them with boldness, since the controlling power came now in the hands of skippers and boatswains and pilots. Therefore also the stand on the Pnyx, which had stood so as to look off towards the sea, was afterwards turned by the thirty tyrants so as to look inland, because they thought that maritime empire was the mother of democracy, and that oligarchy was less distasteful to tillers of the soil.

Plutarch's story about the Thirty Tyrants turning the stand on the Pnyx to face the countryside, rather than the sea, has been questioned on various grounds. Yet, as Shear suggests, "archeological excavation has shown that the meeting place of the *ekklesia* was rebuilt at just this time and the orientation of the structure was reversed" (Shear 2011: 177–78).

When the Thirty rose to power, oligarchic hostility toward Piraeus and the sea turned destructive.[41] During their reign, the Thirty committed three acts

---

41. In what follows, I concentrate primarily on the rule of the Thirty in 404/403. On the relationship between the Four Hundred and Piraeus: von Reden (1995: 29); Garland (1987:

that are best understood as parts of a coherent attempt to cripple Piraeus: they auctioned off for destruction Piraeus' shipsheds, destroyed a series of proxeny decrees, and persecuted wealthy metics.

First, the Thirty auctioned off for destruction Piraeus' shipsheds (Isoc. 7.66). As Garland explains (1987: 96), "ranked by Demosthenes (22.76) alongside the Parthenon, the Propylaia and the Stoas as among the finest architectural achievements of the fifth-century democracy, the Periclean shipsheds allegedly cost 1000 T to build (Isoc. 7.66). Their destruction by the Thirty was a calculated act of sabotage intended to scupper Athens' navy, since triremes required a thorough overhauling in dry docks during the six winter months that they were not on active service." But sabotage does not do justice to the significance of the act. In fact, the Thirty were broke, but shipyards that cost 1,000 T to build were auctioned off for only three talents in order to be destroyed.[42]

Second, the Thirty destroyed a number of proxeny decrees—arrangements whereby a foreigner was recognized as a public guest of a state on account of services performed for the benefits of the state's citizens (on *proxenia*: Mack 2015; cf. chapter 4). Proxeny decrees embodied the city's commitment to foreigners. As Culasso Gastaldi (2004) noted, the destruction of the proxeny decrees was part of a broader process of retrenchment away from Piraeus and its connection with the fifth-century democracy.

Finally, the Thirty persecuted and expropriated Athens' wealthy metics (Xen. *Hell.* 2.3.21; cf. [Arist.] *Ath.Pol.* 35.4):

> [The Thirty] put many people to death out of personal enmity, and many also for the sake of securing their property. One measure that they resolved upon, in order to get money to pay their guardsmen, was that each of their number should seize one of the metics residing in the city, and that they should put these men to death and confiscate their property.

Taken in isolation, the actions against metics may simply suggest that the Thirty were predatory rulers with a short-term horizon. However, if we consider the Thirty's treatment of metics alongside their treatment of Piraeus' shipsheds and proxeny decrees, a different picture emerges.

31–32). The limited information we have concerning the rule of the Five Thousand (in 410) does not allow me to reach any robust conclusions about their attitude towards Piraeus and the sea.

42. Whereas we lack direct evidence of the Thirty's destruction of commercial facilities, it seems reasonable to suppose, in line with the other evidence discussed so far, that they were either destroyed or allowed to decay.

Why did the Thirty seek to undermine, if not openly destroy the infrastructure and manpower of Piraeus, which could have provided much-needed revenue to their government? Widespread oligarchic hostility toward the sea provides the necessary background to contextualize the tyrants' actions. But the severity of these actions cannot be fully justified either as an instantiation of oligarchic hostility, or simply as the behavior of predatory rulers.

I suggest instead that the Thirty's actions against Piraeus are best viewed as a strategic move to remain in power. As political scientist Bruce Bueno de Mesquita (2003: 8–9) suggests, "every political leader faces the challenge of how to hold onto his or her job. The politics behind survival in office is . . . the essence of politics. The desire to survive motivates the selection of policies and the allocation of benefits; it shapes the selection of political institutions and the objectives of foreign policy; it influences the very evolution of political life." If the destruction of Piraeus damaged the oligarchs—preventing them from exploiting the harbor's resources—it damaged the democrats more. Without Piraeus, the Thirty could always expropriate those who still owned stuff in Athens, as they in fact did. The democrats, on the other hand, lacking the expropriation option and without Piraeus, had no alternative sources of revenue at their disposal.[43]

The Thirty's attack on the infrastructure and manpower of Piraeus, then, was a paroxystic reaction to a broadly felt hostility toward the harbor and its people expressed by antidemocratic writers and politicians throughout the classical period. But, perhaps more cogently, it was an instance of the logic of political survival—a calculated strategy to weaken the democratic opposition's political comeback by undermining their economic base.

The logic of political survival would have had consequences for the polis' prosperity. An oligarchic Athens faced two possible growth scenarios. First, in the absence of Piraeus, the oligarchy could have relied on alternative resources to boost growth, such as expropriations, financial support from Sparta or Persia, or the exploitation of other natural resources, for example the silver mines. However, whereas expropriations and foreign support were short-term

---

43. During the civil war, as soon as the democrats could, they took the high-risk/high payoff option of moving their base from Phyle, in the mountains far from the sea, to Piraeus. In line with the interpretation provided above, this move can be interpreted in terms of military strategy to reveal the democrats' willingness to mobilize the remaining population there. However, it seems also reasonable to assume that the occupation of Piraeus meant to signal that democratic victory would mean a recommitment to Piraeus—both to sea power and maritime commerce. Similarly, democratic opposition to the Four Hundred mobilized from Piraeus: Garland (1987: 32).

solutions, the mines also would have required conspicuous investments after a decade of disuse.[44] Had the oligarchs chosen the path of boosting Athens' silver exports, two major problems remained. First, how to import grain to feed the population. Second, how to import wood necessary to mining operations (Bresson 2016: 74).[45] In the absence of a powerful navy capable of fighting piracy and other threats to maritime commerce, Athenian oligarchs would have had to rely on some other state.

Second, the oligarchs could have restored Piraeus after quashing the democratic opposition. But if the oligarchs had waited too long, other harbors would have likely stepped into the vacuum created by Piraeus' absence, as Rhodes did after the Macedonian occupation of Athens in the third century. Moreover, under an oligarchy, Piraeus would have hardly become the trading center that it was in the fifth century (or in the fourth century under the restored democracy). A functioning Piraeus required the active participation of categories of people—namely, the Athenian lower classes and metics—that the oligarchs would have had a hard time credibly committing to, especially after the persecutions of the Thirty.

There are many moving pieces in a counterfactual reconstruction such as the one presented above. It is therefore not my goal to put the question of growth-*cum*-oligarchy in Athens to rest. However, if my reconstruction is plausible, then we might conclude that whereas oligarchy could have survived in a predatory, low-growth environment, high and sustained growth required a functioning Piraeus.

5.2.d. Conclusion

In this section, I tried to assess counterfactually how Athens would have fared under an oligarchic government. I argued that Athens' prosperity in the fourth century depended in meaningful ways on Piraeus because the harbor was

---

44. Expropriation is unlikely to be a sustaining wealth generating strategy anywhere, but especially in a porous sociopolitical environment like Hellas (Ober 2015a; Arcenas 2018), where people (especially noncitizens) can move fairly freely from one polis to another. As to foreign support, the Persian stance of funding Greek states to play them against one another (cf. ch. 4) suggests that the Persian would have continued to fund Athens only as long as it was in their interest. Sparta may have been a more generous donor, but supporting oligarchy at Athens may have soon proved to be a task beyond its purse.

45. Clearly, without Piraeus, Athens would not have been able to play host for the largest eastern Mediterranean market, which would have affected the volume of economic activity and the value of the city's exports.

critical to Athens' security, revenues, and grain supply. I put pressure on the argument that Piraeus' success would have simply carried over from the fifth century into the fourth. Piraeus was a fine harbor, located in a favorable geographic position. But geography per se cannot explain Piraeus' success, even in the fifth century.

Piraeus' prominence depended not only on geography, but also on additional factors. For Amit, these factors were the harbor's infrastructure, Athens' prosperity and its role in attracting rich foreigners, the absence of competitors, and finally the city's reputation. In this section, I showed that none of these factors survived intact the late fifth-century crisis. In terms of infrastructure, whatever the Athenians had built, the Peloponnesian War, the civil war, and the Thirty had largely destroyed. Rich foreigners had been persecuted and killed under the Thirty, and many fled the city.[46] The absence of competitors is an ex-post fallacy. In the year 403, it was perhaps less than obvious that Sparta, or Thebes, or Corinth would fail to take Athens' place as at the helm of Greece. If they didn't, it was due as much to Athens' quick recovery, as it was to her enemies' failure. Finally, had Athens not recovered, the owl would have yielded to more powerful coinages, as it did after Athens fell under Macedonian rule. The same, I suggest, goes for Piraeus.

Given the extent of the damage the harbor suffered in the late fifth century, a functioning Piraeus required major investments in infrastructure and institutional capacity. An oligarchic government would not have been able to invest in Piraeus as much as it was needed to return the harbor to a position of primacy in the Aegean.

But how much better did the democracy do, compared to a counterfactual oligarchy? In figure 5.2, I attempt to put some, admittedly impressionistic, numbers on a counterfactual oligarchic growth path and compare it with available evidence for Athens' fourth-century growth under the democracy. Given the nature of the evidence for both counterfactual and actual growth rates, figure 5.2 is meant to provide only a broad outline of Athenian performance in comparative perspective.

Data for Athenian growth under the democracy are proxied by Ober's data on Athens' General Income (2015a: 245; 2015b: 499).[47] I add a data point for the year 400, assuming that state income after the Peloponnesian War would have equaled state income after Chaeronea—that is, according to

---

46. Although we know from multiple sources that some stayed in Athens and fought alongside the democratic opposition to oust the Thirty (cf. ch. 4).

47. I do not include Ober's estimates for minting fees because they are only guesses.

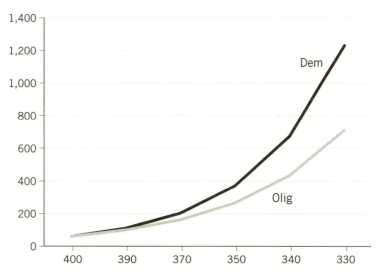

FIGURE 5.2. Athens' growth: democracy vs. oligarchy

Plutarch (*Mor.* 842F), sixty talents. For the 370s, 350s, 340s, and 330s, I employ Ober's numbers, assessing state income at 600 T; 130 T; 400 T; and 1,200 T, respectively.

Data for Athenian growth under a counterfactual oligarchy is also proxied by state income, and based on the following assumptions. A counterfactual fourth-century oligarchy would have relied primarily on the Laurion silver mines as a source of income. We lack direct evidence that would allow us to estimate how effectively an oligarchy would have exploited the mines because, when the oligarchic regimes of the Four Hundred and the Thirty took power in the last decade of the fifth century, the mines were shut down. However, there does not seem to be any compelling reason to suppose that an oligarchic government in the fourth century would have been hostile to mining in principle (as it would have been hostile to the sea and Piraeus). In addition to the mines, the oligarchs could have continued to fund their operations through expropriations or benefited from Persian (or Spartan) support, as the democracy did during the Corinthian War. These latter revenue streams would have fluctuated in ways that make an estimate exceedingly difficult. I speculate, perhaps generously, that from a low of 60 T in the year 400 (the same estimate that I used earlier for the democracy), state revenue would have risen quickly to 160 T (in the 390s). 160 T is the amount that, according to Crosby (1950), the mines yielded around the year 350, when Athens intensified their exploitation. From there, I assume that

Athens' growth under an oligarchy would have steadily risen. To approximate the rate of growth throughout the fourth century, I rely on Ober's (2008: 47) calculations of the relative capacity of Athens' highest-performing oligarchic neighbor: Corinth. Based on these calculations, an oligarchic Athens would have fared about 60% as well as democratic Athens did, which yields 720 T in the 330s.

Conclusion

HOW DID the Athenians build a stable, growth-enhancing constitution? In this book, I argued that the process of constitution building in Athens featured a series of steps. The first was the elaboration of a collective consensus on the principles of a new constitutional order. At the end of the fifth century, external pressures exacerbated underlying defects in the fifth-century democratic structure, causing its collapse. After the collapse, a series of democratic and oligarchic governments rose to power, but failed to return stability to an increasingly divided polis. As they reacted against the excesses of democracy and oligarchy, the Athenians collectively defined the minimal conditions that a governmental structure needed to display to command their consent. The consensus was enshrined in the notion of patrios politeia, which encompassed a series of critical elements. First, it established a connection between a desirable form of government and a shared past, whose features were essential to a shared future. These features were coherent enough to eliminate various alternatives— some, like divine kingship or one-man rule, more obvious than others, like dominion of one class or group over another. These features were also action-guiding. The consensus identified the body of Athens' laws, now made more coherent and publicly accessible, as a set of bright lines to guide behavior, and it elevated the courts as the authoritative body to interpret and modify such laws. The consensus on patrios politeia fostered stability against a background of civil war and violence because it was grounded on the notion of legality, and not on the unique legitimacy of the interests of one of the warring parties—masses or elites, democrats or oligarchs. Harkening back to the lawgiver Solon—the man who, standing among competing factions "as a wolf among dogs," (cf. chapter 1) had returned stability to the polis in the archaic period—the Athenian consensus struck a balance among diverging interests.

The second step was making the consensus self-enforcing through institutional reforms. The reforms addressed the pitfalls of the regimes that rose and fell during the tumultuous last decade of the fifth century. Against the fifth-century democracy's inability to credibly commit to policy, the Athenians introduced another legislative institution and new procedural rules to regulate lawmaking and legal change. Against the lawless behavior of the ruling oligarchs, the reforms defined personal and economic rights for all citizens, created robust institutional channels to enforce those rights, and bestowed the responsibility to protect them on all citizens.

The third step was to use the new constitution as a framework to negotiate the competing demands of social order and growth. Policy-making in the fourth century reveals the existence of a trade-off of inclusion in Athens' institutional development. On the one hand, the Athenians strove to protect the fragile balance of power between the interests of masses and elites by limiting access to political institutions. On the other hand, they sought to incentivize economic activity by extending access to economic, legal, and social institutions to selected categories of noncitizens, while giving them reasons to trust a constitutional system that made it very hard to revoke privileges on a whim.

Social scientists should pay attention to premodern case studies like Athens for three reasons. First, premodern case studies can contribute to theory building. My account of Athens' constitutional struggles, for example, stresses the role of consensus-building for constitutional stability, and the process of gradual and instrumental extension of institutional access as a pathway to political and economic development. Both processes are usually hard to flesh out in more complex institutional settings.

Second, premodern case studies offer a critical out-of-sample testing ground for modern theories. For example, the case of ancient Athens puts pressure on theories of institutional development that focus on state capacity (Hobbes 1994 [1651]; Weber 1965 [1919]; Tilly 1990; Morris 2014) or liberal institutions (Fukuyama 1992; 2011; 2014; Diamond 2008). Athens did not establish institutions associated with contemporary liberal democracy, such as free and fair elections in which most long-term adult residents could participate. Athens also did not establish institutions associated with the modern concept of rule of law. Finally, Athens did not develop state institutions that kept citizens "in awe," monopolizing the legitimate use of violence (Carugati, Ober, and Weingast 2019). And yet, the polis sustained high levels of growth (for premodern standards) and a cohesive nonauthoritarian government, while providing a sizeable basket of social goods to a large portion of the population. Athens, then, looks fairly developed in historical context. But the polis' development rested on institutions that differed remarkably from those of contemporary countries. Consider, for example, the concept of rule of law. As we saw in chapter 2, Athens' constitutional reforms measure well against thick definitions of rule of law that emphasize aspects like generality, publicity, clarity, and general applicability (e.g. Fuller 1964; World Justice Project). But the Athenian rule of law did not feature independent judiciaries, judicial precedent, or a police force. Similarly, although the Athenian constitution was an unwritten set of rules enforced collectively by laypeople, it was nonetheless successful in promoting long-term stability.

Third, the payoff of elevating premodern case studies as comparative evidence on a par with modern cases is quite large for both development theorists and practitioners. Without developing strongly centralized state institutions or liberal values, Athens was a large participatory democracy capable of providing important social goods—for example, legality, order, stability, security of person and property, and fair distribution of material goods—to both citizens and (some) noncitizens. If these goods represent a meaningful level of development, then we must strive to articulate a more robust theory of institutional development capable of explaining premodern, as well as modern, cases. Moreover, because institution building in the real world relies on inadequate theories, this book's findings have implications for development practitioners as well. In particular, the story of Athens suggests that institution-building efforts need not be solely concerned with centralized state institutions and ever more complex institutional and constitutional arrangements. In sum, premodern case studies provide an invaluable and largely untapped body of empirical evidence to better understand the range of institutional structures capable of sustaining valuable social goods that we normally associate uniquely with contemporary Western institutions.

But can we compare modern and premodern societies without introducing anachronisms that invalidate the results? First, Athens was awfully small compared to modern countries. Second, its inhabitants were homogeneous in terms of language, culture, and religion. Third, Athens' political and economic development coexisted with exclusionary practices—including slavery and the exclusion of women from the political process. I discuss each issue in turn.

Athens was certainly small compared to most contemporary nations.[1] With a population of approximately 250,000 people and a territory of around 2500 square kilometers, the polis was a bit less populous than the pacific island of Vanuatu and a bit smaller than the European state of Luxembourg. However, Athens was also far too large to fit the model of a face-to-face society—a society where individuals know one another intimately and interact frequently and closely (Ober 1989a; contra Finley 1973a). Moreover, the Athenians had no

---

1. In the Hobbesian/Olsonian tradition, size introduces problems of collective action that are answered, ordinarily, through authority relations (Olson 1965). The Greek world does not fit this paradigm (Ober 2015a).

means or technology to communicate at a distance. Therefore, in Athens, as in modern countries, social cooperation required formal institutional structures to bridge the distance, geographic as well as epistemic, among actors.[2]

Second, for modern standards, Athens was an extremely homogeneous society. In fact, the Athenians shared language, culture, and religion with one another, and with many other Greeks. Since the end of World War II, the political economy of development has identified ethnicity and religion among the primary drivers of civil conflict and instability (but see the landmark work of Fearon and Laitin 2003).[3] But the fact that Athenian society was homogeneous in these respects does not mean that sources of conflict were absent. In fact, in Athens, as elsewhere in Greece, other cleavages—such as socioeconomic inequality and differing views of how best to govern a society—were primary drivers of unrest and civil war.

Last but not least, I must address the issues of exclusion and exploitation. In 1960, M. I. Finley asked if Greek civilization was based on slave labor and found that it was. This answer was part of Finley's influential but now outdated theory of the Greek economy as radically embedded in social structures that thwarted innovation, investment, entrepreneurship, and ultimately growth. Because one important part of Finley's argument (economic stagnation) has been refuted, other components stand on shakier ground. The question of whether the Greek economy relied on exploitative practices (and to what extent it did) awaits a new theory of ancient-slavery-as-exploitation that is compatible with the finding of sustained growth. This task goes well beyond the scope of this book. However, we know that slavery in Athens was not a monolithic institution: some slaves enjoyed privileges not warranted by their social condition, while others were brutally exploited.[4]

---

2. By "epistemic distance" I mean that, in non-face-to-face societies, people do not know enough about each other to build trust and overcome collective action problems in the absence of formal institutions.

3. Other important work challenges ethnicity as the critical variable in decisions about taxation (Kasara 2007) and collective action (Habyarimana et al. 2007), and even puts pressure on the ability of individuals to correctly ascribe ethnicity (Habyarimana et al. 2005).

4. As I mentioned in chapter 4, economic activity in labor-intensive sectors such as mining relied heavily on slave labor. However, in other areas of the economy, exploitation was much less pervasive. Moreover, some categories of Athenian slaves performing economically productive or administrative functions enjoyed forms of freedom, economic independence, and protections not warranted by their social condition. These include *chōris oikountes*, slave bankers, and publicly owned slaves (Jacob 1928; Todd 1993; E. Cohen 1992; Hunter 2006; Kamen 2013; Ismard 2015).

Beside slavery, other forms of exclusion also stand out. Most notably, the right to participate in politics was restricted to adult male citizens. Women, children, resident aliens, and foreigners all lived under a government that they neither consented to, nor shaped. The issue of the exclusion of women from political as well as economic rights cannot be brushed aside as an essential feature of a premodern society. In fact, the reflection of Athenian philosophers (notably, Plato in the *Republic*) and the practice of other Greek states (notably, Sparta's extension of economic rights to women) suggest that the exclusion of women was not part of the *zeitgeist*, but a societal choice. But this choice, I argue, is similar to the choice of granting privileges to some but not other slaves, or the choice of excluding some but not all noncitizens from economic, legal, and social institutions. These choices are all instances of trade-offs of inclusion emerging from attempts to square conflicting demands without undermining the bases of social cooperation. Instead of an insurmountable obstacle to comparison, then, these forms of exclusion, and the degrees to which they were or were not overcome, can shed much needed light on what it takes to build inclusive institutions.

In what follows, I distill some preliminary lessons from the Athenian constitution-making process. I began, and I conclude, with the case of Myanmar. The victory of Aung San Suu Kyi's National League for Democracy in the 2015 election marked an important step toward peace and democratization in Myanmar. Yet, both the transition and the pacification of the country hang in the balance. Most readers will be familiar with the events surrounding the Rohingya crisis—and the opprobrium that such events generated the world over. But the Rohingya crisis is one of many obstacles on Myanmar's road to peace and stability. I argued in the introduction that another one of these obstacles is the 2008 constitution, because of the power that it bestows on Myanmar's armed forces, and because of the absence of a meaningful engagement with ethnic demands.

Constitutional reforms are high on Aung San Suu Kyi's agenda—but direct action has proved ineffective (for example, a constitutional referendum was scheduled for May 2015, but it was never held). Negotiations have since then taken the form of a political dialogue. So far, three much-publicized "21st Century Panglong" conferences were held in August 2016, May 2017, and July 2018. By appealing to the spirit of Panglong, Aung San Suu Kyi is seeking to strengthen the legitimacy of the negotiation process and her role in it. But both the specific focus of the reforms (most notably, the provision that prevents Aung San Suu Kyi from becoming president) and the choice of the legislator of the past (Aung San, whose record with the ethnic minorities was at best mixed) hardly suggest a commitment to a process that can meaningfully account for the interests of all parties.

The case of Athens suggests that for Myanmar to achieve a lasting peace more steps will need to be taken. First, an agreement must be reached on the basic principles that are to guide the peace process and the reforms. There is some sense, at least in words (in both the Nationwide Ceasefire Agreement and the Framework for Political Dialogue), that the actors are willing to respect a general principle of legality, at least when it comes to choosing the path of peaceful negotiation over violence. Moreover, there is also some sense that the actors are willing to commit to an inclusive process of negotiation, one that meaningfully considers the interests of relevant parties—the NLD, the Tatmadaw, and the ethnic minorities. Second, and perhaps most urgently, institutions must be created to make the commitment to respecting those principles credible. Only when an institutional structure that makes it very costly for all actors to renege is established can the parties hope to conduct effective negotiation on tough constitutional issues, like federalism and full civilian control of the government. Productive negotiation on these issues, the case of Athens further suggests, will require defining tradeoffs of inclusion to increase well-being without jeopardizing the fragile balance of power among the groups. Key to an effective constitutional reform process will be to identify which package of goods each party is bringing to the negotiation table, and to trade access to those goods, as the Athenians once did, to make all parties well off.

If we discount the evidence from the premodern world, we forfeit the chance to learn from groups that faced many of the challenges that we still face today and whose experience reminds us that there is no single road to building flourishing societies.

Piraeus' Geography

WAS PIRAEUS' success in the fifth century a product of its natural endowments?[1] Given the high costs that the transport of goods over land entails, access to the sea constituted an advantage for any polis. But in the archaic and classical period, the vast majority of the settlements were situated either on islands or along (or in the vicinity of) the coast (Hansen and Nielsen 2004; Ober 2015a). Therefore, access to the sea per se represented a rather small advantage for any individual polis. Yet, the physical environment contributed to rendering some places on the Greek coastline more hospitable than others, shaping the poleis' incentives to transform particular areas into port facilities.

In section A.1, I analyze topographic, oceanographic, and meteorological conditions in the Aegean and show that the Saronic Gulf was a natural sweet spot for navigation. In section A.2, I compare Piraeus with the harbors of Athens' Saronic rivals—Aegina, Corinth, and Megara—and suggest that Piraeus enjoyed some advantage only over Aegina and Corinth, but not over Megara. In section A.3, I reconstruct the early history of Piraeus, which reveals that until the early classical period (ca. 490s), Piraeus was a marshy area unfit for construction and human habitation.

A.1. Aegean Navigation

In his 2001 study of the role of the physical environment in ancient Greek seafaring, Jamie Morton illustrates how interactions between the topography of the coastline, the patterns of winds and currents, and the prevailing

1. Piraeus is a natural deep-water port, but ancient ships did not require deep-water ports: Pomey (2011).

meteorological conditions created a series of threats to ancient mariners—from surging headlands to windy straits.[2]

Headlands were particularly dangerous due to the deep faulting of the Greek coastline.[3] The irregular seabed punctuated by submerged ridges and sea-washed rocks interfered with wind and current patterns to produce steep and unpredictable waves.[4] Such conditions were particularly challenging around promontories with a NW-SE alignment—notably, in the southern Peloponnese (Akritas, Tainaron, and Malea) and in Chalkidiki (particularly around the peninsula of Mt. Athos). Sections of the coast facing the opposite directions (NE or SW) tended to present instead more uniform fronts, resulting in a "relatively straight, cliff-bound and almost harborless" coastline (Morton 2001: 16)—notably, the flanks of the major promontories of the Peloponnese, the coasts of Thessaly, and the coasts of eastern Euboia.

Eroded areas of the coastline created a similar threat. Where "outcrops of hard durable rock had resisted erosion while the softer rock around them had been worn back along a retreating shoreline" (ibid. 71), the seabed was characterized by submerged rocks and shallow reefs. Good examples of such an eroded coastline were the island of Aegina, and the so-called Hollows of Euboia (on the island's southeastern coast). On the west coast of the Aegean, the dangers from offshore rocks and reefs were compounded by winds (especially the Etesians, the strong summer winds, blowing NE-SW) and currents. On the east coast of the Aegean, the dangers from offshore rocks were as great, but the favorable currents, paired with the different alignment of the promontories (E-W), made coastal navigation relatively safer.

Straits constituted another source of hazard for ancient mariners due to the strength and fluctuations of the currents, the strength of the winds, the number and force of squalls, and the presence of submerged or awash rocks. Examples of dangerous straits are the Hellespont/Bosporos breach; the entrance to the Gulf of Corinth;[5] the Chian and Samian Straits; the straits around Euboia (including the Euripos Strait, located between Chalcis and the mainland, and

2. By describing these constraints, my analysis does not suggest that ancient mariners *avoided* dangerous areas. Instead, I simply show that there were areas in the Aegean that were more hazardous than others.

3. In this appendix, I maintain the transliteration of Greek places as they appear in my sources.

4. Winds and currents around headlands influenced the direction, speed, height, and steepness of the waves. Currents tend to be generally weak in the seas around Greece, but they are stronger around headlands and across straits (see below).

5. Here, dangers were compounded by the presence of tides, otherwise absent in the land-locked Mediterranean: Morton (2001: 45).

the straits to the south and north of the Euboian Channel); the strait separating southern Euboia from the island of Andros (Doro Channel); those separating Andros from Tenos and Tenos from Mykonos; and finally, the areas to the south of the Argolic Peninsula and around the island of Salamis in the Saronic Gulf.[6]

The paradox of ancient navigation in the Aegean was that the strongest winds, the Etesians, blew during the sailing season (the summer), but such winds could suddenly "raise considerable storms, forcing vessels, especially sailing ships, to seek temporary shelter" (Morton 2001: 128). Due to the strength of the Etesians, long-distance navigation required areas that could provide safe havens for mariners in the face of rapidly changing weather conditions, especially in the absence of man-made harbors.[7]

Sheltered areas punctuated the east coast of the Aegean, especially behind islands and promontories projecting westward from Asia Minor. In Greece, the high degree of indentation of the coastline provided a wealth of inlets and bays where ships could find temporary shelter. Worthy of mention are the Bay of Karystos in southwest Euboia; Legrena Bay on the southwest of Sounion and its counterpart on the east coast of the promontory; Koressia on Keos; the Rock of Monemvasia off the Peloponnesian coast; the Euboian Sound (an area that offered particularly effective shelter from the Etesians); and the areas around Hermione (to the south of the Argolic Peninsula), Nauplia (in the Gulf of Argos), and Naupaktos (on the northwest coast of the Corinthian Gulf). Phaleron Bay, located southwest of Athens, formed a long open coast (ca. three kilometers) where a number of ships could be beached and smaller vessels could lie at anchor. Relatively sheltered, especially in the summer, Phaleron was however exposed to the southerly and southwesterly winds, such as the Sirocco.

6. Another potential constraint to navigation was the presence in the Aegean of land and sea breezes: these are localized coastal winds that alternate in a daily cycle due to the different rates at which land and sea heat up during the day and cool off at night. In the summer, sea breezes develop some strength in south-facing bays, such as the Messenian, Laconian, Argolic, and Saronic Gulfs. However, "by timing departures from, and entrance to, harbors to coincide with, respectively, land and sea breezes, the potential difficulties of making these maneuvers against adverse winds . . . were avoided" (Morton 2001: 124).

7. Delos and Samos saw the first attempts at constructing artificial harbors in the eighth/ seventh and sixth century, respectively (for Delos: Casson 1971: 362; for Samos: Hdt. 3.45–60.) It is interesting to note that some of the communities involved in early maritime activity (from the late tenth to the sixth century), such as Zagora on Andros and Emborio on Chios, never developed permanent harbor facilities. This suggests that the existence of man-made harbors was perhaps less crucial to the development of early maritime commerce in the archaic period than it was in the classical period.

Natural harbors were rare in the Aegean, appearing only where the stratification or faulting of the local geology was suitably aligned with oceanographic and meteorological factors (Morton 2011: 108–10). Examples of such natural harbors can be found at Emborios on Chios, in the region of Torone in the Chalkidiki (Calm Harbor), at Perachora in the Corinthian Gulf, and in the harbors of Zea and Mounichia (two of the three harbors that made up Piraeus). Some prominent harbor areas—for example Piraeus, Mytilene, and Minoa (the port of Megara)—owed their existence to the deposition of sediments from river mouths (Morton 2001: 136). But in other areas along the Greek coastline, deposition did not have equally beneficial effects. Along much of the west coast of the Peloponnese, for example, coastlands tended to be flat, sandy, and marshy.[8]

In sum, the interaction of geomorphologic, oceanographic, and meteorological factors created a highly fragmented coastline that presented ancient mariners with many threats to navigation, and only a few particularly favorable areas: most notably, the Euboian Sound and the Saronic Gulf. This conclusion confirms the existence of a link between maritime proficiency and geographic location. Chalcis and Eretria (perhaps even Lefkandi)—the poleis that in the mid-eighth century developed trade relations with the Levant and sent out colonies in Italy—and Athens, Aegina, Megara, and Corinth—the second-generation maritime powers (seventh/sixth century)—were all located in these sweet spots.[9]

A.2. Piraeus' Rivals

If the Saronic Gulf presented particularly favorable conditions for navigation in the Aegean, did Piraeus enjoy a natural advantage over the harbors of Athens' Saronic rivals—Aegina, Corinth, and Megara?

8. I discuss the depositional history of Piraeus and Minoa below.

9. The reasons behind the shift from the Euboean Sound to the Saronic Gulf as the hub of the Aegean in the early archaic period are beyond the scope of my investigation. However, the evidence suggests that while the Euboian Sound offered particularly effective protection against the Etesians, the area also presented mariners with two main obstacles. First, the narrow channels at its northern and southern points of entry constituted particularly dangerous areas. Second, periods of calm were frequent, suggesting that the area may have enjoyed *too much* protection against the northeasterly winds (Morton 2001: 103).

A.2.a. Aegina

In the seventh and sixth centuries, Aegina—or, as Plutarch's Pericles apostrophized it, "the eyesore of Piraeus" (Plut. *Per.* 8.5, trans. Perrin 1916; Arist. *Rhet.* 1411a15)—was a power to be reckoned with. Although the island was tiny and its territory barren, Aegina took advantage very early on of her favorable location in the middle of the Saronic Gulf. Like Megara and Corinth, Aegina was a major player in the early phase of Greek commercial expansion in the Mediterranean. But unlike Megara and Corinth, Aegina did not send out colonies in the eighth and seventh centuries. Rather than exploiting their position to attract traders and fostering commerce, the Aeginetans chose the path of harassment and disruption, becoming notorious as pirates. As Figueira (1981: 202, 203) put it, "Aegina is ideally placed to intercept shipping coming up or down the Saronic Gulf... the association of the Aeginetans with piracy is scarcely to be doubted." Aegina's advantage vis-à-vis her rivals, therefore, may have depended on privileging defense over accessibility, and predation over trade.[10] Such a configuration, in turn, may have prevented the tiny island from substantially expanding in the direction of commercial activity.

A.2.b. Corinth

Corinth is located in a favorable position between the Corinthian and the Saronic Gulfs. However, the geography of the region and the location of its harbors suggest that the polis may have had easier access to the former than to the latter. As Salmon (1984: 31) remarks, "this greater convenience of western than of eastern communications by sea from the city was partially responsible for the concentration of Corinthian commercial interests in the west."

Yet, in the early sixth century, the Corinthians built both a harbor at Lechaion on the Gulf of Corinth (the landing closest to the city) and the *diolkos*—the paved track-way that connected the Gulf of Corinth with the Saronic Gulf. The *diolkos* has commonly been regarded as a thoroughfare for long-distance commercial traffic that benefited Corinth through transit tolls and portage fees (Verdelis 1956; cf. Salmon 1984: 136–39). Such an interpretation suggests that the incentives to access the Saronic Gulf offset the expenses of construction. In fact, navigation around the Peloponnese and through the mouth of the Gulf

---

10. This is consistent with an interpretation of Aeginetan harbor facilities as indicating the marginality of commerce to the early Aeginetan community. Figueira (1981: 190–92) attempts to disprove this point, but offers little evidence in support of an alternative thesis.

of Corinth entailed formidable obstacles and thus high transportation costs. However, while the construction of the *diolkos* itself may have constituted a sunk cost that the Corinthians were eager to take on, the transport of boats and goods across the Isthmus by land entailed conspicuous additional costs to merchants (Corinthians or otherwise). Focusing on these logistical challenges, scholars have questioned the interpretation of the *diolkos* as a highway for commercial traffic directed to the west (Casson 1971; Pettegrew 2011). For Pettegrew (2011: 552), "The *diolkos* did not mainly facilitate international trade but served Corinth's regional needs of communication and transport, and the commercial properties of the isthmus lay less in its facility as a thoroughfare than in its double *emporion*."[11] The location of Corinth at the crossroad of eastern and western trade routes, favorable though it may have been overall, may ultimately have compelled the city to divide its energies on two fronts. This, in turn, may have weakened Corinth's position in the Saronic Gulf.

A.2.c. Megara

Like the island of Aegina, Megara controlled a small and relatively barren territory. This lack of resources may have been among the factors that led to the polis' early expansion toward the sea in the mid-seventh century. Megara, like Corinth, was one of the first Greek poleis to send out colonies, particularly in the Propontis and in Sicily (Murray 1983: 103, 114). Like Corinth, Megara enjoyed a strategic position between the Peloponnese and the rest of mainland Greece, and between the Corinthian and the Saronic Gulfs. Unlike Corinth, however, Megara was better situated on the shores of the Saronic Gulf. Here, the harbors of Nisaia and Minoa, protected by the island of Salamis, enjoyed a particularly favorable (that is, easily defensible and easily accessible) position.

Established or expanded in the seventh century, the harbors of Nisaia and Minoa share some striking features with Piraeus, such as their proximity to the urban center and their location in a marshy area that was the result of depositional processes (Legon 1981: 91; Morton 2001: 136). Further analysis of the

11. The *emporia* in question are Lechaion (on the Corinthian Gulf) and Kenchreai (on the Saronic Gulf). Hesychius (s.v. "diolkos") defined the *diolkos* as the place from Lechaion to Kenchreai. Geography makes Hesychius' suggestion doubtful (the distance from Lechaion to Kenchreai is much greater than that between the points where the isthmus runs at its narrowest, which is where the *diolkos* was actually built). In fact, excavations have established that the landing of the *diolkos* on the side of the Corinthian Gulf was north of Lechaion (Verdelis 1956). The landing on the Saronic Gulf has not been discovered, but educated guesses place it north of Isthmia (Pettegrew 2011).

harbors is however complicated by the fact that the precise location of both Nisaia and Minoa has never been securely established (Legon 1981: 27–32; Morton 2001: 136; Lazenby 2004: 55). Nonetheless, we do know that Nisaia, like Piraeus, was fortified and connected to the city through Long Walls, although the construction occurred only relatively late, in the early 450s (Legon 1981: 27).

Despite its favorable geography and early successes, the power and prosperity of Megara was greatly curtailed toward the end of the sixth century by both internal dissensions and increasing competition from the polis' direct rivals, particularly Corinth and Athens (Trever 1925). The Athenian capture of Salamis between the archonship of Solon (594) and the rule of Pisistratus (560s–520s) was only a prelude to the struggle that took place later on between the two poleis for the control of the Hellespont.[12] The struggles of the sixth century marked a turning point in the power relationship between Athens and Megara, as well as in the subsequent development of the two poleis. In their aftermath, Megara was no longer a major player, while Athens began her ascent as the greatest naval and commercial power of the classical period. Interestingly, when Athens defeated Megara for control of the Saronic Gulf and the Aegean, Piraeus was still an unhealthy marsh.

A.3. Piraeus' Late Development

In prehistoric times, the stretch of land where Piraeus now lies was an island. The island was progressively joined to the mainland through the accretion of sediments deposited by the Kephisos and Ilissos Rivers.[13] In the Bronze Age, Piraeus seems to have been largely insignificant. While Phaleron—a long beach landing located to the south of Piraeus—played an important role, Porto Rafti (later to become part of the deme of Prasiai, situated on the eastern shores of Attica) likely constituted the principal port of Attica.[14] After a long period of retrenchment toward the territory of Athens and its immediate surroundings

12. Hornblower (1991: 139ff.) has linked the development of Piraeus directly to the Athenian capture of Salamis. He suggests that, "the use of Piraeus was unthinkable as long as Salamis opposite was in hostile, specifically Megarian, hands" (cf. Morton 2001: 107, n. 61).

13. Geological evidence supports Strabo's etymological speculations according to which the name Piraeus comes from the adverb *peran*, meaning "on the other side," "across" (Strabo. *Geog.* 1.3.18; cf. Morton 2001: 29; Garland 1987: 7). Images are available from Goiran et al. (2011) at: http://geology.gsapubs.org/content/39/6/531/F5.expansion.html.

14. Evidence of a Mycenean settlement is limited to a single burial at Charavgi dated to LHIIIB. The importance of Porto Rafti emerges from archeological finds (220 burials revealing connections of the area with Egypt and the Levant) and from Greek mythology (myth of Erysichthon—cf. Apollod. 3.14.2; Paus. 1.31.2). Phaleron too was celebrated in myth (as the place

during the Iron Age, new settlements sprang up along the western coast of Attica between 760 and 700. These included Phaleron, Trachones, Helleniko, Aliki, Voula, Vouliagmeni, and Vari.[15] Piraeus was not among them.

In the sixth century, when Athens began to take her first steps toward the sea with an expedition to Sigeion (on the south side of the entrance to the Hellespont, probably shortly before the archonship of Solon in 594) and later, with the capture of Salamis, Phaleron was the primary point of access to the sea (Garland 1987: 11; Cary 1949: 77). After the conquest of Salamis, more ports sprang up on the west coast of Attica, in Eleusis, Keratsini, Voula, and Sounion. Piraeus, once again, was not among them.[16]

Still in the early classical period, the area around Piraeus was considered unfit for both construction and human habitation (Garland 1987: 7).[17] A suggestive piece of evidence that captures Piraeus' marginality before the classical period is Herodotus' *Histories*, where the historian mentions Piraeus only once, as a substitute for a cardinal point (8.85).

---

where Theseus set sail for Crete: Plut. *Thes.* 22.1; and where Menesthus left for Troy: Hom. *Il.* 2.556). Some prosperous chamber tombs were also found there: Garland 1987: 11.

15. Middle Geometric expansion toward the coast: cemetery at Palaia Kokkinia (Coldstream 1968; 1977). Late Geometric settlements: Garland (1987: 11).

16. Similarly, when, under the Pisistratids, Athens extended her presence in the north Aegean, it was still the bay of Phaleron, not Piraeus, that witnessed Athenian ships take the sea.

17. Piraeus might not have been prime real estate, but a sizeable settlement in the area predated the expansion of the harbor: Traill (1975); Garland (1987; 14, 59).

Piraeus' History

AFTER ITS development in the 490s, Piraeus quickly became the principal hub of Aegean and Eastern Mediterranean trade. Was Piraeus' success in the fifth century sufficient to ensure its success after the fifth century?

I track the development of Piraeus and Athens, from the fifth century until the twentieth century CE. The investigation is subject to two major caveats concerning chronology and the availability of data. First, I divided the history of Piraeus and Athens into four periods: 1) the classical period (fifth and fourth century); 2) the Hellenistic and Roman periods (third century–fourth century AD); 3) the Byzantine and Ottoman periods (fourth century AD–1834); and finally, 4) the period after the proclamation of Greek independence (1834–twentieth century). Throughout the four periods, the physical environment (topography, oceanography, and meteorology) remained constant (Morton 2001). However, if navigation and shipbuilding technology remained constant throughout antiquity (that is, periods #1 and 2: W. V. Harris 2011: 11; Scheidel 2011), both changed dramatically from the fifteenth century onward (Unger 1980: ch. 5). These changes spread fast across Europe and the Mediterranean and it is hard to evaluate whether and to what extent they affected the relative importance of individual harbors.[1]

Second, the frequency and quality of data varies dramatically throughout the period under consideration. If relatively abundant quantifiable evidence is available for the classical period, later periods offer only sparse, largely qualitative evidence. The variation is starkest between the classical and the

---

1. The problem is compounded by the interaction of the two factors. After the fifteenth century, shipbuilding and navigation techniques evolved, but the problem of assessing the relative importance of Piraeus before and after this time is magnified by the tremendous shift brought about by the opening of Atlantic sea routes. I attempt to control for changes in trading patterns by expanding the temporal frame.

Hellenistic and Roman period, where it coincides with a tremendous shift in the geopolitical center of gravity of the Mediterranean due to Alexander's conquests. Expanding the temporal frame is thus necessary to rule out evidentiary biases. Once we do so, a clear pattern emerges. The parallel rise and fall of Athens and Piraeus throughout history suggest that the diminished importance of the city and the harbor that we observe at the end of the classical period was not a singular occurrence due to geopolitical shifts, but an instance of an otherwise consistent phenomenon.

B.1. The Classical Period

According to Ober (2008), in the period between 508 and 322, Athens was the highest performing polis in the Greek world. Ober measures Athens' success in term of state capacity as proxied by aggregate military activity, public buildings, and domestic programs (2008: ch. 2). The data shows that Athens' capacity began to increase in the middle of the sixth century, peaked in the 430s, and declined sharply during the late fifth-century crisis, only to rise again sharply and then steadily (with a setback after the Social War of 357–355) until the Macedonian conquest.

In order to measure Piraeus' success in the same period, I choose a series of proxies that are relatively independent of Ober's state capacity measures. In other words, I attempt to measure Piraeus' success based on its performance as a harbor, not as an extension of the polis of Athens. Having defined a good harbor as a place that is easy to reach and easy to defend, I proxy Piraeus' success in the classical period via four measures: population size (both citizens and metics); security (walls); capacity (warships); and volume of trade (taxes on imports and exports).[2]

B.1.a. Population

Reconstructing the entire population of Piraeus would require data on all the categories of people that resided in Athens' harbor town—that is, citizens, metics, foreign merchants, and slaves. However, we know virtually nothing about foreigners and slaves, whose numbers are likely to have fluctuated conspicuously and frequently over time. As a result, for the purposes of this investigation, I focus on citizens and metics.

---

2. More explicitly, population size and volume of trade reflect the "easy-to-reach" part of the definition, while security and capacity reflect the "easy-to-defend" part.

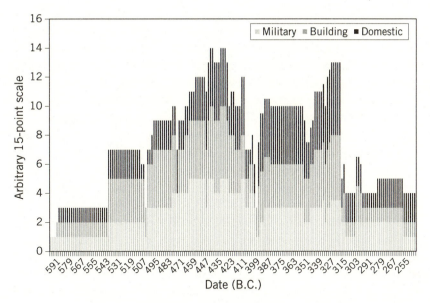

FIGURE B.1. Athenian state capacity (600 to 250): Ober (2008)

B.1.A.I. CITIZENS

Needless to say, we have no direct evidence for the citizen population of Piraeus at any point in time during the classical period. However, following Ober's (2008) methodology, I reconstruct a baseline number from the number of councilors (*bouleutai*, sing. *bouleutēs*) representing the deme of Piraeus in the Athenian Council of Five Hundred (*Boulē*).[3]

Ober (2008: 141) suggests that the deme of Prasiai, whose *bouleutic* quota was three delegates, had an average population of two hundred adult males. This

---

3. Following the reforms of Cleisthenes in the year 508, citizen representation in the Council of Five Hundred depended on deme population. The problem of estimating population numbers based on the *Bouleutic* quota (the number of councilors each deme sent to the *Boulē*) is that the quota was never modified throughout the classical period to respond to demographic variations (Hansen 1999: 249). Moreover, evidence from funerary inscriptions reveals that Athenian citizens who resided in other Attic demes lived (and were buried) in Piraeus (Garland 1987: 60). There are, however, insurmountable difficulties in estimating their numbers and how such numbers varied over time. For the purposes of this investigation, I limit myself to acknowledging the existence of this problem. For the composition of Piraeus' population: Grigoropoulos (2009); von Reden (1995); Garland (1987); Dicks (1968); Panagos (1968); Amit (1965). I return to these issues in section B.1.a.iv.

number yields a ratio of sixty-seven adult male citizens per *bouleutēs*, matching a total adult male population of roughly 33,500 citizens. These numbers are roughly consistent with late fourth-century estimates, but underestimate fifth-century population figures (Hansen 1999: 92). I therefore modify Ober's calculations by introducing variations consistent with known demographic fluctuations.

Following Hansen, I assume that the total Athenian male population in the 430s was sixty thousand people, yielding a ratio of 120 people per *bouleutēs*; in the 400s, total male population probably declined to twenty-five thousand, yielding a ratio of fifty people per *bouleutēs*; by the 330s, population averaged ca. thirty thousand, yielding a ratio of sixty people per *bouleutēs* (Hansen 1988). In 317, Demetrius of Phalerum's census suggests that the citizen population was twenty-one thousand, yielding a ratio of forty-two people per *bouleutēs*.

We know that, throughout the classical period, the sizeable deme of Piraeus sent to the Council nine *bouleutai* (Garland 1987: 59; cf. Traill 1975). Based on these numbers, Piraeus' adult male population in the classical period fluctuated between 540 (in the 330s) and 1,080 (in the 430s) adult males, reaching a low of 450 in the post-Peloponnesian War period and declining further after Athens' defeat at Amorgos (378 adult males).

In the demographic structure of Athens, the ratio of males to total population has been estimated at about one-third (Hansen 1999: 93). Therefore, 450 to 1,080 adult males correspond to a total citizen population in the deme of Piraeus, including women and children, ranging between 3,240 in the 430s and 1,620 in the 330s, reaching lows of 1,350 in the 400s and 1,134 in 317.

B.1.A.II. METICS

Estimating the metic population of Piraeus presents even thornier issues. According to Hansen (1999: 93), "in contrast to the number of citizens, which was stable and roughly stationary, that of metics must have varied according to circumstances: peace and prosperity brought many metics to Athens, but they vanished again in any long war or crisis." Assessing these fluctuations based on the ancient evidence, however, is very difficult.

The only figure available for the classical period is in Thucydides (2.31.2), who reports that three thousand metic hoplites served alongside an Athenian contingent during the invasion of Megara in 431. General estimates of their total strength in this period have produced a range of 28,000 to 30,000 metics living in Attica (including men, women, and children).[4] Whitehead (1986: 83–84) has calculated that of the 366 metics whose deme of residence is known,

---

4. Garland (1987: 61). Gomme (1933: 26) estimates 28,500.

sixty-nine (ca. 20%) were registered in Piraeus. Combined, these numbers give us an estimate of the total metic population in Piraeus of about five thousand to six thousand in the 430s.[5]

In 317, Demetrius' census revealed that the metic population in Athens had dropped to ten thousand, suggesting (keeping constant the fifth-century ratio of metics living in Athens and metics living in Piraeus) that Piraeus' metic population was about two thousand people in the 310s.

B.1.A.III. POPULATION: CONCLUSIONS

According to these figures, in the 430s the population of Piraeus including citizen and metic men, women, and children, numbered approximately 8,240–9,240. To his estimate, we must add an unknown number of slaves and foreigners. With Hansen (2008: 267), I estimate the boost at 10%. The grand total adds up to a population of around 9,064–10,164 people in the 430s (ca. 9,100–10,200).

Using the available data about citizens and metics drawn from Demetrius of Phalerum's census and employing the same boost (10%) for slaves and foreigners, I estimate the population of Piraeus in 317 at 3,447 people (ca. 3,500).

In the absence of direct evidence for the metic population in Piraeus the 330s, I assume that their numbers roughly matched mid-fifth-century levels. Such an assumption is consistent with the primary role of Piraeus in both periods.[6] As a result, I assess Piraeus' total population in the 330s at 7,282–8,382 (ca. 7,300–8,400).

For the early fourth century, the problem of estimating the metic population may prove unsolvable. On the one hand, we know that some metics stayed in Athens during the last years of the fifth century. A number of them were

5. Consistent with Garland (1987: 61). If these estimates are correct, and if we maintain the ratio of males to total population that we assumed as valid for Athenian citizens, then we obtain a number of adult male metics living in Piraeus of about 1,700–2,000.

6. Garland (1987: 61; cf. Clerc 1893: 375ff.) thinks that Piraeus' metic population never again reached fifth-century levels. This assumption is grounded on Isocrates' assertion that metics had left Piraeus after the Social War and Xenophon's suggestions for incentivizing metics to do business in Athens. Whereas the former does not mean that Athens suffered from lack of metics for long after the Social War, the latter suggests that Athens should incentivize *more* metics to come to Athens. Contra Garland, one may equally speculate that, in the 330s, when Piraeus was again a hub of Aegean commerce and many new incentives were put in place to foster commerce, the number of metics even exceeded mid-fifth-century levels. Given the speculative nature of these reflections, however, I simply assume that numbers in the 330s matched those in the 430s.

persecuted by the Thirty, some stuck around even after the persecutions to fight with Thrasybulus for democracy, as discussed in chapters 2 and 4. When the civil war ended, some may have returned. How many, however, is anyone's guess. On the other hand, Isocrates' statement that after the Social War metics and foreigners left Athens suggests that they may have behaved similarly in the aftermath of the Peloponnesian War. In the absence of direct evidence, I slash the number of metics that resided in Piraeus in the 430s in half and assume that in 400, the metic population of Piraeus was around 2,500–3,000. I also slash in half the percentage boost of slaves and foreigners (to 5%, assuming that slaves were probably forced to stay in Athens, whereas foreigners experienced no such compulsion). Total population figures thus amount to 4,043–4,568 in 400 (ca. 4,000–4,600).

B.1.A.IV. CAVEATS

The population estimates I presented above are not meant to provide an accurate overall estimate of the population of Piraeus. First, the fact that the Cleisthenic reforms predate the development of the harbor necessarily leads to underestimating actual population numbers. Although Piraeus was a sizeable settlement already before the fifth century, it is likely that after the construction of the Long Walls and the development of Athens' navy and commercial harbor, a greater number of people—Athenians and non-Athenians alike—moved their families and/or their trade to Piraeus. However, the *bouleutic* quota was never modified to match such demographic fluctuations. Second, the quota only refers to Athenian residents in Piraeus, and thus excludes Athenians who lived in Piraeus, but were registered in other demes. As a result, my overall estimates cannot but produce a low (perhaps very low) assessment. [7]

For comparison, Garland (1987: 58) and Morris (2005: 15) estimate population numbers for Piraeus at thirty thousand and twenty-five thousand, respectively. If we employ Hansen's shotgun method, we obtain a middle-range result between my estimates and those of Morris and Garland. The intramural area occupied around three hundred hectares (of which one-third occupied by domestic settlements: Hansen and Nielsen 2004: 636). With an estimated population density ranging from 150 hectares (Hansen's own shotgun estimate: 1988; 2006a; 2008) and 170 hectares (with Travlos 1988), we obtain a total population of 15,000–17,000.

Given such large variations, is there any value in these calculations? My estimates aim at diachronically benchmarking population counts in order to

---

7. For this reason, when my calculations provide a range, I plot the higher estimate.

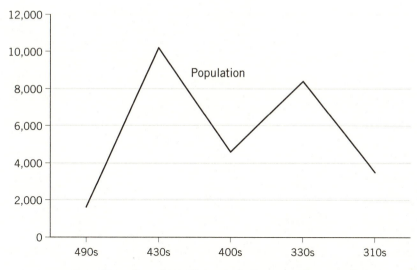

FIGURE B.2. Piraeus' population. X axis: years; Y axis: population numbers.

provide quantifiable assessments of broad population trends as a proxy for the harbor's success. The margin of error, large though it may be, remains equally large across the period. Moreover, as we will see, the trends emerging from population estimates mirror the trends emerging from other proxies. For these reasons, I suggest that, for the limited purposes of this investigation, such numbers are instructive.

The results are plotted in figure B.2.[8]

B.1.b. Security

I proxy security through a relatively straightforward measure: walls. The literary sources document the construction and destruction of the walls of Athens with surprising regularity, which allows us to track the state of the Long Walls throughout the classical period.

Built between the 490s and the 440s (with the later addition of the Eetionea fort under the government of the Four Hundred in the year 411/400: Thuc. 1. 107.1; 8. 90–94), the Long Walls were destroyed at the end of the Peloponnesian War, when the Spartan siege forced Athens to capitulate and surrender

8. I calculate Piraeus' population in 500 based on van Wees' (2013: 91) estimate of thirty thousand citizens at the end of the sixth century and no metic population, consistent with the lack of development of Piraeus' infrastructure.

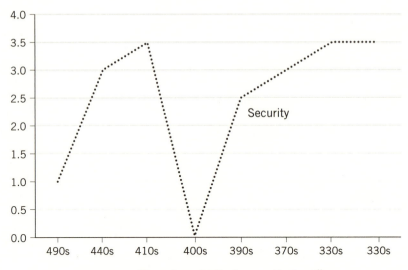

FIGURE B.3. Piraeus' security. X axis: years; Y axis: walls.

in the year 404 (Xen. *Hell.* 2.2.20). By the year 391, Conon had rebuilt the walls, which remained in place throughout the fourth century, and beyond (Xen. *Hell.* 4.8.9; Diod. 14.85; cf. Garland 1987: 14–57, 163–69).[9] After the Battle of Chaeronea (in the year 338), the walls of Mounichia and Eetionea were refurbished.

The results are plotted in figure B.3.[10]

B.1.c. Capacity

I proxy Piraeus' capacity by the number of warships built during the classical period. Ideally, we would use the number of both warships and commercial ships that Piraeus could host, but we have very scanty information concerning commercial ships.[11]

9. The only addition of note is that, after Sphodrias' raid (in the year 378), the Athenians built gates around Piraeus (Xen. *Hell.* 5.4.34).

10. Figure keys: 0=no walls; 1=wall around Piraeus; 2=North Wall and Phaleric Wall (in the 450s) / Walls around Asty and Piraeus after 228); 2.5=North Wall, South Wall, Phaleric Wall, no gates (between 394 and 387); 3=North Wall, South Wall, and Phaleric Wall, gates; 3.5=North Wall, South Wall, Phaleric Wall, fortification of Eetionea/repairs to Eetionea and Mounichia (337).

11. The lack of information concerning merchant ships, paired with the absence of a state-owned merchant fleet makes general estimates impossible (Amit 1965: 15–18). The population

According to van Wees (2013: 66; cf. Amit 1965: 18–19), in the archaic period, "the Athenian navy . . . did not lag behind the general trend of development in Greece, but consisted of 50 triremes by 500 BC, and 70 by 490. Under Themistocles, its size was more than doubled by the building of another 100 triremes, and the last-minute construction of another 30 triremes in 480 brought the total up to 200 at the time of the Persian invasion." In the year 446, after the (alleged) ratification of the Thirty Years' peace, Athens built an additional one hundred ships, bringing the total up to three hundred, which was still the grand total in the year 421 (Garland 1987: 96; cf. Thuc. 2.13.8–9; Xen. *Anab.* 7.1.27; Aeschin. 2. 175).

In the course of the Sicilian expedition (415–413) Athens lost 170 ships (Thuc. 6.43.1; 7.16.2 and 7.20.2). In the year 411, Athens built a new fleet of 104 ships (Thuc. 8.30.2), and in the year 406, when Conon was blockaded off of Mytilene, the Athenians sent another squadron of 110 triremes (Garland 1987: 97). At the Battle of Aegospotami, Athens mustered 180 ships, but the following year, after Athens' final defeat in the Peloponnesian War, the city surrendered all of her ships except for twelve.[12]

By the time of the foundation of the Second Athenian Confederacy, Athens had rebuilt one hundred ships. From then on, according to Garland (1987: 97–98) "the naval lists show a steady build-up," reaching a peak of about 420 ships in the year 325. At Amorgos, Athens lost 170 ships and the rest came under control of Macedon (Habicht 1997: 39).[13]

The results are plotted in figure B.4.

---

of the city of Athens could also be used to proxy for Piraeus' capacity, since once Athens' population reached about ten thousand people, its continued growth depended on imports through Piraeus.

12. In both Amit's and Garland's narratives, it remains unclear what happened to the 130 ships that survived the Sicilian expedition. Thucydides' (8.1.2) statement that the Athenians realized after Sicily that "they had not sufficient ships in their docks" suggests that either the fleet of three hundred ships had suffered losses between 421 and 415 or that the remaining 130 ships were employed to protect Attica, Euboea, and Salamis as they did under Pericles (Thuc. 2.24.2). For the purposes of this reconstruction, I add the 104 ships built in 411 to the 130 ships that survived the Sicilian expedition.

13. The Athenians deployed 170 ships at Amorgos, probably "the largest naval expedition ever" (Garland 1987: 100). The ships that the Macedonians did not destroy at Amorgos probably remained in the Athenian docks and came under the control of Antipater. Of the approximately four hundred ships in 330 and 325, eighteen were quadriremes in 330, while fifty were quadriremes and seven were quinquiremes in 325.

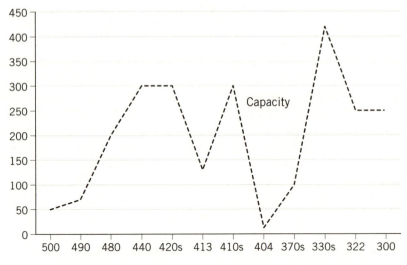

FIGURE B.4. Piraeus' capacity. X axis: years; Y axis: number of ships.

B.1.d. Volume of Trade

In order to calculate the volume of trade that passed through Piraeus, taxes collected in the harbor constitute a preferred measure.[14] But although we are relatively well informed of the kind of taxes collected in Piraeus, we have little data.

According to Boeckh (1842), custom duties were raised both from the harbor—in the form of custom duties on imports and exports, and fees paid for foreign ships docked in the harbor—and from the markets—in the form of taxes on the sale of goods consumed in the country, and fees paid for the right of selling in the market (the latter probably paid only by aliens). Imports and exports were subject to a duty of 2% (of which the tax on grain was farmed separately). An additional tax of 1% was levied upon vessels (and individuals?) for the use of the harbor. Xenophon mentions another duty for permission to deposit commodities in the warehouses and magazines. Finally, we hear of a

14. Following Xenophon's advice to boost the role of Piraeus as a commercial center (*Por.* 3.13), another rough measure would be the number and size of commercial buildings, such as "lodging-houses for ship-owners near the harbors, and convenient places of exchange for merchants, also hotels to accommodate visitors." However, it is formidably difficult to track down the diachronic development of such buildings and to match buildings to their functions through the literary sources and the archaeological record.

tax on sales levied in the market, although we know nothing about its nature or its profitability.[15]

For the purposes of this reconstruction, I proxy volume of trade based on the limited direct evidence for the *pentēkostē*—the 2% tax on import and export. We know from Andocides (1.133–4) that the tax was farmed in 402/401 and 401/400 and yielded thirty talents and thirty-six talents, respectively. With Isager and Hansen, I add to these numbers ten talents generated by the grain trade, obtaining a total of forty talents in 402/401 and forty-six talents in 401/400.[16] The small volume of profits is consistent with Athens' low profile at the end of the Peloponnesian War. In times of prosperity, we must assume with Boeckh that custom duties would have been "far more productive" (1842: 318; cf. Ober 2015b: 509).

In fact, for the fourth century, Amemyia (2007: 110) calculates that the total volume of imports and exports, including grain, would have yielded around 5,520 T. Taxed at 2%, Piraeus' trade yielded a total of 110 T/yr. Amemyia does not specify when in the fourth century his estimates apply. Conservatively, I assume that his numbers reflect the situation in the 340s, when Athens recovered from the Social War, but before the Lycurgan era.

Calculating the yield of the import-export tax in the fifth century is more complicated. Strauss (1987a: 50; cf. Hopper 1979: 100) estimates volume of imperial trade in 413 at eighteen thousand talents (the number reflects the volume of trade in all ports of the empire). For Hopper, 25% of imperial trade (or 4,500 T) was generated by Piraeus. If taxed at 2%, Piraeus' trade would have yielded ninety talents.[17]

The results are plotted in figure B.5.[18]

15. In addition, we hear of two temporary taxes: a 5% tax levied for a few years after 415 on "commodities exported or imported by sea in the states of the subject allies," and a tax of 10% levied by the Athenians at Byzantium beginning in 409 (Boeckh 1842: 325).

16. Andocides' passage implies that volume of trade (without grain) in 401/400 amounted to 1,800 T. Isager and Hansen (1975: 52) add five hundred talents generated by the grain trade and come up with a total of 2,300 T for the year 401/400.

17. The *pentēkostē* was introduced in the early fourth century. According to Woolmer (2016: 70), in the fifth century, "prior to the outbreak of the Peloponnesian War, the standard Athenian tax on trade had been levied at 1% ad valorem, a rate that remained unchanged until 413 BCE when the Athenians implemented an emergency 5% tax on all maritime trade conducted in all harbors of the empire." Therefore, because imports and exports were not taxed at 2% in the fifth century, this result should not be taken as reflecting accurate income numbers for the fifth century.

18. In the Hellenistic period, the Macedonian occupation of Piraeus and the geopolitical shift brought about by Alexander's conquest determined a rapid decline in the prosperity of

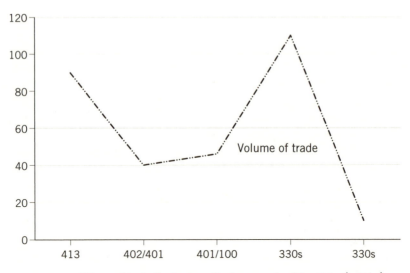

FIGURE B.5. Volume of trade. X axis: years; Y axis: proceeds of the 2% tax (in T/yr).

B.1.e. Conclusion

If we compare Ober's measures of Athens' performance with the data I collected for Piraeus, it is clear that the city and the harbor followed broadly similar paths. According to figure B.1, Athens' performance increased throughout the sixth century, peaked in the 430, declined abruptly toward the end of the Peloponnesian War, only to rise again at the beginning of the fourth century. Despite a setback in the years of the Social War (357–355), the polis' performance peaked again in the 330s, and declined after the Battles of Amorgos and Crannon.

The same goes for Piraeus (see figure B.6). After the foundation of the harbor in the 490s, Piraeus' performance peaked in the 430s, and declined abruptly after the defeat of Athens in the Peloponnesian War. In the 330s, Piraeus was once again a highly performing harbor. After the 330s, the proxies for security and (to a lesser extent) capacity remained high, which is consistent with the Macedonian occupation of the harbor and its transformation into a naval base (on which more below). Population and volume of trade, however, declined.

Piraeus (Garland 1987: 46). To convey this decline, and in the absence of direct evidence, I arbitrarily set the number for the year 300 at ten talents. I come back to the history of Piraeus in the Hellenistic period in the next section.

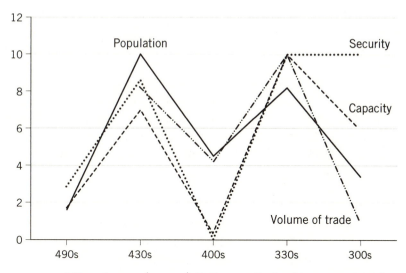

FIGURE B.6. Piraeus' success (490–300). X axis: years; Y axis: arbitrary ten-point scale.

B.2. The Hellenistic and Roman Periods

As the classical period faded into the world of Alexander, Greece began to play a smaller and smaller role in the geopolitics of the Mediterranean. As Ober has recently argued, the Macedonian conquest did not coincide with a collapse of Greek civilization. Yet, as his index of development shows (2015a: 3), Greece's prosperity began to decline.[19] By the end of the Roman period, population and consumption levels in core Greece had tumbled to lows seen last during the Iron Age. Athens, we may surmise, broadly followed this path. How did Piraeus fare in this period?

Classical scholarship has long employed the evidence from funerary inscriptions to suggest that the size of the population of Piraeus sharply declined during the Hellenistic period (Garland 1987; Panagos 1968; Dicks 1968; Kahrstedt 1954). In fact, between the third and the first century, the number of inscriptions dropped dramatically from 110 inscriptions representing sixty different Greek and non-Greek states, to thirty-four inscriptions representing only eighteen states (cf. Garland 1987: 64–65).

But the use of funerary *stēlai* to estimate population numbers has been recently questioned. For Grigoropoulos (2009), in order to estimate demographic trends through the epigraphic records, the evidence of funerary inscriptions

19. During the Hellenistic and Roman periods, Greece's center of gravity shifted away from Athens and toward Northern Greece and the Peloponnese (Mackil 2013).

ought not to be taken at face value (coarse straight count), but evaluated through cross-checks using different kinds of inscriptions.[20] Based on this method, the picture he derives is one of population growth, particularly in the Roman period.

When we look at Grigoropoulos' numbers more closely, however, it is possible to formulate a series of observations. First, Grigoropoulos' estimates are consistent with short-term fluctuations already documented in previous scholarship. The first occurred between the first and third century CE (when we have thirty-eight funerary inscriptions representing ten states).[21] The second occurred under the Roman emperor Constantine. According to Dicks (1968: 147), "In 86 B.C. Sulla ravaged Piraeus destroying the arsenal and docks, but although Strabo dismissed it as an unimportant village, it seems to have revived early in the Imperial era and served as a base for Constantine's fleet in A.D. 322." Notwithstanding these short-term variations, whose magnitude is inscrutable from the available evidence, the general trend is one of overall population decline after the Battle of Amorgos in 322 (Day 1942: 271–79).

The picture that emerges from population numbers is consistent with the different role that Piraeus played in post-classical times. In the Hellenistic and Roman periods, Piraeus was no longer a commercial hub, but a ship-building center (especially at the beginning of the Hellenistic period) and a military stronghold (under the Macedonians and the Roman emperor Constantine). So much so that, as Garland (1987: 47) pointed out, information about Piraeus in the post-classical era is largely confined to the role of the harbor as a strategic stronghold in the military history of Athens and her *hēgemons*.

The declining importance of Piraeus as a commercial center is also reflected in the emerging prominence of other ports in the Aegean, notably Delos, Alexandria, and Rhodes. At the Battle of Pydna in 168, the Romans defeated the Macedonians and progressively established their control over Greece (completing the task in 146, with the destruction of Corinth). After Pydna, Athens gained control of Delos. In the words of Panagos (1968: 130), "pour satisfaire

20. Such as *ephēbic* (from the *ephēbeia*, the training of youth as soldiers) and *bouleutic* (from the *Boulē*, or Council of Five Hundred) inscriptions. According to Grigoropoulos, funerary evidence can be trusted only when the percentages of names from each deme recorded on all types of inscriptions show small deviations.

21. Note, however, that these numbers reflect an increase in the number of Athenian citizens registered in Piraeus, which may indicate a decline in the metic and foreign population: Garland (1987).

les Grecs et châtier les Rhodiens qui s'étaient mis contre eux, ils [i.e. the Romans] cédèrent aux Athéniens les îles de Lemnos et de Délos qui leur avaient jadis appartenu et que le Macédoniens venaient de perdre. En octroyant Délos aux Athéniens qui étaient très experts, les Romains cherchaient ainsi à affaiblir économiquement Rhodes qu'ils convoitaient."[22] Yet, in doing so, the Romans complicated things for the Athenians. In fact, "Après l'annexion de Délos, les Athéniens se trouvèrent dans l'obligation, sous la pression du nouvel ordre de choses, de contribuer au développement du nouveau port au détriment du Pirée."[23] But there were additional reasons that made Delos less than a boon for Athens.

The island of Delos had been bestowed on Athens, "with the stipulation that it was to be a free port" (Day 1942: 51). As a result, Athens could not extract rents in the form of taxes. In addition, "when the Romans required the native Delians to depart from the island, they allowed them to take away their moveable property. But difficulties arose over the interpretation of the property included under the stipulation laid down by the Romans" (ibid.). Athens thus inherited a harbor she could not derive taxes from, and a series of legal disputes that required the arbitration of the Achaean League and the Romans to solve. As Polybius (30.21; trans. Shuckburgh 1889) caustically noted, in acquiring Delos, the Athenians "got the wolf by the ears."

In the course of the Hellenistic and Roman periods, the development of other major ports, most notably at Alexandria and Rhodes, further contributed to Piraeus' demise. In 86, the Sullan sack of Athens coincided with an abrupt decline in the prosperity of both Athens and Piraeus, which continued throughout Roman times.[24]

To sum up, the fortunes of Piraeus and Athens declined after Amorgos. The decline continued throughout the Hellenistic and Roman eras, albeit punctuated by ephemeral revivals when the *hēgemon* of the day chose Piraeus as a military base.

---

22. "To satisfy the Greeks and chastise the Rhodians who opposed them, the Romans ceded to Athens the islands of Lemnos and Delos, which they had previously controlled and which the Macedonians had just lost. In granting Delos to the Athenians who were experts, the Romans also sought to economically weaken Rhodes, which coveted it."

23. "After the annexation of Delos, the Athenians found themselves compelled, under the pressure of the new order of things, to contribute to the development of the new port to the detriment of Piraeus."

24. Panagos (1968: 134) sees another short-term revival of Piraeus in the period of the Mithridatic Wars, before the final onslaught by Sulla in 86.

B.3. The Byzantine and Ottoman Periods

The Byzantine and Ottoman periods offer a particularly interesting counterfactual. Unlike in Hellenistic and early Roman times, when the center of gravity of Mediterranean commerce shifted away from the Aegean (first toward the east, with Alexander's conquests, and then toward the west, with Rome), in the period from the fourth century to the nineteenth century CE Greece was again the epicenter of great empires. Athens and Piraeus, however, literally disappear from the evidence. For Dicks (1968: 147), "with the increasing significance of Constantinople and Salonica throughout the Byzantine civilization, both Athens and Piraeus were reduced to provincial status and there was little development, a feature which continued throughout the period of Turkish domination (1456–1829). In the Middle Ages, Piraeus was known as Porto Leone and in 1834, when Athens became capital of Greece, hardly a house stood in the town."

Dicks' conclusions find support in the evidence provided by shipbuilding manuals and archaeological investigations of Attica, as well as discussions of medieval and early modern voyages (Pryor and Jeffrey 2006; Pryor 1988; Unger 1980). Unger's work on shipbuilding, for example, emphasizes the enhanced centrality of Byzantium and Cyprus in the control of Eastern Mediterranean commercial trade routes. During the Byzantine period, the conflict between Byzantines and Arabs progressively shifted the center of gravity of Mediterranean commerce away from the Eastern Mediterranean and toward the Italian cities, particularly Venice and Genoa. Finally, the global reach of maritime trade, made possible by innovation in shipbuilding and navigation techniques in the fifteenth and sixteenth century, determined the increasingly provincial status of the Mediterranean (Unger 1980: chs. 2, 4, and 5).

Seeking a more fine-grained explanation for the absence of Piraeus and Athens from the records, however, one must also take into account the biases arising from archeological practice. The reports of the excavations of the British School at Athens emphasize the difficulties of reconstructing what Eugenia Drakopoulou (2009: 146–47) has termed the "puzzle . . . of the buildings of Athens in the Byzantine era and during the Ottoman occupation . . . the reasons for this difficulty are more or less known. The present image of Athens is mainly the result of buildings from two historical periods: antiquity, Greek and Roman, and the modern period, that is, the last two centuries. The long intermediary Byzantine and Ottoman periods are indicated by just a few monuments, mainly churches." This state of things is due in part to the fact that Byzantine and Ottoman "buildings, fortifications, residences and many Christian churches were demolished for town planning and residential reasons."

Even taking such biases into account, the evidence suggests that throughout this long stretch of time—roughly from the fifth through the mid-nineteenth century—Athens and Piraeus are conspicuous only for their absence.

B.4. The Period of Greek Independence

Population figures for the area around Piraeus in the late nineteenth and throughout the twentieth century give a sense of the magnitude and the pace of change after independence. As Dicks (1968: 147) remarked, "Piraeus... played a large part in the revival of Athens. Resettled by islanders with the trading instincts of the ancient metics it grew rapidly throughout the latter part of the nineteenth century. The population, which did not exceed 4,000 in 1840, rose from 11,000 in 1870 to 75,000 in 1907, and this figure was increased threefold by the refugee settlement of 1922." From 1840 to 1907, the population of Piraeus increased from four thousand to seventy-five thousand and reached an all-time peak in 1922 (225,000 people) due to the influx of Greek refugees from Asia Minor after the Greco-Turkish War. Between 1922 and 2000, population numbers did not diverge significantly from an average of 180,000–190,000 people. In recent times, however, the population of the port town experienced a contraction that continues to this day (ca. 160,000 people).

Population figures thus reflect the enhanced role of the settlement. But other proxies speak to the harbor's renewed commercial importance. At the time of independence, Piraeus was a village populated by fishers. Soon after, it grew to become the largest Greek seaport and one of the largest seaports in the Mediterranean Sea basin. Moreover, in addition to its central role as a passenger port, Piraeus is today one of the top-ten container ports in Europe. The enhanced importance of Piraeus in the nineteenth and twentieth century can hardly be linked to a revival of Mediterranean commerce vis-à-vis global trade, or to a revival of Greece vis-à-vis other Mediterranean countries. The evidence points instead to the revival of Athens as the capital of the newly independent kingdom as the crucial factor in the revival of Piraeus.[25]

25. In order to further support this point, one could a) compare the development of Nafplio (Greece's capital between 1821 and 1834) and Athens, and of the cities' harbors, across the period of the war of independence (that is before and after 1834); or b) investigate the development of Thessaloniki (which was Greece's primary port in the Byzantine and Ottoman periods and today Greece's second port) and ask: had Thessaloniki become the new capital of Greece, what would have happened to Piraeus? Whereas Nafplio's geography suggests that the territory would have hardly provided a good spot for a capital, the case of Thessaloniki constitutes a more interesting challenge. These comparisons are, however, beyond the scope of this appendix.

Acemoglu, D., S. Naidu, P. Restrepo, and J. A. Robinson. 2014. "Democracy Does Cause Growth." NBER working paper.

Acemoglu, D., and J. A. Robinson. 2006. *Economic Origins of Dictatorship and Democracy*. New York: Cambridge University Press.

Acemoglu, D., and J. Robinson. 2012. *Why Nations Fail*. New York: Crown Publishers.

Acemoglu, D., and J. Robinson. 2016. "Paths to Inclusive Political Institutions." In *Economic History of Warfare and State Formation*, edited by Jari Eloranta, Eric Golson, Andrei Markevich, and Nikolaus Wolf. Springer.

Ackerman, B. 1991. *We the People*. Cambridge, MA: Harvard University Press.

Andocides. 1968. *Minor Attic Orators in Two Volumes. Volume 1: Antiphon Andocides*. Translated by K. J. Maidment. Cambridge, MA: Harvard University Press; London: William Heinemann, Ltd.

Aghion, Ph., A. Alesina, and F. Trebbi. 2004. "Endogenous Political Institutions." *Quarterly Journal of Economics* 119(2), 565–611.

Akrigg, B. 2007. "The Nature and Implications of Athens' Changed Social Structure and Economy." In R. Osborne, *Debating the Athenian Cultural Revolution: Art, Literature, Philosophy, and Politics 430–380 BC*. Cambridge: Cambridge University Press.

Akrigg, B. 2011. "Demography and Classical Athens." In C. Holleran and A. Pudsey, *Demography and the Graeco-Roman World: New Insights and Approaches*. Cambridge: Cambridge University Press.

Almeida, J. A. 2003. *Justice as an Aspect of the Polis Idea in Solon's Political Poems: A Reading of the Fragments in Light of the Researches of New Classical Archaeology*. Leiden, Netherlands: Brill.

Alston, Eric, and T. Ginsburg. 2017. "Playing for Constitutional Time: Interim Constitutions and Transitional Provision." In *The Timing of Lawmaking*, edited by Saul Levmore and Frank Fagan. Edward Elgar.

Alston, L. J., M. andré Barreto Campelo de Melo, B. Mueller, and C. Pereira. 2016. *Brazil in Transition: Beliefs, Leadership, and Institutional Change*. Princeton: Princeton University Press.

Alston, L., B. Mueller, T. Nonnenmacher, and E. Alston. 2018. *Institutional and Organizational Analysis: Concepts and Applications*. Cambridge: Cambridge University Press.

Amemiya, T. 2007. *Economy and Economics of Ancient Greece*. London: Routledge.

Amit, M. 1965. *Athens and the Sea*. Collection Latomus.

Anderson, G. 2005. "Before Turannoi Were Tyrants: Rethinking a Chapter of Early Greek History." *Classical Antiquity* 24(2), 173–222.

Anderson, G. 2009. "The Personality of the Greek State." *Journal of Hellenic Studies* 129, 1–22.

Andrewes, A. 1954. *Probouleusis: Sparta's Contribution to the Technique of Government.* Oxford: Clarendon Press.

Ansolabehere, S. 2006. "Voters, Candidates, and Parties." In B. R. Weingast and D. A. Wittman, *The Oxford Handbook of Political Economy.* Oxford: Oxford University Press.

Arcenas, S. 2018. *Stasis: The Nature, Frequency, and Intensity of Political Violence in Ancient Greece.* PhD Dissertation, Stanford University.

Aristotle. 1934. *Aristotle in 23 Volumes. Volume 19.* Translated by H. Rackham. Cambridge, MA: Harvard University Press; London: William Heinemann, Ltd.

Aristotle, and Stephen Everson. 1996. *The Politics, and the Constitution of Athens.* Cambridge: Cambridge University Press.

Armitage, D. 2017. *Civil Wars. A History in Ideas.* New York: Alfred A. Knopf.

Arnaoutoglou, I. 2003. *Thusias heneka kai sunousias: Private Religious Associations in Hellenistic Athens.* Athens: Academia Athenon.

Asheri, D. 1980. "La colonizzazione greca." In *La Sicilia antica,* edited by E. Gabba and G. Vallet 1, 89–142. Naples.

Badian, E. 1995. "The Ghost of Empire: Reflections on Athenian Foreign Policy in the Fourth Century BC." In *Die athenische Demokratie im 4. Jahrhundert v. Chr.,* edited by Walter Eder, 79–106. Stuttgart: Steiner.

Bang, P. F. 2009. "Labor: Free and Unfree." In *A Companion to Ancient History,* edited by A. Erskine. Wiley-Blackwell.

Barro, R. J. 1997. *Determinants of Economic Growth: A Cross-Country Empirical Study.* Cambridge, MA: M.I.T. Press.

Baum, M. A., and D. A. Lake. 2003. "The Political Economy of Growth: Democracy and Human Capital." *American Journal of Political Science* 47(2), 333–47.

Berent, M. 1996. "Hobbes and the 'Greek Tongues.'" *History of Political Thought* 17, 36–59.

Berent, M. 1998. "*Stasis,* or the Greek Invention of Politics." *History of Political Thought* 19, 331–62.

Berent, M. 2000a. "Anthropology and the Classics: War, Violence and the Stateless *Polis.*" *Classical Quarterly* 50, 257–89.

Berent, M. 2000b. "Sovereignty: Ancient and Modern." *Polis* 17, 2–34.

Berent, M. 2004. "In Search of the Greek State: A Rejoinder to M. H. Hansen." *Polis* 21, 107–46.

Berger, S. 1992. *Revolution and Society in Greek Sicily and Southern Italy.* Stuttgart: Steiner.

Bergh, A., and C. H. Lyttkens. 2014. "Measuring Institutional Quality in Ancient Athens." *Journal of Institutional Economics* 10(2), 279–310.

Bers, Victor. 2009. *Genos Dikanikon: Amateur and Professional Speech in the Courtrooms of Classical Athen..* Washington, DC: Center for Hellenic Studies, Trustees for Harvard University.

Bitros, George C., and Anastassios D. Karayiannis. 2010. "Morality, Institutions and the Wealth of Nations: Some Lessons from Ancient Greece." *European Journal of Political Economy* 26(1), 68–81.

Black, D. 1948. "On the Rationale of Group Decision-Making." *Journal of Political Economy* 56(1), 23–34.

Blamire, A. 2001. "Athenian Finance, 454–404 BC." *Journal of the American School of Classical Studies at Athens* 70(1), 99–126.

Blok, J., and A.P.M.H. Lardinois. 2006. *Solon of Athens: New Historical and Philological Approaches.* Leiden, Netherlands: Brill.

Boardman, J., I. Edwards, N. Hammond, and E. Sollberger, eds. 1982. *The Cambridge Ancient History.* Cambridge: Cambridge University Press. doi:10.1017/CHOL9780521224963.

Boeckh, A. 1842. *The Public Economy of Athens.* Second edition. London: J. W. Parker.

Boegehold, A. L. 1996. "Resistance to Change in the Law at Athens." In *Dēmokratia: A Conversation on Democracies, Ancient and Modern,* edited by Josiah Ober and Charles W. Hedrick. Princeton: Princeton University Press.

Boix, C. 2003. *Democracy and Redistribution.* Cambridge: Cambridge University Press.

Bonner, R. J., and G. Smith. 1938. *The Administration of Justice from Homer to Aristotle.* Chicago: University of Chicago Press.

Bresson, A. 2016. *The Making of the Ancient Greek Economy: Institutions, Markets, and Growth in the City-States.* Princeton: Princeton University Press.

Brun, P. 1983. *Eisphora-Syntaxis-Stratiotika.* Annales Litteraires de l'Universite de Besancon, 284.

Brunt, P. A. 1972. *Social Conflicts in the Roman Republic.* New York: Norton.

Brunt, P. A. 1987 [1971]. *Italian Manpower, 225 BC–AD 14.* Cambridge: Cambridge University Press.

Buchanan, J., and G. Tullock. 1962. *The Calculus of Consent—Logical Foundations of Constitutional Democracy.* Ann Arbor: University of Michigan Press.

Bueno de Mesquita, B., et al. 2003. *The Logic of Political Survival.* Cambridge, MA: M.I.T. Press.

Burke, E. 1984. "Eubulus, Olynthus, and Euboea." *TAPA* 114, 111–20.

Burke, E. 1990. "Athens after the Peloponnesian War: Restoration Efforts and the Role of Maritime Commerce." *Classical Antiquity* 9(1), 1–13.

Burke, E. 1992. "The Economy of Athens in the Classical Era: Some Adjustments to the Primitivist Model." *TAPA* 122, 199–226.

Burke, E. 2010. "Finances and the Operation of the Athenian Democracy in the 'Lycurgan Era.'" *American Journal of Philology* 131(3), 393–423.

Calvert, R. L. 1985. "Robustness of the Multidimensional Voting Model: Candidate Motivations, Uncertainty, and Convergence." *American Journal of Political Science* 29(1), 69–95.

Canevaro, M. 2011. "The Twilight of Nomothesia." *Dike* 14, 55–85.

Canevaro, M. 2013a. "Nomothesia in Classical Athens: What Sources Should We Believe?" *Classical Quarterly* 63(1), 139–60.

Canevaro, M. 2013b. *The Documents in the Attic Orators. Laws and Decrees in the Public Speeches of the Demosthenic Corpus.* Oxford: Oxford University Press.

Canevaro, M. 2015. "Making and Changing Laws in Classical Athens." In *The Oxford Handbook of Ancient Greek Law,* edited by Edward M., Harris and Mirko Canevaro. Oxford: Oxford University Press.

Canevaro, M. 2016. "The Procedure of Demosthenes' *Against Leptines*: How to Repeal (and Replace) an Existing Law." *Journal of Hellenic Studies* 136.

Canevaro, M. 2018a. "The Authenticity of the Document at Dem. 24.20–3, the Procedures of Nomothesia and the So-Called ἐπιχειροτονία τῶν νόμων." *Klio* 100(1), 70–124.

Canevaro, M. 2018b. "Majority Rule vs. Consensus: The Practice of Deliberation in the Greek Poleis." In *Ancient Greek History and Contemporary Social Science,* edited by M. Canevaro, B. Gray, A. Erskine, and J. Ober. Edinburgh Leventis Studies. Edinburgh: Edinburgh University Press.

Canevaro, M., and E. M. Harris. 2012. "The Documents in Andocides' *On the Mysteries.*" *Classical Quarterly* 62, 98–129.

Canevaro, M., and E. M. Harris. 2017. "The Authenticity of the Documents at Andocides' *On the Mysteries* 77–79 and 83–84." *Dike* 18.

Carawan, Edwin. 1998. *Rhetoric and the Law of Draco.* Oxford: Oxford University Press.

Carawan, E. 2002. "The Athenian Amnesty and the Scrutiny of the Laws." *Journal of Hellenic Studies* 122.

Carawan, E. 2007. "The Trial of the Arginusai Generals and the Dawn of 'Judicial Review.'" *Dike* 10.

Carawan, E. 2012. "The Meaning of *me mnesikakein.*" *Classical Quarterly* 62(2), 567–81.

Carawan, E. 2013. *The Athenian Amnesty and Reconstructing the Law.* Oxford University Press.

Cargill, J. 1981. *The Second Athenian League: Empire or Free Alliance?* Berkeley: University of California Press.

Carugati, F. 2015. *In Law We Trust (Each Other).* PhD dissertation, Stanford University.

Carugati, F. 2019a. Working paper. "Constitution and Consensus: The Institutional Foundations of Democratic Stability."

Carugati, F. 2019b. "Tradeoffs of Inclusion: Development in Ancient Athens." Forthcoming. *Comparative Political Studies.*

Carugati, F., R. Calvert, and B. R. Weingast. 2019. Working paper. "Judicial Review by the People Themselves: Democracy and the Rule of Law in Ancient Athens."

Carugati, F., G. Hadfield, and B. R. Weingast. 2015. "Building Legal Order in Ancient Athens." *Journal of Legal Analysis* 7(2), 291–324.

Carugati, F., and J. Ober. 2020. "Democratic Collapse and Recovery: Athens 413–403." In D. Moss, A. Westad, and A. Fung, *When Democracy Breaks.* The Tobin Project.

Carugati, F., J. Ober, and B. R. Weingast. 2016. "Development and Political Theory in Classical Athens." *Polis: The Journal for Ancient Greek Political Thought* 33(1), 71–91.

Carugati, F., J. Ober, and B. R. Weingast. 2019. "Is Development Uniquely Modern? Athens on the Doorstep." *Public Choice.* https://doi.org/10.1007/s11127-018-00632-w.

Carugati F., and M. Pyzyk. Working paper. "Supply and Demand in Processes of State Formation: Evidence from Ancient Greece."

Carugati, F., and B. R. Weingast. 2018. "Rethinking Mass and Elite: Decision-Making in the Athenian Law-Courts." In *Ancient Greek History and Contemporary Social Science*, edited by M. Canevaro, B. Gray, A. Erskine, and J. Ober. Edinburgh Leventis Studies. Edinburgh: Edinburgh University Press.

Cary, M. 1949. *The Geographic Background of Greek and Roman History.* Oxford: Clarendon Press.

Casson, L. 1971. *Ships and Seamanship in the Ancient World.* Princeton: Princeton University Press.

Cawkwell, G. L. 1973. "The Foundation of the Second Athenian Confederacy." *Classical Quarterly* 23(1).

Cawkwell, G. L. 1981. "Notes on the Failure of the Second Athenian Confederacy." *Journal of Hellenic Studies* 101, 40–55.

Christ, M. R. 1998. *The Litigious Athenian.* Baltimore: Johns Hopkins University Press.

Christ, M. R. 2007. "The Evolution of the Eisphora in Classical Athens." *Classical Quarterly* 57(1), 53–69.

Clerc, M. 1893. *Les Métèques athéniens: étude sur la condition légale, la situation morale et le rôle social et économique des étrangers domiciliés àAthènes*. Paris: Thorin and fils.

Cloché, P. 1960. "Les hommes politiques et la justice populaire dans l'Athènes du IVe siècle." *Historia: Zeitschrift für Alte Geschichte* 9(1).

Cohen, D. 1995. *Law, Violence, and Community in Classical Athens*. New York: Cambridge University Press.

Cohen, E. 1973. *Ancient Athenian Maritime Courts*. Princeton: Princeton University Press.

Cohen, E. 1992. *Athenian Economy and Society: A Banking Perspective*. Princeton: Princeton University Press.

Cohen, E. 1994. "Status and Contract in Fourth-Century Athens: A Reply to Stephen C. Todd." In *Symposion 1993*. Köln, 141–52.

Coldstream, J. N. 1968. *Greek Geometric Pottery: A Survey of Ten Local Styles and Their Chronology*. London: Methuen.

Coldstream, J. N. 1977. *Geometric Greece*. New York: St. Martin's Press.

Collier, P. 1999. "On the Economic Consequences of Civil War." *Oxford Economic Papers* 51, 168–83.

Collier, P. 2000. "Doing Well Out of War: An Economic Perspective." In *Greed and Grievance: Economic Agendas in Civil Wars*, edited by Mats Collier and David M. Malone. Lynne Rienner, 91–112.

Collier, P., and A. Hoeffler. 1998. "On the Economic Causes of Civil War." *Oxford Economic Papers* 50, 563–73.

Conophagos, C. E. 1980. Le Laurium antique, Athens.

Cox, G. W., D. North, and B. Weingast. 2012. "The Violence Trap: A Political-Economic Approach to the Problem of Development." Available at http://papers.ssrn.com/sol3/papers. cfm?abstract_id=2370622.

Crosby, M. 1950. "The Leases of the Laureion Mines." *Hesperia* 19, 189–312.

Crosby, M. 1957. "More Fragments of Mining Leases from the Athenian Agora." *Hesperia* 26, 1–23.

Culasso Gastaldi, E. 2004. *Le prossenie ateniesi del IV secolo a.C.: gli onorati asiatici. Fonti e studi di storia antica; 10*. Alessandria: Edizioni dell'Orso.

Davies, J. Kenyon. 1971. *Athenian Propertied Families, 600–300 B.C.* Oxford, Clarendon Press.

Davies, J. K. 1981. *Wealth and the Power of Wealth in Classical Athens*. Reprints edition. Salem, NH: Ayer Co.

Davies, J. 2004. "Athenian Fiscal Expertise and Its Influence." In *Mediterraneo Antico, Pisa: Istituti editoriali e poligrafici internazionali*, Anno VII, Fascicolo 2.

Day, J. 1942. *An Economic History of Athens under Roman Domination*. New York: Columbia University Press.

De Angelis, F. 2000. "Estimating the Agricultural Base of Greek Sicily." *Papers of the British School at Rome* 68, 111–48.

De Angelis, F. 2006. "Going against the Grain in Sicilian Greek Economics." *Greece and Rome* 53(1), 29–47.

De Angelis, F. 2010. "Reassessing the Earliest Social and Economic Development in Greek Sicily." In *Mitteilungen des Deutsches Archaeologisches Institut. Rome* 116, 21–53.

De Angelis, F. 2016. *Archaic and Classical Greek Sicily: A Social and Economic History*. New York: Oxford University Press.

De Ligt, L., and S. J. Northwood. 2008. "Introduction: New Approaches to the Demographic, Agrarian, and Political History of the Middle and Late Republic." In *People, Land and Politics. Demographic Developments and the Transformation of Roman Italy 300 BC–AD 14*. Edited by L. de Ligt and S. J. Northwood. Leiden: 1–14.

Demosthenes. Online. Loeb Classical Library. https://www.loebclassics.com/browse?t1=author.demosthenes.

Dermineur, E. 2014. "Single Women and the Rural Credit Market in 18th Century France." *Journal of Social History* 48(1), 175–99.

de Ste. Croix, G.E.M. 1956. "The Constitution of the Five Thousand." *Historia: Zeitschrift für Alte Geschichte* 5(1), 1–23.

de Ste. Croix, G.E.M. 1981. *The Class Struggle in the Ancient Greek World: From the Archaic Age to the Arab Conquests*. Ithaca, NY: Cornell University Press.

Diamond, L. Jay. 2008. *The Spirit of Democracy: The Struggle to Build Free Societies throughout the World*. New York: Holt Paperbacks.

Dickinson, O.T.P.K. 1994. *The Aegean Bronze Age*. Cambridge: Cambridge University Press.

Dicks, T.R.B. 1968. "Piraeus: the Port of Athens." *Town Planning Review* 39(2), 140–48.

Dillery, J. 1993. "Xenophon's 'Poroi' and Athenian Imperialism." *Historia: Zeitschrift fur Alte Geschichte*.

Diodorus Siculus. 1989. *Diodorus of Sicily in Twelve Volumes*. Translated by C. H. Oldfather. Vol. 4–8. Cambridge, MA: Harvard University Press; London: William Heinemann, Ltd.

Dixit, A. K. 2004. *Lawlessness and Economics: Alternative Modes of Governance*. Princeton: Princeton University Press.

Doucouliagos, H., and M. A. Ulubaşoğlu. 2008. "Democracy and Economic Growth: A Meta-Analysis." *American Journal of Political Science* 52(1), 61–83.

Downs, A. 1957. *An Economic Theory of Democracy*. New York: Harper and Row.

Drakopoulou, E. 2009. "British School at Athens Research on Byzantine Attica." *British School at Athens Studies* 17, 145–51.

Easterly, W., and R. Levine. 1997. "Africa's Growth Tragedy: Policies and Ethnic Divisions." *Quarterly Journal of Economics* 112(4).

Eder, W., 1995. *Die athenische Demokratie im 4. Jahrhundert v. Chr.: Vollendung oder Verfall einer Verfassungsform?: Akten eines Symposims 3.-7. August 1992, Bellagio*. Stuttgart: F. Steiner.

Edwards, I., C. Gadd, N. Hammond, and E. Sollberger. 1973. *The Cambridge Ancient History*. Cambridge: Cambridge University Press. doi:10.1017/CHOL9780521082303.

Elkins, Z., T. Ginsburg, and J. Melton J. 2009. *The Endurance of National Constitutions*. Cambridge: Cambridge University Press.

Elster, J. 1993. "Constitution-Making in Eastern Europe: Rebuilding the Boat in the Open Sea." *Public Administration* 71(1/2), 169–217.

Elster, Jon. 1995. "Forces and Mechanisms in the Constitution-Making Process." *Duke Law Journal* 45, 364–96.

Elster, Jon. 2000. "Arguing and Bargaining in Two Constituent Assemblies." *University of Pennsylvania Journal of Constitutional Law* 2, 345–421.

Engen, D. Tai. 2010. *Honor and Profit: Athenian Trade Policy and the Economy and Society of Greece, 415–307 B.C.E.* Ann Arbor: University of Michigan Press.

Erdkamp, P. P. 1998. *Hunger and the Sword.* J. C. Gieben: Amsterdam.

Faraguna, M. 1992. *Atene nell'età di Alessandro: problemi politici, economici, finanziari.* Rome: Accademia Nazionale dei Lincei.

Faraguna, M. 2003. "Alexander and the Greeks." In *Brill's Companion to Alexander the Great,* edited by Joseph Roisman, 99–130. Leiden, Netherlands: Brill.

Fawcett, P. 2016. "When I Squeeze You with Eisphorai: Taxes and Tax Policy in Classical Athens." *Hesperia* 85, 153–99.

Fearon, J. 2011. "Self-Enforcing Democracy." *Quarterly Journal of Economics* 126(4).

Fearon, J. D., and D. D. Laitin. 2003. "Ethnicity, Insurgency, and Civil War." *American Political Science Review* 971(1), 75–90.

Feng, Y. 2003. *Democracy, Governance, and Economic Performance: Theory and Evidence.* Cambridge, MA: M.I.T. Press.

Fenoaltea, S. 1984. "Slavery and Supervision in Comparative Perspective: A Model." *Journal of Economic History* 44, 635–68.

Figueira, T. J. 1981. *Aegina, Society and Politics.* Arno Press.

Figueira, T. J. 1998. *The Power of Money: Coinage and Politics in the Athenian Empire.* Philadelphia: University of Pennsylvania Press.

Finley, M. I. 1951. *Studies in Land and Credit in Ancient Athens, 500–200 B.C.: The Horos-Inscriptions.* New Brunswick, NJ: Rutgers University Press.

Finley, M. I. 1960. "Was Greek Civilization Based on Slave Labor?" In *Slavery in Classical Antiquity: Views and Controversies.* Cambridge: W. Heffer.

Finley, M. I. 1973a. *Democracy Ancient and Modern.* New Brunswick, NJ: Rutgers University Press.

Finley, M. I. 1973b. *The Ancient Economy.* University of California Press.

Finley, M. I. 1975. *The Use and Abuse of History.* New York: Penguin Books.

Finley. M. I. 1981 [1978]. "The Fifth Century Athenian Empire: A Balance Sheet." In *Imperialism in the Ancient World,* edited by P.D.A. Garnsey and C. R. Whittaker. Cambridge: Cambridge University Press.

Finley, M. I. 1985. *Ancient History: Evidence and Models.* New York: Penguin Books.

Finley, M. I. 1999. *Ancient Economy.* Updated edition. Berkeley: University of California Press.

Flament, Ch. 2007. "L'atelier athénien: réflexions sur la 'politique monétaire' d'Athènes à l'époque classique." In *Liber amicorum Tony Hackens,* edited by Gh. Moucharte et al. Louvain-la-Neuve, 1–10.

Fleck R. K., and F. A. Hanssen. 2006. "The Origins of Democracy: A Model with Application to Ancient Greece." *Journal of Law and Economics* 49(1), 115–46.

Fleck, R. K., and F. A. Hanssen. Forthcoming. *Engineering the Rule of Law in Ancient Athens.* The Journal of Legal Studies.

Flower, H. 2010. "Rome's First Civil War and the Fragility of Republican Political Culture." In *Citizens of Discord: Rome and Its Civil Wars,* edited by B. W. Breed, C. Damon, and A. Rossi. Oxford: Oxford University Press.

Forsdyke, S. 2005. *Exile, Ostracism, and Democracy: The Politics of Expulsion in Ancient Greece.* Princeton: Princeton University Press.

Forsdyke, S. 2012. *Slaves Tell Tales*. Princeton: Princeton University Press.

Forsdyke, S. 2018. "Ancient and Modern Conceptions of the Rule of Law." In *Ancient Greek History and Contemporary Social Science*, edited by M. Canevaro, B. Gray, A. Erskine, and J. Ober. Edinburgh Leventis Studies. Edinburgh: Edinburgh University Press.

Frazer, B. L. 2009. "A History of Athenian Taxation from Solon to the Grain Tax Law of 374/3 B.C." PhD dissertation, University of California, Berkeley.

Frier, B. W., and D. P. Kehoe. 2007. "Law and Economic Institutions." In *The Cambridge Economic History of the Greco-Roman World*, edited by W. Scheidel, I. Morris, and R. P. Saller. Cambridge: Cambridge University Press, 113–43.

Fuks, A. 1953. *The Ancestral Constitution: Four Studies in Athenian Party Politics at the End of the Fifth Century B.C.* London: Routledge and Paul.

Fuks, A. 1984. *Social Conflict in Ancient Greece*. Jerusalem: Magnes Press, Hebrew University.

Fukuyama, F. 1992. *The End of History and the Last Man*. New York: Free Press.

Fukuyama, F. 2011. *The Origins of Political Order*. New York: Farrar, Strauss, and Giroux.

Fukuyama, F. 2014. *Political Order and Political Decay: From the Industrial Revolution to the Globalization of Democracy*. New York: Farrar, Straus, and Giroux.

Fuller, Lon L. 1964. *The Morality of Law*. New Haven: Yale University Press.

Gabrielsen, V. 1994. *Financing the Athenian Fleet*. Baltimore: Johns Hopkins University Press.

Gabrielsen, V. 2007. "Brotherhoods of Faith and Provident Planning: The Non-Public Associations of the Greek World." *Mediterranean Historical Review* 22(2), 183–210.

Gabrielsen, V. 2013. "Finance and Taxes." In *A Companion to Ancient Greek Government*. Oxford: Wiley.

Gabrielsen, V. 2016. "Associations, Modernization and the Return of the Private Network in Athens." *In Die Athenische Demokratie im 4. Jahrhundert: Zwischen Modernisierung und Tradition*, edited by Claudia Tiersch. Steiner, Stuttgart.

Gagarin, Michael. 1981. *Drakon and Early Athenian Homicide Law*. New Haven: Yale University Press.

Gagarin, M. 1986. *Early Greek Law*. University of California Press.

Gagarin, M. 2005. "Early Greek Law." In M. Gagarin and D. Cohen, *The Cambridge Companion to Ancient Greek Law*. Cambridge: Cambridge University Press.

Gagarin, M. 2008. *Writing Greek Law*. Cambridge: Cambridge University Press.

Gardner, P. 1913. "Coinage of the Athenian Empire." *Journal of Hellenic Studies* 33, 147–88.

Garland, R. 1987. *The Piraeus. From the 5th to the 1st Century B.C.* Ithaca, NY: Cornell University Press.

Garnsey, P. 1988. *Famine and Food Supply in the Graeco-Roman World*. Cambridge: Cambridge University Press.

Gehrke, H.-J. 1985. *Stasis: Untersuchungen zu den inneren Kriegen in den griechischen Staaten des 5. und 4. Jahrhunderts v. Chr.* München: Beck.

Geraghty, R. M. 2007. "The Impact of Globalization in the Roman Empire, 200 BC–AD 100." *Journal of Economic History* 67(4).

Gerring, J., et al. 2005. "Democracy and Economic Growth: A Historical Perspective." *World Politics* 57(April), 323–64.

Ginsburg, T., and A. Z. Huq. 2016. *Assessing Constitutional Performance*. New York: Cambridge University Press.

Ginsburg, Tom, and Aziz Z. Huq. 2018. *How to Save a Constitutional Democracy.* Chicago and London: University of Chicago Press.

Goiran, J-P., et al. 2011. "Piraeus, the Ancient Island of Athens: Evidence from Holocene Sediments and Historical Archives." *Geology* 39(6), 531–34.

Goldsmith, R. W. 1984. "An Estimate of the Size and Structure of the National Product of the Early Roman Empire." *Review of Income and Wealth* 30, 263–88.

Goldstone, J. 2002. "Efflorescences and Economic Growth in World History." *Journal of World History* 13, 323–89.

Gomme, A. W. 1933. *The Population of Athens in the 5th and 4th Centuries B.C.* Oxford: B. Blackwell.

Gonzalez de Lara, Yadira, Avner Greif, and Saumitra Jha. 2008. "The Administrative Foundations of Self-Enforcing Constitutions." *American Economic Review* 98(2): 105–9.

Goodell, T. D. 1893–94. "An Athenian Parallel to a Function of Our Supreme Court." *Yale Review* 2.

Goodwin, W. W. 1895. "The Athenian *Graphē Paranomōn* and the American Doctrine of Constitutional Law." *TAPA* 26, lx-lxi.

Gottesman, A. 2014. *Politics and the Street in Democratic Athens.* Cambridge: Cambridge University Press.

Gowder, P. 2014. "Democracy, Solidarity, and the Rule of Law: Lessons from Athens." *Buffalo Law Review* 62(1).

Gowder, Paul. 2016. *The Rule of Law in the Real World.* New York: Cambridge University Press.

Grandjean, C. 2006. "Athens and Bronze Coinage." In *Agoranomia.* American Numismatic Society, 99–108.

Granovetter, M. 1973. "The Strength of Weak Ties." *American Journal of Sociology* 78(6), 1360–80.

Greif, A. 1998. "Self-Enforcing Political Systems and Economic Growth: Late Medieval Genoa." In R. H. Bates, *Analytic Narratives.* Princeton: Princeton University Press.

Greif, A., and D. D. Laitin. 2004. "A Theory of Endogenous Institutional Change." *American Political Science Review* 98(4).

Griffin, S. M. 1996. *American Constitutionalism: From Theory to Politics.* Princeton: Princeton University Press.

Grigoropoulos, D. 2009. "The Population of the Piraeus in the Roman Period: A Re-Assessment of the Evidence of Funerary Inscriptions. *Greece and Rome* 56(2), 164–82.

Haber, S., and V. Menaldo. 2011. "Do Natural Resources Fuel Authoritarianism? A Reappraisal of the Resource Curse." *American Political Science Review.*

Habicht, C. 1997. *Athens from Alexander to Antony.* Cambridge, MA: Harvard University Press.

Habyarimana, J., M. Humphreys, J. N. Posner, and J. M. Weinstein. 2005. "Ethnic Identifiability: An Experimental Approach." http://www.columbia.edu/~mh2245/papers1/ID_paper.pdf.

Habyarimana, J., M. Humphreys, J. N. Posner, and J. M. Weinstein. 2007. "Why Does Ethnic Diversity Undermine Public Goods Provision?" *American Political Science Review* 101(4), 709–25.

Hadfield, G., and B. R. Weingast. 2012. "What Is Law? A Coordination Model of the Characteristics of Legal Order." *Journal of Legal Analysis* 4(2), 471–514.

Hadfield, G., and B. R. Weingast. 2013. "Law without the State: Legal Attributes and the Coordination of Decentralized Collective Punishment." *Journal of Law and Courts* 1(1), 3–34.

Hadfield, G., and B. R. Weingast. 2014. "Microfoundations of the Rule of Law." *Annual Review of Political Science* 17, 21–42.

Halkos, George E., and Nickolas C. Kyriazis. 2010. "The Athenian Economy in the Age of Demosthenes: Path Dependence and Change." *European Journal of Law and Economics* 29, 255–77.

Hall, J. M. 2007. *A History of the Archaic Greek World, ca. 1200–479 BCE.* Malden, MA: Blackwell Publications.

Hansen, M. H. 1974. *The Sovereignty of the People's Courts in Athens in the Fourth Century BC and the Public Action against Unconstitutional Proposals.* Odense University Press.

Hansen, M. H. 1975. *Eisangelia: The Sovereignty of the People's Court in Athens in the Fourth Century BC and the Impeachment of Generals and Politicians.* Odense University Press.

Hansen, M. H. 1978. "Nomos and Psephisma in Fourth-Century Athens." *Greek, Roman, and Byzantine Studies* 19.

Hansen, M. H. 1979a. "Did the Athenian Ecclesia Legislate after 403/2?" *Greek, Roman, and Byzantine Studies* 20.

Hansen, M. H. 1979b. "Misthos for Magistrates in Fourth-Century Athens?" *Symbolae Osloenses* 54.

Hansen, M. H. 1984. "The Number of Rhetores in the Athenian Ecclesia, 355–322 B.C." *Greek, Roman, and Byzantine Studies* 25.

Hansen, M. H. 1985. "Athenian Nomothesia." *Greek, Roman, and Byzantine Studies* 26, 345–71.

Hansen, M. H. 1986. *Demography and Democracy: The Number of Athenian Citizens in the Fourth Century B.C.* Herning, Denmark: Systime.

Hansen, M. H. 1987a. "Graphē Paranomōn against Psēphismata Not Yet Passed by the Ekklesia." *CandM* 38.

Hansen, M. H. 1987b. *The Athenian Assembly in the Age of Demosthenes.* Blackwell.

Hansen, M. H. 1988. *Three Studies in Athenian Demography.* Copenhagen, Denmark: Munksgaard.

Hansen, M. H. 1989a. "Was Athens a Democracy?" *Classical Review* 40(1).

Hansen, M. H. 1989b. "Solonian Democracy in Fourth Century Athens." *CandM* 40.

Hansen, M. H. 1990a. "Diokles' Law and the Revision of the Athenian Corpus of Laws in the Arconship of Eucleides." *CandM* 41.

Hansen, M. H. 1990b. *Review Article: Ober, J. 1989 Mass and Elite in Democratic Athens.* Princeton: Princeton University Press.

Hansen, M. H. 1999. *The Athenian Democracy in the Age of Demosthenes.* University of Oklahoma Press.

Hansen, M. H. 2002. "Was the Polis a State or a Stateless Society?" In *Even More Studies in the Ancient Greek Polis*, edited by Thomas H. Nielsen. Acts of the Copenhagen Polis Centre [CPC] 6, 17–47.

Hansen, M. H. 2006a. *The Shotgun Method: The Demography of the Ancient Greek City-State Culture.* Columbia: University of Missouri Press.

Hansen, M. H. 2006b. *Studies in the Population of Aigina, Athens and Eretria.* Copenhagen, Denmark: Kongelige Danske Videnskabernes Selskab.

Hansen, M. H. 2008. "An Update on the Shotgun Method." *Greek, Roman, and Byzantine Studies* 48, 259–86.

Hansen, M. H. 2016. "The Authenticity of the Law about Nomothesia Inserted in Demosthenes against Timokrates 33." *Greek, Roman, and Byzantine Studies* 56, 594–610.

Hansen, M. Herman, and T. Heine Nielsen. 2004. *An Inventory of Archaic and Classical Poleis.* Oxford: Oxford University Press.

Hanson, V. D. 1998. *Warfare and Agriculture in Classical Greece.* Revised edition. Berkeley: University of California Press.

Hanssen, F. A., and R. K. Fleck. 2012. "On the Benefits and Costs of Legal Expertise: Adjudication in Ancient Athens." *Review of Law and Economics* 8, 367–99.

Hanssen, F. A., and R. K. Fleck. 2013. "How Tyranny Paved the Way to Democracy: The Democratic Transition in Ancient Greece." *Journal of Law and Economics* 56, 389–416.

Hardin, R. 1989. "Why a Constitution?" In *The Federalist Papers and the New Institutionalism,* edited by Bernard Grofman and Donald Wittman. New York: Agathon Press.

Hardin, R. 1999. *Liberalism, Constitutionalism, and Democracy.* Oxford University Press.

Harding, Ph. 1987. "Metics, Foreigners or Slaves? The Recipients of Honours in IG II² 10." *Zeitschrift für Papyrologie und Epigraphik* 67.

Harding, Ph. 1995. "Athenian Foreign Policy in the Fourth Century." *Klio* 77, 105–25.

Harris, E. M. 1990. "The Constitution of the Five Thousand." *Harvard Studies in Classical Philology* 93, 243–80.

Harris, E. M. 1994. "Law and Oratory." In I. Worthington, *Persuasion: Greek Rhetoric in Action.* London: Routledge.

Harris, E. M. 2006a. *Democracy and the Rule of Law in Classical Athens: Essays On Law, Society, and Politics.* Cambridge: Cambridge University Press.

Harris, E. M. 2006b. "The Rule of Law in Athenian Democracy. Reflections on the Judicial Oath." *Dike* 9.

Harris, E. M. 2007a. "Did the Athenian Courts Attempt to Achieve Consistency? Oral Tradition and Written Records in the Athenian Administration of Justice." In *Politics of Orality,* edited by Craig Cooper. Leiden, Netherlands: Brill, 343–70.

Harris, E. M. 2007b. "Who Enforced the Law in Classical Athens?" In *Symposion 2005: Vorträge zur griechischen und hellenistischen Rechtsgeschichte,* edited by Eva Cantarella. Wien: Verlag der Österreichischen Akademie der Wissenschaften, 159–76.

Harris, E. M. 2013. *The Rule of Law in Action in Democratic Athens.* Oxford University Press.

Harris, E. M., D. M. Lewis, and M. Woolmer, eds. 2016. *The Ancient Greek Economy.* Cambridge: Cambridge University Press.

Harris, W. V. 2011. "Introduction." In *Maritime Technology in the Ancient Economy: Ship-Design and Navigation,* edited by W.V. Harris and K. Iara. Portsmouth, RI: Journal of Roman Archaeology.

Harrison, A.R.W. 1955. "Law Making at Athens and the End of the Fifth Century BC." *Journal of Hellenic Studies* 75.

Herman, G. 1995. "Honour, revenge and the State in Fourth-Century Athens." In *Die athenische Demokratie im 4. Jahrhundert v. Chr.: Vollendung oder Verfall einer Verfassungsform?: Akten eines Symposims 3.-7. August 1992, Bellagio,* edited by W. Eder and C. Auffarth. Stuttgart: F. Steiner, 43–60.

Herman, G. 1996. "Ancient Athens and the Values of Mediterranean Society." *Mediterranean Historical Review* 11, 5–36.

Herodotus, Robert B. Strassler, and Andrea L. Purvis. 2007. *The Landmark Herodotus: The Histories.* New York: Pantheon Books.

Hignett, C. 1952. *A History of the Athenian Constitution to the End of the Fifth Century B.C.* Oxford: Clarendon Press.

Hin, S. 2013. *The Demography of Roman Italy: Population Dynamics in an Ancient Conquest Society, 201 BCE–14 CE.*

Hobbes, T., and E. M. Curley. 1994 [1651]. *Leviathan: With Selected Variants from the Latin Edition of 1668.* Indianapolis: Hackett Publication Co.

Hopkins, K. 1978. *Conquerors and Slaves.* Cambridge: Cambridge University Press.

Hopkins, K. 1980. "Taxes and Trade in the Roman Empire (200 B.C.–A.D. 400)." *Journal of Roman Studies* 70, 101–25.

Hopper, R. J. 1953. "The Attic Silver Mines in the Fourth Century B.C." *ABSA* 48, 200–254.

Hopper, R. J. 1979. *Trade and Industry in Classical Greece.* London: Thames and Hudson.

Hornblower, S. 1983. *The Greek World, 479–323 BC.* London: Methuen.

Hornblower, S. 1991. *A Commentary on Thucydides.* Oxford University Press.

Hotelling, Harold. 1929. "Stability in Competition." *Economic Journal* 39(153), 41–57. doi:10.2307/2224214.

Humphrey, J. William. 2006. *Ancient Technology.* Westport, CT: Greenwood Press.

Hunter, V. 1994. *Policing Athens: Social Control in the Attic Lawsuits 420–320 BC.* Princeton: Princeton University Press.

Hunter, V. 2006. "Pittalacus and Eucles: Slaves in the Public Service of Athens." *Mouseion* 6.

Huntington, S. P. 1968. *Political Order in Changing Societies.* New Haven: Yale University Press.

Imai, K., and J. M. Weinstein. 2000. "Measuring the Economic Impact of Civil War." CID Working Paper No. 51.

Isager S., and M. H. Hansen. 1975. *Aspects of Athenian Society in the Fourth Century B.C.* Translated by J. Hsiang. Odense, 1975 (1972), 42–50.

Ismard, P. 2010. *La cité des réseaux. Athènes et ses associations, vie-ier siècle av. J.-C.* Paris: Publications de la Sorbonne.

Ismard, P. 2015. *La démocratie contre les experts: les esclaves publics en Grèce ancienne.* Paris: Seuil.

Isocrates. 1980. *Isocrates in Three Volumes.* Translated by George Norlin. Cambridge, MA: Harvard University Press; London: William Heinemann, Ltd.

Jacob, O. 1928. *Les esclaves publics a Athene.* Liege.

Johnstone, S. 1999. *Disputes and Democracy: The Consequences of Litigation in Ancient Athens.* Austin: University of Texas Press.

Jones, A.H.M. 1957. *Athenian Democracy.* Oxford.

Jongman, W. 2007. "Consumption in the Early Roman Empire." In *The Cambridge Economic History of the Greco-Roman World*, edited by W. Scheidel, I. Morris, and R. P. Saller. Cambridge: Cambridge University Press.

Joyce, C. 2008. "The Athenian Amnesty and Scrutiny of 403." *Classical Quarterly* 58(2), 507–18.

Joyce, C. 2014. "...And 'All the Laws' (Andocides, On the Mysteries 81–2): A Reply to E. Carawan." *Antichthon* 48, 37–54.

Joyce, C. 2015. "Oaths (ὅρκοι), Covenants (συνθῆκαι) and Laws (νόμοι) in the Athenian Reconciliation Agreement of 403 BC." *Antichthon* 49, 24–49.

Kadens, E. 2015. "The Medieval Law Merchant: The Tyranny of a Construct." *Journal of Legal Analysis* 7(2), 251–89.

Kagan, D. 1987. *The Fall of the Athenian Empire.* Ithaca, NY: Cornell University Press.

Kahrstedt, U. 1954. *Das wirtschaftliche Gesicht Griechenlands in der Kaiserzeit. Kleinstadt, Villa und Domäne.* Bern.

Kaiser, B. A. 2007. "The Athenian Trierarchy: Mechanism Design for the Private Provision of Public Goods." *Journal of Economic History* 67(2), 445–80.

Kalimtzis, K. 2000. *Aristotle on Political Enmity and Disease: An Inquiry into Stasis.* Albany: State University of New York Press.

Kamen, D. 2013. *Status in Classical Athens.* Princeton: Princeton University Press.

Kang, S., and J. Meernik. 2005. "Civil War Destruction and the Prospects for Economic Growth." *Journal of Politics* 67(1), 88–109.

Karachalios, Foivos Spyridon. 2013. *The Politics of Judgment: Dispute Resolution and State Formation from the Homeric World to Solon's Athens.* http://purl.stanford.edu/cn134tw2820.

Karayiannis, A., and A. Hatzis. 2012. "Morality, Social Norms and the Rule of Law as Transaction Cost-Saving Devices: The Case of Ancient Athens." *European Journal of Law and Economics* 33(3), 621–43.

Kasara, K. 2007. "Tax Me if You Can: Ethnic Geography, Democracy, and the Taxation of Agriculture in Africa." *American Political Science Review* 101(1), 159–72.

Kay, P. 2014. *Rome's Economic Revolution.* First edition. Oxford: Oxford University Press.

Kierstead, J. C. 2013. *A Community of Communities: Associations and Democracy in Classical Athens.* PhD dissertation, Stanford University.

Knutsen, C. H. 2012. "Democracy and Economic Growth: A Survey of Arguments and Results." *International Area Studies Review* 15(4), 393–415. https://doi.org/10.1177/2233865912455268.

Kraay, C. M. 1976. *Archaic and Classical Greek Coins.* London: Methuen and Co.

Kramer, L. 2004. *The People Themselves: Popular Constitutionalism and Judicial Review.* New York: Oxford University Press.

Kremmydas, C. 2012. *A Commentary on Demosthenes' Against Leptines.* Oxford.

Krentz, P. 1980. "Foreigners against the Thirty: IG II2 10 Again." *Phoenix* 34.

Krentz, P. 1982. *The Thirty at Athens.* Ithaca, NY: Cornell University Press.

Krentz, P. 1986. "The Rewards for Thrasyboulos' Supporters." *ZPE* 62.

Kroll, J. H. 1972. *Athenian Bronze Allotment Plates.* Cambridge, MA: Harvard University Press.

Kroll, J. H. 2011. "The Reminting of Athenian Silver Coinage, 353 B.C." *Hesperia* 80(2), 229–59.

Kron, G. 2011. "The Distribution of Wealth in Athens in Comparative Perspective." *Zeitschrift für Papyrologie und Epigraphic* 179, 129–38.

Kron, G. 2014. "Comparative Evidence and the Reconstruction of the Ancient Economy: Greco-Roman Housing and the Level and Distribution of Wealth and Income." In *Quantifying the Greco-Roman Economy and Beyond,* edited by François de Callataÿ. Bari: Edipuglia.

Kuran, T. 1991. Now Out of Never. The Element of Surprise in the East European Revolutions of 1989. *World Politics* 44(1), 7–48.

Kuran, T. 1995. *Private Truths, Public Lies: The Social Consequences of Preference Falsification.* Cambridge, MA: Harvard University Press.

Kylander, M. E., et al. 2005. "Refining the Pre-Industrial Atmospheric Pb Isotope Evolution Curve in Europe Using an 8000 Year Old Peat Core from NW Spain." *Earth and Planetary Science Letters* 240(2), 467–85.

Kyriazis, N. 2009. "Financing the Athenian State." *European Journal of Law and Economics* 27.

Kyriazis, N., and E.M.L. Economou. 2013. "Social Contract, Public Choice, and Fiscal Repercussions in the Athenian Democracy." *Theoretical and Practical Research in Economic Fields* 4(1), 61–76.

Lagia, A. 2015. "Diet and the Polis: An Isotopic Study of Diet in Athens and Laurion during the Classical, Hellenistic, and Imperial Roman Periods." In *Archaeodiet in the Greek World: Dietary Reconstruction from Stable Isotope Analysis*, edited by Anastasia Papathanasiou, Michael P. Richards, and Sherry C. Fox. *Hesperia Supplement* 49.

Lambert, S. D. 1997. *Rationes Centesimarum: Sales of Public Land in Lykourgan Athens*. Amsterdam: Gieben.

Lambert, S. D. 2017. *Inscribed Athenian Laws and Decrees in the Age of Demosthenes*. Leiden, The Netherlands: Brill.

Lane, M. 2016. "Popular Sovereignty as Control of Office-Holders." In *Popular Sovereignty in Historical Perspective*, edited by R. Bourke and Q. Skinner. Cambridge: Cambridge University Press.

Langdon, M. 1991. "The Poletai Records." *Athenian Agora* 19, 55–143.

Lanni, A. 2004. "Arguing from 'Precedent': Modern Perspectives on Athenian Practice." In *The Law and the Courts in Ancient Greece*. Duckworth.

Lanni, A. 2006. *Law and Justice in the Courts of Classical Athens*. Cambridge: Cambridge University Press.

Lanni, A. 2009. "Social Norms in the Courts of Ancient Athens." *Journal of Legal Analysis* 1(2), 691–736.

Lanni, A. 2010. "Judicial Review and the Athenian 'Constitution,'" *Harvard Law School Public Law and Legal Theory Working Paper Series*, Paper No. 10–21.

Lanni, A. 2012. "Publicity and the Courts of Classical Athens." *Yale Journal of Law and the Humanities* 24, 119.

Lanni, A. 2016. *Law and Order in Ancient Athens*. New York: Cambridge University Press.

Lanni, Adriaan M., and Adrian Vermeule. 2012. "Constitutional Design in the Ancient World." *Stanford Law Review* 64 (907).

Lanni, Adriaan, and Adrian Vermeule. 2013. "Precautionary Constitutionalism in Ancient Athens." *Cardozo Law Review* 34, 893.

Lazenby, J. F. 2004. *The Peloponnesian War: A Military Study*. London: Routledge.

Leão, D. Ferreira, and P. J. Rhodes. 2015. *The Laws of Solon: A New Edition with Introduction, Translation and Commentary*. London: I. B. Tauris.

Legon, R. P. 1981. *Megara: The Political History of a Greek City-State to 336 B.C.* Ithaca: Cornell University Press.

Levitsky, S., and D. Ziblatt. 2018. *How Democracies Die*. First edition. New York: Crown.

Lewis, D. 1973. "The Athenian Rationes Centesimarum." In *Problèmes de la terre en Grèce ancienne*, edited by M. I. Finley. Paris: Mouton.

Lewis, D. 1974. "Entrenchment-Clauses in Attic Decrees." In Donald William Bradeen, Malcolm Francis McGregor, and Benjamin Dean Meritt, *[Phoros (Romanized Form)]; Tribute to Benjamin Dean Meritt*. Locust Valley, NY: J. J. Augustin.

Lewis, D. 2013. "Slave Marriages in the Laws of Gortyn: A Matter of Rights?" *Historia* 62(4), 390–416.

Lewis, S. 2009. *Greek Tyranny*. Exeter, Devon, UK: Bristol Phoenix Press.

Lintott, A. W. 1971. "Lucan and the History of the Civil War." *Classical Quarterly* 21(2), 488–505.

Lintott, A. 1982. *Violence, Civil Strife, and Revolution in the Classical City, 750–330 B.C.* Baltimore: Johns Hopkins University Press.

Lintott, A. W. 1999. *Violence in Republican Rome.* Oxford: Oxford University Press.

Linz, J. J. 1978. *The Breakdown of Democratic Regimes: Crisis, Breakdown and Reequilibration.* Baltimore: Johns Hopkins University Press.

Lipset, S. M. 1959. "Some Social Requisites of Democracy: Economic Development and Political Legitimacy." *American Political Science Review* 53(1).

Loening, T. C. 1987. *The Reconciliation Agreement of 403/402 BC in Athens.* Stuttgart: Franz Steiner Verlag Wiesbaden.

Loraux, N. 2002. *The Divided City.* New York: Zone Books.

Lyttkens, C. H. 1991. "A Predatory Democracy? An Essay on Taxation in Classical Athens." *Explorations in Economic History* 31, 62–90.

Lyttkens, Carl Hampus. 2008. "Institutions, Taxation, and Market Relationships in Ancient Athens." Working Papers 9. Lund University, Department of Economics.

Lyttkens, C. H. 2010. "Institutions, Taxation and Market Relationships in Ancient Athens." *Journal of Institutional Economics* 6(4).

Lyttkens, C. H. 2006. "Reflections on the Origins of the Polis. An Economic Perspective on Institutional Change in Ancient Greece." *Constitutional Political Economy* 17, 31–48.

Lyttkens, C. H. 2013. *Economic Analysis of Institutional Change in Ancient Greece.* Routledge.

MacDowell, D. M. 1975. "Law-Making at Athens in the 4th Century BC." *Journal of Hellenic Studies* 95, 62–74.

MacDowell, D. M. 1978. *The Law in Classical Athens.* Cornell University Press.

Mack, W. J. 2015. *Proxeny and Polis: Institutional Networks in the Ancient Greek World.* First edition. Oxford: Oxford University Press.

Mackil, E. 2004. "Wandering Cities: Alternatives to Catastrophe in the Greek Polis." *American Journal of Archaeology* 108(4).

Mackil, E. 2013. *Creating a Common Polity. Religion, Economy, and Politics in the Making of the Greek Koinon.* University of California Press.

Maddison, A. 2007. *Contours of the World Economy, 1–2030 AD: Essays in Macro-Economic History.* Cambridge.

Markle, M. M. 1985. "Jury Pay and Assembly Pay at Athens." *Crux,* 265–97.

Mayer, E. 2012. *The Ancient Middle Classes.* Harvard University Press.

Mazarakis-Ainian, A. 1997. *From Rulers' Dwellings to Temples: Architecture, Religion and Society in Early Iron Age Greece (1100–700 B.C.).* Jonsered: Paul Åströms Förlag.

McCannon, B. C. 2012. "The Origin of Democracy in Athens." *Review of Law and Economics* 8, 531–62.

Meiggs R., and D. Lewis. 1969. *Greek Historical Inscriptions.* Oxford.

Meritt, B. D. 1933. *Hesperia* 2(2).

Millett, P. 1991. *Lending and Borrowing in Ancient Athens.* Cambridge: Cambridge University Press.

Milgrom, P. R., D. C. North, and B. R. Weingast. 1990. "The Role of Institutions in the Revival of Trade: The Law Merchant, Private Judges, and the Champagne Fairs." *Economics and Politics* 2, 1–23. doi:10.1111/j.1468-0343.1990.tb00020.x.

Millett, P. C. 2000. "Mogens Hansen and the Labeling of Athenian Democracy." In *Polis and Politics: Studies in Ancient Greek History*, edited by P. Flensted-Jensen, M. H. Hansen, T. H. Nielsen, and L. Rubinstein. Museum Tusculanum Press, 337–62.

Mittal S., and B. Weingast. 2013. "Self-Enforcing Constitutions: With an Application to Democratic Stability in America's First Century." *Journal of Law, Economics, and Organization* 29(2), 278–302.

Monson, A., and W. Scheidel, eds. 2015. *Fiscal Regimes and the Political Economy of Premodern States*. Cambridge University Press.Morris, I. 1998. "Archaeology as a Kind of Anthropology (A Response to David Small)." *Democracy 2500? Questions and Challenges*, edited by Ian Morris and Kurt A. Raaflaub. Dubuque, IA: Kendall/Hunt, 229–39.

Morris, I. 1999. "Foreword." In M. I. Finley, *The Ancient Economy*. Updated edition. Berkeley: University of California Press.

Morris, I. 2004. "Economic Growth in Ancient Greece." *Journal of Institutional and Theoretical Economics* 160(4), 709–42.

Morris, I. 2005. *The Growth of Greek Cities in the First Millennium BC*. Princeton/Stanford Working Papers in Classics.

Morris, I. 2009a. "The Eight-Century Revolution." In Raaflaub, Kurt A., and Hans van Wees, A Companion to Archaic Greece. Chichester, UK: Wiley-Blackwell.

Morris, I. 2009b. *The Greater Athenian State*. In Morris and Scheidel, *The Dynamics of Ancient Empires*. Oxford, 99–177.

Morris, I. 2010. *Why the West Rules—for Now: The Patterns of History, and What They Reveal about the Future*. London: Profile Books.

Morris, I. 2013. *The Measure of Civilization: How Social Development Decides the Fate of Nations*. Princeton: Princeton University Press.

Morris, I. 2014. *War! What Is It Good For?* Farrar, Straus, and Giroux.

Morris I., and B. Powell. 2006. *The Greeks: History, Culture, and Society*. Second Edition. Pearson.

Morton, J. 2001. *The Role of the Physical Environment in Ancient Greek Seafaring*. Leiden, Netherlands; Boston: Brill.

Murdoch, J. C., and T. Sandler. 2002. "Economic Growth, Civil Wars, and Spatial Spillovers." *Journal of Conflict Resolution* 46 (1), 91–110.

Murdoch, J. C, and T. Sandler. 2004. "Civil Wars and Economic Growth: Spatial Dispersion." *American Journal of Political Science* 48, 138–51.

Murray, O. 1993. *Early Greece*. Second edition. Cambridge, MA: Harvard University Press.

Nathan, Laurie, and Monica Duffy Toft. 2011. "Correspondence: Civil War Settlements and the Prospects for Peace." *International Security* 36(1), 202–10.

Negretto, Gabriel L. 2013. *Making Constitutions: Presidents, Parties, and Institutional Choice in Latin America*. Cambridge: Cambridge University Press.

Nicolet, C. 1994. "Economy and Society, 133–43 BC." In *The Cambridge Ancient History, Volume IX: The Last Age of the Roman Republic, 146–43 BC*, edited by J. A. Crook et al. Second edition. Cambridge.

North, D. C. 1993. "Institutions and Credible Commitment." *Journal of Institutional and Theoretical Economics* 149(1), 11–23.

North, D., B. Wallis, and J. Weingast. 2009. *Violence and Social Orders*. Cambridge: Cambridge University Press.

North, D., and B. Weingast. 1989. "Constitutions and Commitment." *Journal of Economic History* 49(4).

Ober, J. 1989a. *Mass and Elite in Democratic Athens*. Princeton: Princeton University Press.

Ober, J. 1989b. "The Nature of Athenian Democracy." *Classical Philology* 84(4).

Ober, J. 1996. *The Athenian Revolution: Essays on Ancient Greek Democracy and Political Theory*. Princeton: Princeton University Press.

Ober, J. 1998. *Political Dissent in Democratic Athens: Intellectual Critics of Popular Rule*. Princeton: Princeton University Press.

Ober, J. 2000. "Quasi-Rights: Participatory Citizenship and Negative Liberties in Democratic Athens." *Social Philosophy and Policy* 17(1), 27–61. doi:10.1017/S0265052500002521.

Ober, J. 2002. "Social Science History, Cultural History, and the Amnesty of 403." *Transactions of the American Philological Association* 132, 127–37.

Ober, J. 2007. "I Besieged that Man: Democracy's Revolutionary Start." In K. A. Raaflaub, J. Ober, and R. W. Wallace, *Origins of Democracy in Ancient Greece*. 2007. Berkeley: University of California Press.

Ober, J. 2008. *Democracy and Knowledge*. Princeton: Princeton University Press.

Ober, J. 2010. "Wealthy Hellas." *Transactions of the American Philological Association* 140(2), 241–86.

Ober, J. 2015a. *The Rise and Fall of Classical Greece*. Princeton: Princeton University Press.

Ober, J. 2015b. "Fiscal Policy in Classical Athens." In *Fiscal Regimes and the Political Economy of Premodern States*, edited by Andrew Monson and Walter Scheidel. Cambridge: Cambridge University Press.

Ober, J. 2017. "Inequality in Late-Classical Democratic Athens: Evidence and Models." In *Democracy and Open Economy World Order*, edited by G.C. Bitros and N.C. Kyriazis. New York: Springer.

Ober J. 2019. *The Greeks and the Rational*. Fall 2019 Sather Lectures. In progress.

O'Donnell, G. A. 1973. *Modernization and Bureaucratic-Authoritarianism: Studies in South American Politics*. Berkeley: Institute of International Studies, University of California.

Olson, M. 1965. *The Logic of Collective Action: Public Goods and the Theory of Groups*. Cambridge, MA: Harvard University Press.

Ordeshook, P. C. 1992. "Constitutional Stability." *Constitutional Political Economy* 3, 137-175.

Ordeshook, P. 1993. "Some Rules of Constitutional Design." In E. Frankel Paul, F. Dycus Miller, and J. Paul, *Liberalism and the Economic Order*. Cambridge.

Osborne, M. J. 1981. *Naturalization in Athens*. Brussels.

Osborne, R. 2003. "Changing the Discourse." In *Popular Tyranny, Sovereignty and Its Discontents in Ancient Greece*, edited by K. Morgan. University of Texas Press.

Osborne, R. 2009. *Greece in the Making, 1200–479 BC*. Second edition. London: Routledge.

Osborne, Robin. 2010. *Athens and Athenian Democracy*. Cambridge: Cambridge University Press.

Ostwald, M. 1986. *From Popular Sovereignty to the Sovereignty of Law*. University of California Press.

Panagos, C. T. 1968. *Le Pirée; étude économique et historique depuis les temps les plus anciens jusqu'à la fin de l'Empire romain*. Athens.

Papazarkadas, N. 2011. *Sacred and Public Land in Ancient Athens*. Oxford: Oxford University Press.

Parker, A. J. 1992. *Ancient Shipwrecks of the Mediterranean and the Roman Provinces*. Oxford.

Persson, Torsten, and Guido E. Tabellini. 2003. *The Economic Effects of Constitutions*. Cambridge, MA: M.I.T. Press.

Pettegrew, D. K. 2011. "The *Diolkos* of Corinth." *American Journal of Archaeology* 115(4), 549–74.

Phillips, D. D. 2013. *The Law of Ancient Athens*. Ann Arbor: University of Michigan Press.

Piérart, M. 2000. "Qui étaient les nomothètes à l'époque de Démosthène?" In *La codiication des lois dans l'antiquité*, edited by E. Lévy. Paris, 229–56.

Pitsoulis, A., 2011. "The Egalitarian Battlefield: Reflections on the Origins of Majority Rule in Archaic Greece." *European Journal of Political Economy* 27, 87–103.

Plato, John M. Cooper, and D. S. Hutchinson. 1997. *Complete Works of the Athenians*. Available at http://myweb.ttu.edu/gforsyth/00.htm.

Plutarch. 1914. *Plutarch's Lives. Volume 2*. Translated by Bernadotte Perrin. Cambridge, MA: Harvard University Press; London: William Heinemann, Ltd.

Plutarch. 1916. *Plutarch's Lives. Volume 3*. Translated by Bernadotte Perrin. Cambridge, MA: Harvard University Press; London: William Heinemann, Ltd.

Plutarch. 1918. *Plutarch's Lives. Volume 6*. Translated by Bernadotte Perrin. Cambridge, MA: Harvard University Press; London: William Heinemann, Ltd.

Polybius. 1889. *Histories*. Translated by Evelyn S. Shuckburgh. London and New York: Macmillan. Reprint Bloomington, 1962.

Pomey, P. 2011. "L'évolution des techniques de construction navale et l'économie maritime." In *Maritime Technology in the Ancient Economy: Ship-Design and Navigation*, edited by W. V. Harris and K. Iara. Portsmouth, RI: Journal of Roman Archaeology.

Pritchard, D. 2010. "Costing the Armed Forces of Athens during the Peloponnesian War." *Ancient History* 37(2).

Pritchard, D. 2015. *Public Spending and Democracy in Classical Athens*. Austin, TX: University of Texas Press.

Pryor, J. 1988. *Geography, Technology, and War: Studies in the Maritime History of the Mediterranean, 649–1571*. Cambridge.

Pryor, J. H., and E. Jeffrey. 2006. *The Age of the Dromon: The Byzantine Navy ca. 500–1204*. Leiden, Netherlands: Brill.

Przeworski, A. 1991. *Democracy and the Market*. New York: Cambridge University Press.

Przeworski, A. 2005. "Democracy as an Equilibrium." *Public Choice* 123(3/4), 253–73.

Przeworski, A. 2006. "Self-Enforcing Democracy." In Barry R. Weingast and Donald A. Wittman, *The Oxford Handbook of Political Economy*. Oxford: Oxford University Press.

Przeworski, A., and F. Limongi. 1993. "Political Regimes and Economic Growth." *Journal of Economic Perspectives* 7(3), 51–69.

Przeworski, A., et al. 2000. *Democracy and Development: Political Institutions and Well-Being in the World, 1950–1990*. Cambridge: Cambridge University Press.

Pseudo-Xenophon, and G. Forsythe. 2001. *The Constitution*.

Pyzyk, M. Working Paper. "Onerous Burdens: Liturgies and the Athenian Elite."

Pyzyk, M. Forthcoming. "Finance, War-Making, and Technē in 4th-Century Greece." In *War in the Ancient World: The Economic Perspective*, edited by Manuela Dal Borgo and Roel Konijnedijk. Cambridge University Press.

Quillin, J. M. 2002. *Achieving Amnesty: The Role of Events, Institutions and Ideas.* TAPA 132, 71–107.

Raaflaub, K. 2006. "Thucydides on Democracy and Oligarchy." In *Brill's Companion to Thucydides,* edited by A. Tsakmakis and A. Rengakos. Leiden, Netherlands: Brill.

Raubitschek, A. E. 1941. *Hesperia* 10.

Ray D., and J. Esteban. 2017. "Conflict and Development." *Annual Review of Economics* 9: 263–93.

Renfrew, C. 1985. *The Archaeology of Cult: The Sanctuary at Phylakopi.* London: British School of Archaeology at Athens.

Rhodes, P. J. 1972a. "The Five Thousand in the Athenian Revolutions of 411 B.C." *Journal of Hellenic Studies* 92, 115–27.

Rhodes, P. J. 1972b. *The Athenian Boule.* Oxford.

Rhodes, P. J. 1980. "Athenian Democracy after 403 B.C." *Classical Journal* 75(4), 305–23.

Rhodes, P. J. 1981. *A Commentary on the Aristotelian Athenaion Politeia.* Oxford: Clarendon Press.

Rhodes, P. J. 1991. "The Athenian Code of Laws 410–399 BC." *Journal of Hellenic Studies,* 110.

Rhodes, P. J. 1998. "Enmity in Fourth Century Athens." In P. Cartledge, P. Millett, and S. von Reden, *Kosmos: Essays in Order, Conflict, and Community in Classical Athens.* Cambridge: Cambridge University Press.

Rhodes, P. J. 2003. "Sessions of Nomothetai in Fourth-Century Athens." *Classical Quarterly* 53(1), 124–29.

Rhodes, P. J. 2010. "Stability in the Athenian Democracy after 403 B.C." In *Zwischen Monarchie und Republik: Gesellschaftliche Stabilisierungsleistungen und Politische Transformationspotentiale in den antiken Stadtstaaten,* edited by B. Linke, M. Meier, and M. Strothmann. Stuttgart: Franz Steiner Verlag.

Rhodes, P. J. 2011. "Appeals to the Past in Classical Athens." In Herman, G., *Stability and Crisis in the Athenian Democracy. Historia Einzelschriften* 220, 13–30.

Rhodes, P. J. 2013. "The Organisation of Athenian Public Finance." *Greece and Rome* 60(2), 203–31.

Rhodes, P. J., and David M. Lewis. 1997. *The Decrees of the Greek States.* Oxford: Clarendon Press.

Rhodes, P. J., and R. Osborne. 2003. *Greek Historical Inscriptions: 404–323 BC.* Oxford: Oxford University Press.

Riess, W. 2012. "Stasis." In *Encyclopedia of Ancient History.* Wiley Online.

Riker, W. 1983. "Political Theory and the Art of Heresthetics." In *Political Science: The State of the Discipline,* edited by A. Finifter. Washington, DC: American Political Science Association, 47–67.

Riker, W. 1984. "The Heresthetics of Constitution-Making: The Presidency in 1787, with Comments on Determinism and Rational Choice." *American Political Science Review* 78, 1–16.

Robertson, N. 1990. "The Laws of Athens, 410–399 B.C." *Journal of Hellenic Studies* 110, 43–75.

Robinson, E. W., ed. 2004. "Democracy in Syracuse, 466–412 BC." In E. W. Robinson, *Ancient Greek Democracy.* Malden, MA: Blackwell Pub.

Robinson, E. W. 2011. *Democracy beyond Athens: Popular Government in Greek Classical Age.* Cambridge: Cambridge University Press.

Robinson, J. A., and R. Torvik. 2016. "Endogenous Presidentialism." *Journal of the European Economic Association* 14(4), 907–42.

Ross, M. L. 2001. "Does Oil Hinder Democracy?" *World Politics* 53(3), 325–61.

Ross, M. L. 2015. "What Have We Learned about the Resource Curse?" *Annual Review of Political Science* 18, 239–59.

Runciman, W. G. 1990. "Doomed to Extinction: The Polis as an Evolutionary Dead-End." *The Greek City*, edited by Oswyn Murray. Oxford: Oxford University Press, 348–67.

Ruschenbusch, E. 1966. *Solōnos Nomoi: die Fragmente des Solonischen Gesetzeswerkes, mit einer Text- und Überlieferungsgeschichte.* Wiesbaden: F. Steiner.

Ruschenbusch, Eberhard. 1978. *Untersuchungen zu Staat und Politik in Griechenland, vom 7.–4. Jh. v. Chr.* Bamberg: AKU Fotodruck GmbH.

Rutter, N. K. 2000. "Syracusan Democracy: 'Most like the Athenian?' " In *Alternatives to Athens*, edited by R. Brock and S. Hodkinson. Oxford, 137–51.

Ruze, F. 1974. "La fonction des probouloi dans le monde grec antique." In W. Seston, *Melanges d'histoire ancienne offerts a William Seston.* Paris: E. de Boccard.

Sachs, J., and A. Warner. 1995. "Natural Resource Abundance and Economic Growth." In *Leading Issues in Economic Development*, edited by G. Meier and J. Rauch. New York: Oxford University Press.

Sachs, J., and A. Warner. 2001. "The Curse of Natural Resources." *European Economic Review* 45 (4–6), 827–38.

Saller, R. 2005. "Framing the Debate over Growth in the Ancient Economy." In Morris and Manning, *The Ancient Economy.* Stanford University Press.

Salmon, J. B. 1984. *Wealthy Corinth.* Oxford University Press.

Sambanis, N. 2004. "Using Case Studies to Expand Economic Models of Civil War." *Perspectives on Politics*, 259–79.

Samons, Loren J. 2000. *Empire of the Owl: Athenian Imperial Finance.* Stuttgart: Steiner.

Schaefer, H. 1954. "Probouleuma." In *Paulys Realencyclopädie der classischen Altertumswissenschaft.* Stuttgart: J.B. Metzler.

Scheidel, W. 2007. "A Model of Real Income Growth in Roman Italy." *Historia: Zeitschrift für Alte Geschichte* 56 (3), 322–46.

Scheidel, W. 2008. "The Comparative Economics of Slavery in the Greco-Roman World." In *Slave Systems: Ancient and Modern*, edited by E. Dal Lago and C. Katsari. Cambridge University Press: Cambridge, 105–26.

Scheidel, W. 2009. "In Search of Roman Economic Growth." *Journal of Roman Archaeology* 22, 46–70.

Scheidel, W. 2010. "Real Wages in Early Economies: Evidence from Living Standards from 1800 BCE to 1300 CE." *Journal of the Social and Economic History of the Orient* 53, 425–62.

Scheidel, W. 2011. "A Comparative Perspective on the Determinants of Scale and Productivity of Roman Maritime Trade in the Mediterranean." In *Maritime Technology in the Ancient Economy: Ship-Design and Navigation*, edited by W.V. Harris and K. Iara. Portsmouth, RI: Journal of Roman Archaeology.

Scheidel, W., and S. J. Friesen. 2009. "The Size of the Economy and the Distribution of Income in the Roman Empire." *Journal of Roman Studies* 99, 61–91.

Scheidel, W., I. Morris, and R. P. Saller. 2007. *The Cambridge Economic History of the Greco-Roman World.* Cambridge: Cambridge University Press.

Schelling, T. 1966 [1960]. *Strategy of Conflict.* New York: Oxford University Press.

Schmitt, Carl. 2004. *Legality and Legitimacy*. Translated by Jeffrey Seitzer. Durham, NC: Duke University Press.

Schneider, H. 2007. "Technology." In W. Scheidel, I. Morris, and R. P. Saller, *The Cambridge Economic History of the Greco-Roman World*. Cambridge: Cambridge University Press, 144–72.

Schofield, Norman. 2006. *Architects of Political Change: Constitutional Quandaries and Social Choice Theory*. Cambridge: Cambridge University Press.

Schwartzberg, Melissa. 2004. "Athenian Democracy and Legal Change." *American Political Science Review* 98(2), 311–25.

Schwartzberg, Melissa. 2007. *Democracy and Legal Change*. Cambridge [England]: Cambridge University Press.

Schwartzberg, M. 2013a. "Was the *Graphē Paranomōn* a Form of Judicial Review?" *Cardozo Law Review* 34.

Schwartzberg, M. 2013b. *Counting the Many: The Origins and Limits of Supermajority Rule*. Cambridge: Cambridge University Press.

Sealey, R. 1975. Constitutional Changes in Athens in 410 B.C. *California Studies in Classical Antiquity* 8, 271–95.

Sealey, R. 1987. *The Athenian Republic. Democracy or the Rule of Law?* Pennsylvania State University Press.

Seager, R. 1994. "The Corinthian War." Edited by D. Lewis, J. Boardman, S. Hornblower, and M. Ostwald. *The Cambridge Ancient History*, 97–119. Cambridge: Cambridge University Press. doi:10.1017/CHOL9780521233484.005.

Shear, J. L. 2011. *Polis and Revolution: Responding to Oligarchy in Classical Athens*. Cambridge: Cambridge University Press.

Shelmerdine, C. W. 2008. *The Cambridge Companion to the Aegean Bronze Age*. Cambridge: Cambridge University Press.

Shipton, K. 2016. "The Silver Mines of 4th C Democratic Athens: An Economic Nexus." In *Die Athenische Demokratie im 4. Jahrhundert: Zwischen Modernisierung und Tradition*, edited by Claudia Tiersch. Steiner: Stuttgart.

Sickinger, James P. 1999. *Public Records and Archives in Classical Athens*. Chapel Hill: University of North Carolina Press.

Simmons, B. A., and Z. Elkins. 2005. "On Waves, Clusters and Diffusion: A Conceptual Framework." *Annals of the American Academy of Political and Social Science* 598, 33–51.

Simonton, M. S. 2012a. "Review of Julia Shear's *Polis and Revolution*." *Bryn Mawr Classical Review*.

Simonton, Matthew. 2012b. *The Rules of the Few: Institutions and the Struggle for Political Order in Classical Greek Oligarchies*. Stanford PhD Dissertation.

Simonton, M. S. 2017. *Classical Greek Oligarchy: A Political History*. Princeton: Princeton University Press. Sinclair, R. K. 1991. *Democracy and Participation in Athens*. First paperback edition (first edition 1988). Cambridge: Cambridge University Press.

Snodgrass, A. M. 1971. *The Dark Age of Greece: An Archaeological Survey of the Eleventh to the Eighth Centuries BC*. Edinburgh: At the University Press.

Snodgrass, A. M. 1980. *Archaic Greece: The Age of Experiment*. London: J. M. Dent and Sons.

Strauss, B. S. 1987a. *Athens after the Peloponnesian War: Class, Faction, and Policy, 403–386 BC*. Ithaca, NY: Cornell University Press.

Strauss, B. 1987b. "Athenian Democracy. Neither Radical, Extreme, nor Moderate." *Ancient History Bulletin* 1.

Stroud, R. S. 1968. *Drakon's Law on Homicide*. Berkeley and Los Angeles: University of California Press.

Stroud, R. S. 1974. "An Athenian Law on Silver Coinage." *Hesperia* 43, 157–88.

Stroud, R. S. 1998. "The Athenian Grain-Tax Law of 374/3 BC." *Hesperia Supplement* 29.

Sundahl, M. J. 2000. *The Use of Statutes in the Seven Extant* Graphē Paranomōn *and* Graphē Nomon Mē Epitēdeion Theinai *Speeches*. Unpublished PhD dissertation, Brown University.

Sundahl, M. J. 2003. "The Rule of Law and the Nature of the Fourth-Century Athenian Democracy." *CandM* 54, 127–56.

Talbert, Richard J. A. 1974. *Timoleon and the Revival of Greek Sicily, 344–317 B.C.* London: Cambridge University Press.

Tan, James. 2017. *Power and Public Finance at Rome, 264–49 BCE*. New York, NY: Oxford University Press.

Tavares, J., and R. Wacziarg. 2001. "How Democracy Affects Growth." *European Economic Review* 45(8), 1341–78.

Taylor, C. 2007a. "A New Political World." In R. Osborne, *Debating the Athenian Cultural Revolution: Art, Literature, Philosophy, and Politics 430–380 BC*. Cambridge: Cambridge University Press.

Taylor, C. 2007b. "From the Whole Citizen Body: The Sociology of Election and Lot in the Athenian Democracy." *Journal of the American School of Classical Studies at Athens* 76(2).

Taylor, C. 2011. "Migration and the Demes of Attica." In C. Holleran and A. Pudsey, *Demography and the Graeco-Roman World: New Insights and Approaches*. Cambridge: Cambridge University Press.

Taylor, C. 2015. "The Diversity of Networks and Communities." In *Communities and Networks in the Ancient Greek World*, edited by C. Taylor and K. Vlassopoulos. Oxford University Press.

Taylor, C. 2016. "Social Dynamics in Fourth Century Athens: Poverty and Standards of Living." In *Athenische Demokratie im 4.Jh: zwischen Modernisierung und Tradition*, edited by C. Tiersch. Stuttgart.

Taylor, C. 2017. *Poverty, Wealth, and Well-being: Experiencing* Penia *in Democratic Athens*. Oxford University Press.

Taylor, C., and Vlassopoulos, K., eds. 2015. *Communities and Networks in the Ancient Greek World*. Oxford University Press.

Taylor, M. C. 2002. "One Hundred Heroes from Phyle." *Hesperia* 71, 377–97.

Teegarden, David A. 2012. "The Oath of Demophantos, Revolutionary Mobilization, and the Preservation of the Athenian Democracy." *Hesperia* 81(3), 433–65.

Teegarden, D. 2014. *Death to Tyrants!: Ancient Greek Democracy and the Struggle against Tyranny*. Princeton: Princetno University Press.

Temin, P. 2006. "Estimating GDP in the Early Roman Empire." In *Innovazione tecnica e progresso economico nel mondo romano*, edited by Lo Cascio. Bari, 31–54.

Temin, P. 2013. *The Roman Market Economy*. Princeton: Princeton University Press.

Thompson, W. E. 1965. "The Date of the Athenian Gold Coinage." *AJP* 86(2), 159–74.

Thompson, W. E. 1966. "The Function of the Emergency Coinage of the Peloponnesian War." *Mnemosyne* 194, 337–43. Fourth series.

Thorne, A. J. 2001. "Warfare and Agriculture: The Economic Impact of Devastation in Classical Greece." *Greek, Roman, and Byzantine Studies* 42, 225–53.

Thucydides, Robert B. Strassler, and Richard Crawley. 1996. *The Landmark Thucydides: A Comprehensive Guide to the Peloponnesian War.* New York: Free Press.

Thür, G. 2006. "Prosklesis." In *Brill's New Pauly, Antiquity Volumes,* edited by Hubert Cancik and Helmuth Schneider. Consulted online on August 12, 2017 http://dx.doi.org/10.1163/1574-9347_bnp_e1010880.

Tilly, C. 1990. *Coercion, Capital and European States.* Blackwell.

Tinker, H., A. Griffin, and S. R. Ashton. 1983. *Burma, the Struggle for Independence, 1944–1948: Documents from Official and Private Sources.* London: H.M.S.O.

Todd, S. C. 1985. *Athenian Internal Politics 403–395 BC with Particular Reference to the Speeches of Lysias.* PhD dissertation, University of Cambridge.

Todd, S. C. 1990. "The Purpose of Evidence in Athenian Courts." In *Nomos: Essays in Athenian Law, Politics, and Society,* edited by Paul Cartledge, Paul Millet, and Stephen Todd, 19–39. Cambridge.

Todd, S. 1993. *The Shape of Athenian Law.* Oxford: Clarendon Press.

Todd, S. 1994. "Status and Contract in Fourth-Century Athens." *Symposion 1993.* Köln, 125–40.

Todd, S. 1996. "Lysias against Nikomachos: The Fate of the Expert in Athenian Law." In *Greek Law in Its Political Setting,* edited by L. Foxhall and A.D.E. Lewis. Oxford: Clarendon Press.

Toft, M. D. 2010. "Ending Civil Wars. A Case for Rebel Victory?" *International Security* 34(4), 7–36.

Traill, J. 1975. "The Political Organization of Attica." *Hesperia Supplement* 14.

Travlos, J. 1988. *Bildlexikon zur Topographie des Antiken Attika.* Tubingen.

Trever, A. A. 1925. "The Intimate Relation between Economic and Political Conditions in History, as Illustrated in Ancient Megara." *Classical Philology* 20(2), 115–32.

Tridimas, G. 2011. "A Political Economy Perspective of Direct Democracy in Ancient Athens." *Constitutional Political Economy* 22, 58–72.

Tridimas, G. 2012. "Constitutional Choice in Ancient Athens: The Rationality of Selection to Office by Lot." *Constitutional Political Economy* 23, 1–21.

Tridimas, G. 2014. "Rent Extraction and Rent Seeking in Ancient Athens." In *The Elgar Companion to Rent Seeking,* edited by A. Hillman and R. Congleton.

Tridimas, G. 2015. "War, Disenfranchisement and the Fall of the Ancient Athenian Democracy." *European Journal of Political Economy* 38(C), 102–17.

Tridimas, G. 2016. "Conflict, Democracy and Voter Choice: A Public Choice Analysis of the Athenian Ostracism." *Public Choice* 170.

Tridimas, G. 2017. "Constitutional Choice in Ancient Athens: The Evolution of the Frequency of Decision Making." *Constitutional Political Economy* 28.

Turchin, P., and W. Scheidel. 2009. "Coin Hoards Speak of Population Declines in Ancient Rome." *PNAS* 106(41), 17276–79.

Tushnet, M. 2009. "The Inevitable Globalization of Constitutional Law." *Virginia Journal of International Law* 49(985).

Unger, R. W. 1980. *The Ship in the Medieval Economy, 600–1600.* London: Croom Helm.

van Alfen, P. G. 2000. "The 'Owls' from the 1973 Iraq Hoard." *AJN* 12, 9–58. Second series.

van Alfen, P. G. 2011. "Hatching Owls." In *Quantifying Monetary Supplies in Greco-Roman Times*, edited by Fr. de Callataÿ and E. Lo Cascio. Pragmateiai, no. 19, Bari.

van Liefferinge, K., et al. 2014. "Reconsidering the Role of Thorikos within the Laurion Silver Mining Area (Attica, Greece) through Hydrological Analyses." *Journal of Archaeological Science* 41.

van Wees, H. 2000. "The City at War." In R. Osborne, *Classical Greece, 500–323 BC.* New York: Oxford University Press.

van Wees, H. 2007. "Stasis Destroyer of Men." In H. van Wees, C. Brélaz, and P. Ducrey, *Sécurité collective et ordre public dans les sociétés anciennes: sept exposés suivis de discussions par Hans van Wees... [et al.]: Vandoeuvres, Genève, 20–24 août 2007.* Geneva: Fondation Hardt.

van Wees, H. 2013. *Ships and Silver, Taxes and Tribute: A Fiscal History of Archaic Athens.* London: I. B. Tauris.

Vandermersch, C. 1994. *Vins et amphores de Grand Grèce et de Sicile IVᵉ–IIIᵉs. avant J.-C.* Naples.

Verdelis, N. M. 1956. "Der Diolkos am Isthmus von Korinth." *Mitteilungen des deutschen Archäologischen Instituts, Athenische Abteilung* 71, 51–59.

Vlassopoulos, K. 2007. "Beyond and Below the Polis." *Mediterranean Historical Review* 22(1).

Vlastos, G. 1952. "The Constitution of the Five Thousand." *AJP* 73, 189–98.

Voigt, S. 1997. Positive Constitutional Economics—a Survey. *Public Choice* 90, 11–53.

Voigt, S. 2011. Positive Constitutional Economics II—a Survey of Recent Developments. *Public Choice* 146, 205–56.

von Reden, S. 1995. "The Piraeus—A World Apart." *Greece and Rome* 42(1), 24–37. Second series.

Wallis, John Joseph. In progress. *Leviathan Denied: Rules, Organizations, Governments, and Social Dynamics.*

Wallace, Robert W. 1989. *The Areopagus Council, to 307 B.C.* Baltimore: Johns Hopkins University Press.

Wallis, J., and D. North. 2013. *Coordination and Coercion.* Paper presented at the All-UC conference, "Historical Perspective on Political Elites and Economic Growth" at Chapman University, May 31 and June 1, 2013. Available at: http://allucgroup.ucdavis.edu/uploads/5/6/8/7/56877229/wallis-north_g-s.chapman.2013.pdf.

Walter, B. F. 1997. "The Critical Barrier to Civil War Settlement." *International Organization* 51(3), 335–64.

Walter, B. F. 2002. *Committing to Peace: The Successful Settlement of Civil Wars.* Princeton: Princeton University Press.

Weber, M. 1965 [1919]. *Politics as a Vocation.* Philadelphia: Fortress Press.

Weingast, B. R. 1997. "The Political Foundations of Democracy and the Rule of Law." *American Political Science Review* 91(2), 245–63.

Weingast, B. R. 2004. "Constructing Self-Enforcing Democracy in Spain." In *Politics from Anarchy to Democracy: Rational Choice in Political Science,* edited by Joe Oppenheimer and Irwin Morris. Stanford: Stanford University Press.

Werhan, K. 2012. "Popular Constitutionalism, Ancient and Modern." *UC Davis Law Review* 46(1).

Westlake, H. D. 1994. "Dion and Timoleon." In *The Cambridge Ancient History,* edited by D. M. Lewis et al. Second edition. Cambridge: Cambridge University Press.

Whitehead, D. 1977 [1968]. *The Ideology of the Athenian Metic.* Cambridge: Cambridge Philological Society.

Whitehead, D. 1984. "A Thousand New Athenians." *LCM* 9.

Whitehead, D. 1986. *The Demes of Attica, 508/7–ca. 250 B.C.: A Political and Social Study.* Princeton: Princeton University Press.

Whitley, J. 1991. *Style and Society in Dark Age Greece: The Changing Face of a Pre-Literate Society, 1100–700 BC.* Cambridge: Cambridge University Press.

Whitley, J. 2001. *The Archaeology of Ancient Greece.* Cambridge: Cambridge University Press.

Wilhelm, A. 1922. *Jahreshefte* 21/22.

Williams, D. 2014. "What's So Bad about Burma's 2008 Constitution? A Guide for the Perplexed." In *Law, Society and Transition in Myanmar,* edited by Crouch Melissa and Tim Lindsey. Hart Publishing.

Wilson, P. 2000. *The Athenian Institution of the Khoregia: The Chorus, the City, and the Stage.* Cambridge: Cambridge University Press.

Wolff, H. J. 1970. " 'Normenkontrolle' und Gesetzesbegriff in der attischen Demokratie." Heidelberg.

Wolpert, A. 2002. *Remembering Defeat, Civil War and Civil Memory in Ancient Athens.* Baltimore and London: Johns Hopkins University Press.

Wolpert, A. 2017. "Thucydides on the Four Hundred and the Fall of Athens." In *The Oxford Handbook of Thucydides,* edited by Sara Forsdyke, Edith Foster, and Ryan Balot. Oxford University Press.

Woolmer, M. 2016. "Forging Links between Regions: Trade Policy in Classical Athens." In *The Ancient Greek Economy,* edited by E. M. Harris, D.M. Lewis, and M. Woolmer. Cambridge: Cambridge University Press.

Xenophon. 1918. *Xenophon in Seven Volumes. Volume 1.* Carleton L. Brownson. Cambridge, MA: Harvard University Press; London: William Heinemann, Ltd.

Xenophon. 1921. *Xenophon in Seven Volumes. Volume 2.* Carleton L. Brownson. Cambridge, MA: Harvard University Press; London: William Heinemann, Ltd.

Xenophon. 1925. *Xenophon in Seven Volumes. Volume 7: Constitution of the Athenians.* Translated by E. C. Marchant and G. W. Bowersock. Cambridge, MA: Harvard University Press; London: William Heinemann, Ltd.

Yunis, H. 1988. "Law, Politics, and the 'Graphē paranomōn' in Fourth-Century Athens." *Greek, Roman and Byzantine Studies* 29:4.

INDEX

access, forms of, 3, 9, 20. *See also* institutions: access to; open access orders

Acemoglu, Daron, 6

Ackerman, Bruce, 5n8

Acropolis, 25, 26, 32, 53, 121

Aegean Sea: Athenian hegemony in, 118–19; constraints of, 160–61, 180, 181n6; map of, 161; navigation of, 160, 179–82; piracy in, 32, 124n28, 162, 183; Piraeus' primacy in, 13, 14, 137, 140, 159–60, 162, 187; topography of, 179–81

Aegina, 160, 162, 179, 180, 182–83

Aeschines, 57n33, 70n57

Agora, 28, 53n24, 54n28, 55, 76, 95; coin-testing in, 77, 111, 119; taxes on metics and foreigners in, 130, 138

Agoratos, 66n48

Alcibiades, 36, 47, 59, 117

Alexander the Great, 11, 188, 197n18, 199

Alexandria, 14, 200, 201

Alston, Eric, et al., 5n9

Amemiya, Takeshi, 133, 197

Amit, Moshe, 158, 170

amnesty agreement, 15, 41, 63–64, 76; as a contractual arrangement, 63; right-of-return clause in, 65–66; Sparta as enforcer of, 15, 63, 66–67

Andocides, 10, 38, 197

Andros, 181

Ansolabehere, Stephen, 90

aphanēs economy, 110

Arcenas, Scott Lawin, 141n2

Archestratus, 56

Archidamian War, 69n52

Archinus, 74n64

Areopagus, Council of, 25, 26; curtailed powers of, 29–30, 49n17, 56–57; expanded powers of, 65n46, 124, 133, 134n53; public ambivalence about, 133

Arginusae trial, 35, 36

Aristides, 31

Aristophanes: *Clouds*, 29; *Lysistrata*, 26; *Wasps*, 86

Aristotle, 10; on rise of the Four Hundred, 48n16, 49, 51; on associations, 87; on Cleisthenes, 26–27; on law-courts, 82; on magistrates, 30; on metics, 113n12; on *patrios politeia*, 74n64; on revenue schemes, 126n33; on the aftermath of the Sicilian defeat, 46; on Solon, 23–24, 57, 105n50; on the Thirty, 56–57, 58–59, 62

Assembly: antecedents of, 24n4; constraints on, 15n27, 35n28, 36, 64–65; coordination with *nomothetai*, 69; Council of Five Hundred relationship to, 26, 28, 94–95; inability to credibly commit of, 34–35, 36, 39, 40, 53, 60, 66, 71n60, 72; defects of, 18, 34–36, 66; dominant speakers at, 29, 77; expenditure reductions for, 124; Four Hundred and, 48–50; naval station authorization by, 137; pay for serving in, 115, 134, 139; Sicilian Expedition debate in, 45; sociological composition of, 83–84, 85; structure of, 24, 28–29

associations, 87–88, 138

Athenian civil war. *See* civil conflict (Athens)

A NOTE ON THE TYPE

This book has been composed in Arno, an Old-style serif typeface in the classic Venetian tradition, designed by Robert Slimbach at Adobe.